Psychology in Organizations

T0326437

Wirtschaftspsychologie

Herausgegeben von Detlev Liepmann

Band 14

PETER LANG

Frankfurt am Main · Berlin · Bern · Bruxelles · New York · Oxford · Wien

Kathrin Heinitz (ed.)

Psychology in Organizations

Issues from an Applied Area

PETER LANG
Internationaler Verlag der Wissenschaften

Bibliographic Information published by the Deutsche Nationalbibliothek
The Deutsche Nationalbibliothek lists this publication in the Deutsche Nationalbibliografie; detailed bibliographic data is available in the internet at <http://www.d-nb.de>.

ISSN 0945-182X
ISBN 978-3-631-57446-1

© Peter Lang GmbH
Internationaler Verlag der Wissenschaften
Frankfurt am Main 2008
All rights reserved.

Printed in Germany 1 2 3 4 5   7

www.peterlang.de

Preface

Life and work in organizations is as many facetted as the life outside the organization. Hence psychologically interesting issues are manifold. This book will give an insight into up-to-date issues of psychology in organizations. Both theoretical and empirical approaches will try to shed light onto a variety of questions that arise in day-to-day organizational work. The authors show different approaches to organizational behavior, these being either reflections of behavior on the individual or on an organizational level of analysis.

One of the recurring topics of organizational psychology is job satisfaction. Miriam Wirth tries to shed light on antecedents of job satisfaction and hereby investigates the paths between cognitive as well as situational variables and job satisfaction.

Leadership, as the second topic of this book, is represented within the studies of organizational behavior by a huge body of research, not only from a psychological but also from an economic point of view. One reason for this is that leadership is often seen as one of the key concepts that explain organizational effectiveness. More recent foci within the studies of leadership are transformational and charismatic leadership. Jens Rowold and Kathrin Heinitz give an insight into one of the theories concerning charismatic leadership, the Conger and Kanungo Model of charismatic leadership. Its assessment as well as the empirical results are presented. A second growing stream of leadership research is presented by Jan Schilling. His chapter on implicit leadership theories poses the question if leadership ratings assess actual leadership behavior or simply show the implicit theory of leadership of those that fill in the questionnaires. Jan Schilling presents the development, structure and functions of implicit leadership as well as their relevance for the practice. The practical relevance of leadership also becomes apparent when discussing its training. Leadership training and coaching have become increasingly important with a more pronounced focus on leadership research. In their chapter, Jens Radstaak and Jens Rowold give an insight into this important business area.

An upcoming topic in the field of organizational behavior is health issues. Ranging from the evaluation of health problems caused by organizational behavior to organizational health programs, research taps a broad variety of questions concerning health behavior and health problems. In this book, Kathrin Heinitz and Detlev Liepmann discuss the chances for health management in the process of personnel and organizational development. Nicole Wundke and Jörg Felfe find an empirical approach to determine the role of individual and organizational interventions in health programs. They furthermore include process variables in order to evaluate their importance for occupational stress management. Dirk Hanebuth gives an extensive overview of the topic of absenteeism including an examination of the context as a whole and the problem of control and background variables.

In the last chapter of this book, Sabine Smolka, Detlev Liepmann, André Beauducel and Yolanda Ortiz-Deutschmann also focus on the individual perspective and discuss the relevance of concepts such as action and state orientation as well as promotion and prevention focus for organizational behavior.

As already mentioned, this book does not intend to give an extensive overview on the field of organizational behavior but shows through several facets that psychological discussion and research of organizational topics is useful and significant.

Berlin, September 2007
Kathrin Heinitz

Contents

Implicit Leadership Theories: Theory, Research, and Application   47

Jan Schilling

Leadership Training and Coaching   63

Jens Radstaak and Jens Rowold

Backgrounds of Absenteeism   115

Dirk Hanebuth

Problem-Oriented Behavior in Organizations   135

Sabine Smolka, Detlev Liepmann, André Beauducel and Yolanda Ortiz-Deutschmann

References   149

Investigating the Paths between Facets of Intelligence, Job Complexity, and Job Satisfaction

Miriam Wirth

1. Job satisfaction

The study of job satisfaction (JS) looks back on a long research tradition, lasting back into the 1970s in Germany and even into the 1930s in the United States. JS nowadays has developed into one of the most extensively researched topics in the field of Industrial and Organizational Psychology due to the recognition of the potential benefits of JS such as positive work attitudes and behavior and increased employee health.

In these days, however, the current business climate as characterized by flexible organizational forms, reorganizing, merging, reductions in staff and macroeconomic uncertainty is a foundation for concern for employees (Felfe & Six, 2006), and may be among the reasons of the overall low level of JS – in Germany, only 12% report high JS (Gallup, 2003).

In light of the devastating ramifications of job dissatisfaction such as turnover or absenteeism it is not surprising that especially the determinants of JS have been in the spotlight of international research interest. In essence, one distinguishes between situational and dispositional determinants; whereas the main emphasis has been put on *situational* determinants such as salary compared to *dispositional* determinants such as personality traits or intelligence.

The question arising in times, in which situational factors are rather unchangeable, is to what degree dispositional factors do play a role concerning JS. Due to the present business climate, characteristics that predispose individuals to deal with new circumstances have become increasingly important. Uncovering the dispositional characteristics in turn would contribute to new insights regarding recruiting and selection of candidates. During interviews, for instance, this would allow to potentially focus on several attributes that have been linked to a higher level of JS (Gerhart, 2005).

The present study focuses on the influence of one cognitive variable that has been less extensively researched in combination with JS, namely intelligence. Following theoretical underpinnings of Ganzach (1998), it is hypothesized that the relationship between intelligence and JS is moderated by one situational variable: job complexity. By reviewing recent literature on the relationships between intelligence, job complexity and JS, the following sections serve as a basis from which the hypotheses are derived.

1.1 Intelligence as a determinant of job satisfaction

The concept of *job satisfaction* has no universally accepted definition, due to its heterogeneous nature. Locke (1976) was among the first who provided a definition of JS by defining the concept as a "…pleasurable or emotional state resulting from the appraisal of one's job or job experiences" (p. 1300). Contemporary definitions of JS emphasize that both cognitive and affective factors influence JS (Brief, 1998). Overall, the various definitions have the common denominator that JS is regarded as an evaluative assessment of the current work situation that contains both cognitive as well as emotional components. In contradiction to past research that mainly put an emphasis on situational factors, recent research increasingly focuses on dispositional factors. One characteristic that has received very limited little research interest so far is intelligence.

Intelligence is widely regarded as a strong determinant of many important outcomes in life such as satisfaction, happiness and wisdom. It is evidenced that intelligence is one of the best predictors of job performance (Bertua, Anderson, & Salgado, 2005; Schmidt & Hunter, 1998) and its relationship to other social advantages such as employment, economic self-sufficiency, affluence, educational achievement, marital stability, legitimacy and lawful behavior is proven (Herrnstein & Murray, 1994). Schmidt and Hunter (2000) even claimed that intelligence is the most important construct in psychology.

Interestingly, however, its influence on JS has rarely been studied. In a longitudinal study investigating predictors of competence and life satisfaction, Kalimo and Vuori (1990) found that intelligence at an age between 8 and 21 years predicted life satisfaction measured at an age between 31 and 44 years. Not only the relationship between intelligence and life satisfaction, but also the link between personal resources and subjective well-being has been a focus of past research. Diener and Fujita (1995) found that several personal resources were more strongly related to subjective well-being than material resources. Among the personal abilities, intelligence proved to be a significant predictor of both life satisfaction ($r = .27$) and subjective well-being ($r = .30$). The authors explained this by a greater progress towards goals leading to the experience of subjective well-being, or satisfaction.

Lately, it has been questioned whether intelligence is not solely related to life satisfaction but to JS as one specific component of life satisfaction as well. The underlying assumption is that intelligence and hence the ability to deal with complex tasks leads to self-actualization processes and to positive evaluations of the workplace. This in turn would amount to a high level of JS.

Previous research concerning the direct relationship between intelligence and JS yielded inconclusive results. Lipsett and Wilson (1954) reported a low positive relationship between mental ability and JS. In contrast, Lam and Chan (1988) found a negative relationship between intelligence and JS in their sample of sheltered workshop clients. This was explained by the fact that less intelligent clients do not have as well defined preferences concerning their work, and those clients with a higher level of intelligence hold too high expectations about their job. Although the explanation seems reasonable, it can be questioned whether these findings derived from individuals with mental retardation (IQ: $M = 58$, $SD = 13.29$) do also apply for individuals with normal intelligence. However, Barrett and Forbes (1980) and Meulmann (1991) successfully replicated the negative relationship between intelligence and JS in their samples with normal intelligence.

Ganzach (1998) found a direct negative relationship between intelligence and JS. Interestingly, though, the negative effect was only present in case that job complexity was held constant and thus the relationship was analyzed *within* occupational groups. The link turned out to be positive when job complexity was varied and hence the relationship was analyzed *between* occupational groups. Glynn (1999) investigated JS of highly intelligent people and found them to be less satisfied than individuals with normal intelligence. Lounsbury (2004) reported a non-significant relationship between intelligence and JS in the whole sample. Contrary to Ganzach, however, he found a significant negative relationship only in the group of hourly employees whereas in the group of managerial employees he found a significant positive relationship. Again others found zero-relationships between intelligence and JS (Bagozzi, 1978; Colarelli, Dean, & Konstans, 1987; Stone, Stone, & Gueutal, 1990).

Ganzach (1998) attributes the inconsistent results to differences in the samples because heterogeneous as well as homogeneous samples with varying levels of occupation were studied. Another potential reason for the contradictory results could be different measures of intelligence used. Furthermore, it could be that intelligence has no direct effect on JS, as presumed by those who compared the influence of intelligence between occupational groups, and hence in combination with job complexity, but that another variable is involved as well and presumably moderates the relationship. In the following section, a hypothesized model that incorporates both intelligence and job complexity as impacts on JS will be presented.

1.2 Hypothesized model: Job complexity as a moderator of the intelligence - job

satisfaction relationship

According to Glynn (1998), two trends can be recognized in JS research that are closely related to the joint influence of intelligence and job complexity on JS. As already mentioned, first, there has been a trend toward the emphasis of situational determinants over dispositional determinants. Second, there has been a trend toward the investigation of JS of employees with less complex jobs. Glynn (1998) assumes that these two trends are entangled and illustrate an interaction between the influence of situational and dispositional variables, and that job complexity needs to be considered as an important influence. As Glynn (1998) puts it, "...individual characteristics *[such as intelligence, comment of the author]* have increasingly greater influence as an individual's position in the organizational hierarchy increases" (p.194). Glynn (1998) therefore concludes that job complexity should be included as an additional variable in the analysis of the relationship between dispositional factors and JS.

In uncovering the paths between intelligence, job complexity, and JS, in the following, first, a closer look will be taken on the direct relationship between intelligence and job complexity. Second, research examining the direct influence of job complexity on JS will be presented.

Job complexity is referred to as the degree to which an employee's job is demanding, challenging, and stimulating (Fried, Haynes, Slowik, Ben-David, & Tiegs, 2001). It includes enhanced work characteristics such as greater control and responsibility (Axtell et al., 2002), as well as variety, autonomy, task identity, feedback, dealing with others, friendship opportunities (Sims, Szilagyi, & Keller, 1979), ambiguity, unpredictability, and uncertainty (Glynn, 1998).

Various researchers have reported strong relationships between intelligence and job complexity (Blackburn & Neumark, 1993; Farkas & Vicknair, 1996; Ganzach & Pazy, 2001). Schröder et al. (1975) assume a ∩- shaped relationship between level of information processing and environmental complexity. Their ∩-shaped hypothesis of cognitive complexity states that information processing reaches a maximum level in case that environmental complexity matches the level of cognitive complexity. Similarly, it stands to reason that the level of intelligence has to be in congruence with the level of job complexity in order to lead to an optimal performance as well as to satisfaction. Recently, Boudreau, Boswell, Judge and Bretz (2001) investigated the role of intelligence in the process of job search and examined what kind of jobs people with differing levels of intelligence were most likely to obtain. They reached the conclusion that individuals with higher cognitive ability engaged more in the process of job search and obtained more complex jobs than less intelligent individuals. From this line of reasoning, the first assumption investigated in the present study is derived:

A_1 Intelligence will be positively related to level of job complexity.

Besides the relationship between intelligence and job complexity, prior evidence suggests that the level of job complexity is related to attitudinal outcomes such as JS. Gardell (1978) reported that job autonomy as one aspect of job complexity was positively correlated with JS. More recently, Eskildsen, Kristensen and Westlund (2003) found a positive relationship between job level and JS, indicating that more complex jobs as characterized by more diversified and challenging tasks contribute to a high level of JS. Grebner, Semmer, Faso, Gut, Kälin and Elfering (2003) replicated the results of Eskildsen et al. (2003) since they also found that job complexity predicted JS in their sample of call centre agents. All in all, the results give rise to the assumption that job complexity is positively related to JS, with employees holding highly complex jobs being more satisfied than those with less complex jobs. Therefore, the following second assumption is analyzed in the present study:

A $_2$ Job complexity will be positively related to job satisfaction.

Taking the links between intelligence and job complexity on the one hand and job complexity and JS on the other hand into consideration, the importance of job complexity regarding the relationship between intelligence and JS becomes obvious.

Recently, the influence of intelligence in combination with job complexity on JS has been investigated (Ganzach, 1998; Lounsbury et al., 2004). In contrast to the majority of dispositional theories on JS, Ganzach (1998) hypothesizes in his causal model that JS is not determined by motivational or affective characteristics but by one cognitive characteristic: intelligence. His causal model is build upon a social-cognitive approach to individual differences and posits that intelligence is both positively as well as negatively associated with JS via two opposing processes. He introduces job complexity as a moderator variable that determines whether intelligence has a positive or negative effect on JS.

On the one hand, intelligence is believed to have a direct negative influence in case that the relationship is analyzed within occupational groups. In this case, the level of job complexity is assumed to be relatively constant, resulting in dissatisfaction of intelligent individuals who tend to desire more complex work. This direct relationship between intelligence and JS is thought to be moderated by job complexity since the more complex the job the less negative the impact of intelligence on JS. This leads to the following third assumption:

A $_3$ Intelligence will have a direct *negative* effect on JS when job complexity is held constant (analyzed within occupations).

Intelligence is thought to increase JS, however, when the level of job complexity is varying, as is the case when the relationship is compared between occupational groups (Ganzach, 1998):

A $_4$ Intelligence will be *positively* related to JS when job complexity is varied (analyzed between occupations).

In the previous assumptions, the emphasis is put on the relationships between general intelligence, job complexity, and JS. Although theoretical approaches as well as empirical evidence give rise to the assumption that facets of intelligence predict real-life criteria even better than general intelligence (Stern & Guthke, 2001), until now, no study has been published that investigated the role of subconstructs of intelligence concerning job complexity and JS.

Stankov (2000) claims that crystallized intelligence (g_c) is a stronger predictor of life events as opposed to fluid intelligence and general intelligence, and even better than socio-economic status. In line with Stankov (2000), Diener and Fujita (1995) found expert knowledge as an indicator of g_c to be significantly related to life satisfaction ($r = .20$) and even more to subjective well-being ($r = .23$). The educated guess can be made whether g_c is even more related to job complexity and JS than fluid or general intelligence. The underlying rationale is that g_c assesses immediate rather than historical or demographic aspects of behavior, and since job complexity and JS are regarded as immediate evaluative reactions of the current job, the rationale seems reasonable. Since the influence of facets of intelligence has not been investigated thus far, the present research stream will be extended by analyses of the following two assumptions:

A 5   Facets of intelligence (i.e. fluid and crystallized intelligence) will explain more variance in job complexity than general intelligence.

A 6   Facets of intelligence (i.e. fluid and crystallized intelligence) will explain more variance in job satisfaction than general intelligence.

2. Method

2.1 Participants

The data for this study stems from a sample of 117 trainees of a large German chemical company. The majority was male (71.8%). The participants ranged from age 17 to 26, with a mean age of 21 years ($SD = 1.91$). Most of the respondents had a Realschule degree (35.9%), followed by those with a Gymnasium degree (33.3%), and a Gesamtschule degree (20.5%). The remaining 10.3% hold a Hauptschule degree. The advantage of using trainees as subjects is that they have some occupational experience on the one hand, but on the other hand, they are not extremely rooted in their job so that extreme dissatisfaction would already have led to an occupational change (Ott, 1980). For this reason, 1st, 2nd and 3rd year trainees from the following five forms of occupational training were used as subjects: lab technician (chemical; 35.9%), production assistant (chemical; 22.2%), electrician (21.4%), industrial clerk for office communications (11.1%), and welding technician (9.4%). Anonymity was assured through the use of code numbers instead of names.

2.2 Measures

Intelligence. Intelligence was measured via the short version of the *Intelligenz-Struktur-Test 2000R* (Amthauer et al., 2001). The IST 2000R is a timed, structural, and status test (Stern & Guthke, 2001) that is based on the HPI model (hierarchical protomodel of intelligence structure research; Amthauer, 1999). The HPI model assumes that intelligent behavior depends on more than just one ability (Holling, Preckel, & Vock, 2004). Following the HPI model, the short version of the IST 2000R contains primary factors and three levels of hierarchy:

three content-based *primary factors* (verbal, numerical, and figural ability), two *second-order factors* (*fluid* (g_f) and *crystallized* (g_c) *intelligence* (Cattell, 1963)), and at the highest level, the factor *general intelligence* (g). The short version of the IST 2000R used in the present study contains one module investigating verbal intelligence (analogies) and numerical intelligence (arithmetic problems), and two modules concerning figural intelligence (figures and matrices). Each module includes 20 items and each item has 4-5 answer choices. In order to measure fluid and crystallized intelligence, two types of knowledge tests (an extension of the IST 2000R) were applied. The two forms differ only with respect to the sequence of the items in order to prevent copying. The knowledge test consists of 46 questions from six different fields: art-literature, geography-history, mathematics, science, economy, and daily life. The IST 2000R yielded satisfying internal consistencies (Cronbach's alpha: α = .71 - .84).

Job Satisfaction. According to Arvey et al. (1989), one-item measures of JS often lack sufficient reliability. Therefore, in the current study, JS was measured by an 18-item self-report questionnaire ("Arbeitszufriedenheit", Felfe, Liepmann, & Resetka, 1996). The reliabilities reported earlier could be replicated in the present sample (Cronbach's alpha: α = .84). The JS questionnaire distinguishes between an *actual* and a *desired* measure of JS, and thus underlies a need-oriented theory of JS suggesting a principle of homeostasis (Schuler, 1993). It includes a range of intrinsic (e. g. autonomy) and extrinsic (e. g. salary) characteristics of the job. Subjects indicate the importance of the characteristics on a 5-point Likert scale ranging from *not at all important* to *extremely important*. General JS is derived from the discrepancy between *actual* and *desired* JS, in a way that positive values of JS represent job dissatisfaction, whereas negative values indicate high JS. It is noteworthy that, while interpreting the results of the analyses, positive correlations represent negative relationships between JS and other concepts and vice versa.

Factor analytic procedures in previous studies produced three subscales referring to the organizational condition, the working atmosphere, and the economic condition. In order to separate the three hypothetical factors included in the questionnaire, a factor analysis with Varimax rotation was applied. The three-factorial structure of the JS questionnaire could not be replicated in the present study, probably due to the rather small sample size. Instead, a 5-factorial structure emerged that explains altogether about 59.5% of the total variance. For this reason, *general* JS, as determined by the difference between *actual* and *desired* JS, is taken as an indicator of JS and is applied in all analyses.

Job Complexity. Several researchers have shown that both subjective and objective measures of job complexity yield the same results (Ganzach, 1998; Xie & Johns, 1995). Therefore, in the present study, a measure of *subjective job complexity* was derived from the participants' evaluation of the complexity of their jobs using a seven item questionnaire. The items represent the factors of the *Job Diagnostic Index* and were translated into German (Sims et al., 1976). The participants were asked to which degree the following aspects are present in their current job: dealing with others, autonomy, feedback, friendship opportunities, task identity, and task variety. Responses were made on a 5-point Likert scale, anchored at 1 (*very little*) and 5 (*very much*), and 1 (*very seldom*) and 5 (*very often*). The ratings were averaged to construct an overall measure of subjective perception of job complexity, because all 7 items measure a unidimensional construct (Bearden & Netemeyer, 1999).

Control Variables. These variables included age, gender, level of education, the last school marks for the subjects German, English, Mathematics, and the average school mark.

3. Results

This section is organized as follows: In the first three parts, descriptive statistics for JS, job complexity, and intelligence are provided. In the remaining parts, the relationships between intelligence, job complexity, and JS are examined. An alpha level of .05 was used for all statistical tests.

3.1 Descriptive statistics

3.1.1 Job satisfaction

Table 1 shows the means of JS, job complexity, IQ, crystallized and fluid intelligence. To assess the differences in the level of JS of different forms of occupational training, one-way analysis of variance (ANOVA) is applied with form of occupational training serving as independent variable and JS as dependent variable. Analysis of the data reveals a significant difference in the level of JS for forms of occupational training, $F(4, 89) = 2.47$, $p = .05$, indicating that forms of occupational training differ with respect to JS. In addition, cluster centre analysis is applied in order to examine whether groups with varying levels of JS can be identified. It reveals three clusters $F(4, 95) = 198.09$, $p < .001$. The majority of the subjects (N = 56; 58.3%) belongs to the cluster of the moderately satisfied ($M = .90$), followed by the dissatisfied ($M = 1.72$; N = 24; 25%). The minority of the subjects (16.7 %) forms part of the group of the highly satisfied ($M = -.04$; N = 16). In sum, most of the trainees report moderate satisfaction, followed by the unsatisfied and the highly satisfied.

3.1.2 Subjective Job Complexity

Again, one-way ANOVA is applied to detect differences in general subjective job complexity between forms of occupational training. Analysis of the data reveals homogeneity of variances, and indicates that subjects regard their jobs as differing concerning complexity $F(4, 89) = 6.88$, $p = .001$. Tukey post-hoc procedure classifies the forms of occupational training into two groups ($p = .053$), indicating that welding technicians rate their job as least complex and constitute the first group ($M = 2.75$), and lab technicians ($M = 3.68$), industrial clerk of office communications ($M = 3.63$), and electricians ($M = 3.29$) rate their job as most complex and constitute the second group. Production assistants ($M = 3.28$) are not assigned to any group.

3.1.3 Intelligence

IQ, fluid and crystallized intelligence, as well as verbal, numerical, and fig-ural ability were calculated according to the manual of the IST 2000R (Am-thauer et al., 2001). IQ is normally distributed in the sample and ranges from 71 to 136 ($M = 101.86$, $SD = 13.17$). One-way ANOVA indicates that subjects from five forms of occupational training differ with respect to all facets of intelli-gence. Subjects from different forms of occupational training are distinguishable concerning IQ $F(4, 112) = 5.71$, $p < .001$ (two-tailed test), crystallized intelli-gence $F(4, 112) = 21.46$, $p < .001$ (two-tailed test), and fluid intelligence $F(4, 112) = 2.69$, $p < .05$ (two-tailed test). Forms of occupational training differs with respect to verbal ability $F(4, 112) = 7.94$, $p < .001$ (two-tailed test), numerical ability $F(4, 112) = 3.38$, $p < .05$ (two-tailed test), and figural ability $F(4, 112) = 3.37$, $p < .05$ (two-tailed test).

Table 1: Means of Job Satisfaction, Job Complexity, IQ scores, and sum scores of Crystallized and Fluid Intelligence per Form of Occupational Training

	JS	JC	IQ	g_c	g_f
1. Welding Technician	1.39	2.75	95.36	88.73	99.55
2. Production Assistant	0.87	3.28	98.23	89.77	101.77
3. Electrician	1.17	3.29	97.24	99.64	99.00
4. Lab Technician	0.94	3.68	108.86	107.67	105.24
5. Industrial Clerk	0.69	3.63	100.92	97.69	102.08

Note. JS = difference between *actual* and *desired* JS. The higher the value, the lower the level of JS; JC = Job complexity, scale 1-5 (1 = low job complexity, 5 = high job complexity); g_c = crystallized intelligence; g_f = fluid intelligence

3.2 Intelligence, job complexity, and job satisfaction

3.2.1 Intelligence and JS

Contrary to the findings of several studies which reached the conclusion that intelligence is negatively correlated to JS when the relationship is examined within occupational groups, this tendency cannot be not found in the present sample. Correlation analysis of the data reveals negative but non-significant cor-relations between all facets of intelligence and JS for welding technicians (e. g. JS & IQ: $r = -.37$, $p = .27$) and electricians (e. g. JS & IQ: $r = -.35$, $p = .087$). Positive but also non-significant correlations between aspects of intelligence and JS are found for production assistants (e. g. JS & IQ: $r = .40$, $p = .088$), lab tech-nicians (e. g. JS & IQ: $r = .12$, $p = .54$), and industrial clerk of office communication (e. g. JS & IQ: $r = .07$, $p = .89$). Since all correlations fail to reach significance, no evidence for assumption A_3 is obtained. No facet of intelligence is significantly correlated with JS; therefore, assumption A_6 is rejected, too.

In order to test for the hypothesized positive effect between intelligence and JS across occupations, those occupations with more than 20 participants were chosen (electricians, production assistants, and lab technicians). For these three occupations, the correlation between occupational intelligence and occupational JS was computed. In contrast to A_4, no significant correlation is found ($r = .08$, $p = .48$).

3.2.2 Intelligence and job complexity

Correlation analysis was applied in order to examine the relationship between intelligence and job complexity. Evidence for assumption A_1 that intelligence is positively associated with job complexity is obtained for only one facet, that is crystallized intelligence (Table 2). Among the intelligence facets, only crystallized intelligence is positively correlated with job complexity, $r(117) = .21$, $p < .05$. Evidence for assumption A_5 stating that facets of intelligence explain more variance in job complexity was obtained since crystallized intelligence explains 4,2% of the variance in job complexity ($\beta = .21$, $p < .05$), whereas IQ only accounts for 1% of variance.

3.2.3 Job complexity and JS

Analyzing the data with Pearson's r reveals a negative correlation between job complexity and the here used measure of JS, $r(90) = -.38$, $p < .001$. Therefore, evidence for assumption A_2 is obtained. The results indicate that job complexity is positively associated with JS, and that the more complex the job, the more satisfied the employee. When the actual JS is taken as an indicator of JS instead of the difference between actual and desired JS, the relationship gets even more pronounced, $r(96) = .51$, $p < .001$.

Table 2: Intercorrelations among the Variables

Variable	1	2	3	4	5	6	7
1. JS							
2. JC	-.38**						
3. IQ	.01	.10					
4. G_c	.06	.21*	.47**				
5. G_f	.02	.03	.95**	.25**			
6. Verb	-.03	.11	.92**	.55**	.83**		
7. Num	.00	.01	.89**	.32**	.93**	.77**	
8. Fig	.01	.00	.65**	.36**	.58**	.51**	.33**

Note. Verb = verbal ability, Num = numerical ability, Fig = figural ability; *p < .05; **p < .001

Taken together, the correlation between job complexity and JS indicates that employees who hold a job at the top of the job rank regarding complexity are more satisfied than those with low complex jobs.

3.2.3 Intelligence, job complexity and JS

Whereas the direct relationships between crystallized intelligence and job complexity and job complexity and JS are significantly positive, contrary to assumption A_3 and A_4, the relationships between intelligence and JS within and between forms of occupational training fail to reach significance. In contrast to the results obtained by Ganzach (1998), job complexity does not seem to moderate the relationship between intelligence and JS in the present sample since there is a zero-relationship between intelligence and JS that does not change when job complexity is included in a linear regression model. Baron and Kenny (1986) suggest that a *moderator* is evidenced in case that a) the direction of the correlation between independent (here: intelligence) and dependant variable (here: JS) changes as a function of the moderating variable (here: job complexity), b) the independent variable and a factor that specifies the appropriate conditions for its operation interact significantly and c) if a relation between two variables is reduced instead of reversed. Since there are no significant correlations found within forms of occupational training, it would not make sense to test whether the non-significant relationships differed between occupational groups and therefore as a function of job complexity.

Instead, the present results suggest that job complexity can be regarded as a *mediator* between intelligence and JS. According to Baron and Kenny (1986), a mediator is evidenced in case that a) variations in the level of the independent variable significantly account for variations in the mediator, b) variations in the mediator significantly account for variations in the dependant variable, and c) when a) and b) are controlled, a previously significant correlation between the independent and dependant variable is no longer significant, with the strongest demonstration of mediation occurring when c) is zero. Since intelligence is significantly related to job complexity and job complexity is significantly related to JS and in line with Bagozzi (1978) and Colarelli et al. (1987) there is a zero-relationship between intelligence and JS, it seems as if job complexity functions as a mediator between intelligence and JS (see Figure 1).

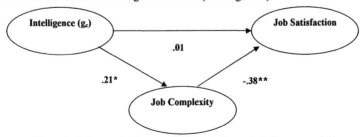

Figure 1. **Job complexity as a mediator between intelligence and JS**

3.3 Evidence for the hypotheses

Regarding the hypotheses, the following conclusions can be drawn: First, evidence for assumption A_1 is obtained, signifying that one facet of intelligence, namely crystallized intelligence, is positively related to level of job complexity. Second, assumption A_2 is proven since job complexity is positively related to JS. Third, assumption A_3 is rejected because there is no direct negative relationship between intelligence and JS within occupational groups. Fourth, contrary to A_4, job complexity is not evidenced as a moderator between intelligence and JS in the present sample but as a *mediator*. Lastly, since crystallized intelligence explains more variance in job complexity compared to general intelligence and fluid intelligence, evidence for assumption A_5 is obtained. No support for assumption A_6 is found because the finding that facets of intelligence, and in particular crystallized intelligence, predict real-life factors even better than general intelligence does not apply for the relationship between facets of intelligence and JS.

4. Discussion

The aim of the present study was to show the substantial relevance and complexity of including both dispositional as well as situational factors in the analysis of the antecedents of JS. Several previous studies found that intelligence as a cognitive influence is related to the level of JS. In addition, the importance of job complexity in the intelligence-JS relationship has repeatedly been reported (Ganzach, 1998; Glynn, 1998; Lounsbury et al., 2003). In the present study, the direct impact of intelligence on JS could not be replicated. Besides aiming at replicating results of earlier studies, this study investigated for the first time the influence of facets of intelligence on job complexity and JS within and between five forms of occupational training. By incorporating facets of intelligence as well as job complexity as determinants of JS, several new and interesting findings emerged.

Overall, the rather low level of JS reported by respondents - only 17% indicated high satisfaction with their current job and 26% even indicated job dissatisfaction - mirrors the current situation in Germany (Gallup, 2003), whole Europe, and the United States (Kristensen et al., 2003). It seems as if job dissatisfaction has become the rule rather than the exception.

Although the present study failed to replicate the direct influence of intelligence on JS as reported by Ganzach (1998), and no support for the findings of Lounsbury et al. (2004) that the relationship was positive for high-complex occupations and negative for low-complex occupations was obtained, direct positive relationships between other study-relevant concepts emerged. Among these, relationships between intelligence and job complexity on the one hand, as well as between job complexity and JS on the other hand were found. Furthermore, the importance of investigating facets of intelligence concerning job complexity became obvious.

4.1 Facets of intelligence as predictors of real-life criteria

The most relevant finding to add value to the present research stream is that, in line with the hypothesis, one facet of intelligence predicted several real-life criteria better than general intelligence as indicated by IQ scores. It seems as if a measure of intelligence that builds upon a hierarchical and faceted model of intelligence that distinguishes between different aspects of intelligence and reduces construct-irrelevant variance (Beauducel, Brocke, & Liepmann, 2001) is a highly valuable instrument in the examination of the relationships between intelligence and real-life criteria like job complexity. Among various facets of intelligence, crystallized intelligence was the only significant correlate of job complexity. This finding indicates that a high level of crystallized intelligence, signifying abilities that stem from acculturation influences, is positively related to the level of complexity of an individual's occupation. However, the causality of the relationship cannot be determined with the present data. Both causal directions are plausible.

On the one hand, it seems logical that the level of crystallized intelligence determines job complexity. The underlying assumption is that individuals who have already acquired knowledge from acculturation influences are more likely to receive a higher education and obtain jobs higher in complexity. The finding that individuals with higher cognitive ability engage more in the process of job search and also obtain more complex jobs supports this causal direction (Boudreau et al., 2001).

On the other hand, the inverse causal direction is also plausible. Job complexity may influence crystallized abilities in a way that a complex and challenging education as well as occupation leads to the acquisition of new knowledge. This causal path is totally in accordance with the theoretical framework on which the concept of crystallized intelligence is built since it is believed to be a product of environmentally varying investments. More precisely, Cattell (1963) suggests that crystallized ability performance is a function of previous time and interest invested in the application of fluid ability, memory, and specific problem solving aids. The finding that crystallized intelligence increases throughout the life span can be regarded as a further indicator for this causal direction (Sternberg, 1999).

Regarding the predictive value of crystallized intelligence, the finding that crystallized intelligence is related to job complexity as one real-life criterion complies with the assumption of Stankov (2000). Further support for the present finding comes from the view that measures of g_c do not assess historical and demographic aspects of behavior but immediate aspects (Stankov, 2000). Yet, the finding that only crystallized intelligence but not fluid intelligence is related to job complexity is surprising since fluid and crystallized ability are highly correlated (Holling et al., 2004). Thus, it would be logical if fluid intelligence was related to job complexity as well. Interestingly, the findings of Beauducel et al. (2001) support the view that especially at young ages, differences between levels of fluid and crystallized intelligence exist. Since the participants of the present study are relatively young and homogenous with respect to age, it is likely that crystallized ability and fluid ability do have differential effects on job complexity.

Taking the above mentioned findings into consideration, it seems as if highly intelligent people are seeking challenges, and therefore hold more complex jobs than individuals with a lower level of (crystallized) intelligence. What theoretical underpinnings do account for this finding?

On a very general explanatory basis, the finding that intelligence is related to job complexity is congruent with both biological and cognitive approaches to *person-environment fit (P-E fit)*, or *person-job fit*. Adapted to the present study, P-E fit refers to the match between an individual's ability and the ability requirements of his or her job. Whereas highly intelligent people are believed to hold complex occupations, individuals with lower intelligence are thought to work in less complex occupations. One general biological approach to P-E fit is the *interaction model* introduced by Stern and Guthke (2001). The authors suggest that genotype or predisposition interact with the environment, signifying that there is interaction between intelligence and level of job complexity. Another more specific approach is that of Arvey (1989) who assumes an *active genotype-environment correlation*. According to Arvey (1989), individuals seek environments that are compatible with their genetic make-ups. Performance as well as JS are optimal if an individual's intelligence is in congruence with the level of environmental complexity in general, and job complexity in particular. All biological approaches regard genetic predispositions as crucial determinants of future levels of job complexity. It is noteworthy, however, that in the present study, only crystallized intelligence was a significant predictor of job complexity. Since crystallized intelligence is thought to increase in the course of life, it would be interesting to determine in future longitudinal studies whether the relationship between crystallized intelligence and job complexity would become even stronger during a longer time span.

The *gravitational hypothesis* is one example of a cognitive approach to PE fit. It posits that individuals sort themselves into jobs that are in accordance with their abilities (Wilk, Desmarais, & Sackett, 1995). In an analysis of two large data sets (N = 11,000), and in line with the results of the present study, Wilk et al. (1995) found that cognitive ability was positively related to movement in job hierarchy over a 5-year period. Other cognitive approaches that do account for the finding are *growth needs/higher-order need satisfaction* approaches (Alderfer, 1969; Hackman & Oldham, 1976). This class of theories puts an emphasis on the fulfillment of personal needs and on self-actualization processes by suggesting that highly intelligent individuals have higher growth needs to be fulfilled compared to less intelligent individuals. Therefore, intelligent individuals seek more complex jobs in order to get the opportunity to fulfill their needs and to self-actualize (Lounsbury et al., 2004). The absence of fit between intelligence and job complexity is believed to result in job dissatisfaction and even in occupational mobility in the long run. Future research should be directed toward the investigation of the causal direction between facets of intelligence and job complexity.

4.2 Job complexity and JS

Besides the finding that intelligence is positively related to job complexity, a positive link between job complexity and level of JS was found. This finding is in line with research conducted by Schneider et al. (1982), Fried et al. (2001), Axtell et al. (2002), and Grebner et al. (2003) who all found job complexity to be positively related to JS. Loher, Noe, Moeller and Fitzgerald (1978) conducted a meta-analysis with 28 studies and reported almost the same correlation ($r = .39$) between job complexity and JS than the one found in the present study ($r = .38$). Similar to the intelligence-job complexity relationship, however, the causal paths between job complexity and JS remain uncertain. It can be assumed that occupations characterized by control, responsibility, variety, and ambiguity as indicators of job complexity lead to a higher challenge and hence higher JS, due to a positive worker experience and psychological well-being. According to several researchers (Csikszentmihalyi, 1988; LeFevre, 1988), involvement in complex work signifies work enhancement and results in JS, and even occasionally in a kind of *flow state*. Oldham, Kulik and Stepina (1991) claim that, whilst experiencing a flow state due to working in jobs with a high level of complexity, employees regard their work as highly absorbing, and are able to block out unwanted or negative stimuli. When a flow state is experienced during work, attention is directed only to the positive aspects of work and this in turn results in the experience of JS.

On the other hand, the reverse causal direction also seems logical in that JS leads to a striving for more complex jobs. If JS always resulted in strivings for more complex jobs, though, employees would continuously change occupation. Once a level of JS was reached, they would seek more complex jobs. Since gravitation toward a more complex job is uncommon in case an incumbent is satisfied with the current job, this causal direction seems less likely than the view that job complexity influences the level of JS.

4.3 Intelligence and JS

As already mentioned above, the hypothesized direct effect of intelligence on JS reported by Ganzach (1998) and Lounsbury et al. (2004) could not be replicated in the present sample. The findings of the present study suggest that JS is not a function of intelligence, therefore not innate, and can be changed. It seems as if the ability to deal with complex tasks and problems does not have an influence on the evaluations of the workplace, and therefore no impact on the level of JS. The establishment and maintenance of JS depends on other factors than intelligence. However, it is noteworthy that other researchers found direct relationships between intelligence and JS. A number of methodological and theoretical reasons will be outlined in the following that do account for the differing results.

Diener and Fujita (1995) provide several reasons for the finding that resources do not predict subjective well-being. Intelligence is regarded as a resource, and since subjective well-being is similar to JS, the reasons presented by Diener and Fujita (1995) will be applied to the present findings.

First, habituation to the level of intelligence may play a role. Similar to individuals adapting to their level of resources, it seems logical that individuals adapt to their level of intelligence, and therefore do not experience a higher level of JS than others (Diener & Fujita, 1995). In line with *multiple discrepancy theory* (Michalos, 1985), which states that happiness is only experienced in case that people perceive recent changes in their resources, the perception of a change in the level of any facet of intelligence is unlikely. Therefore, it is reasonable to assume that intelligence is not directly related to JS.

A second explanation is that intelligence alone is not enough to influence the level of JS, but that resources should be summed. This means that not only intelligence but also other dispositional factors such as personality traits and situational variables should be included in the analysis of the determinants of JS.

Third, it is possible that other factors are more important in the establishment of JS than intelligence. As already mentioned earlier, there is generally no consensus in the academic literature on whether or not intelligence directly impacts the level of JS. Previous studies have yielded contradictory results, with many studies failing to find a link between the two concepts (Bogozzi, 1978; Colarelli et al., 1987). Others found that scores obtained by tests of intellectual ability predicted work behavior across a wide variety of jobs, but it did not predict JS.

Six and Felfe (2004) provide a number of methodological factors as a fourth class that do account for the absence of the expected effect. For instance, regarding the investigation of JS, some individuals may tend to give more positive answers due to anxiety for non-anonymous results and hence organizational consequences. Moreover, items may lead to a more positive evaluation in that incumbents tend to forget negative aspects. In addition, all studies used different measures of intelligence and JS. For instance, some studies relied on one-item measures of JS, and in the present study, an 18-item measure of JS was used. All factors may have contributed to the absence of the expected effect.

Besides methodological reasons, cognitive evaluations may play a role. In particular, individuals tend to evaluate the working situation as more positive as it is in order to resolve cognitive dissonance. Further, socialization processes could attribute to the absence of the expected effect. In case employees notice that their needs cannot be fulfilled in their work situation, they may lower their needs and expectations.

4.4 The mediating role of job complexity

In contrast to the results reported by Ganzach (1998), job complexity did not moderate the relationship between intelligence and JS in the present sample but mediated the relationship. Although there is no direct interaction found in the present sample between person and environment, two other processes suggest that both person and environment indirectly affect JS. First, a person seems to determine his or her environment since there is a relationship between intelligence and job complexity. Second, job complexity as one environmental characteristic seems to determine JS as affective state of the person. Evidence for the gravitational hypothesis was found since people obviously hold occupations in which they fit.

Concerning the mediating effect of job complexity on the relationship between intelligence and JS, two distinct processes are likely. On the one hand, it is possible that the relationship between intelligence, job complexity, and JS is a *top-down* process. It can be assumed that JS is influenced by intelligence via job complexity, in that more satisfied persons get more complex jobs and acquire more knowledge due to their high complex jobs. On the other hand, a *bottom-up* process is likely in that intelligence may determine job complexity and this may result in a higher level of JS (Brief, 1998).

All in all, the results of the present study suggest that JS is directly determined by other variables than intelligence. Especially personality traits as determinants of JS have received some research interest during the last decades. For instance, Judge, Heller and Mount (2002) performed a meta-analysis of 163 samples and found that all Big Five personality traits significantly correlated with JS. Future research should therefore focus on the combined influences of intelligence and personality traits on JS.

4.5 Practical implications

A number of practical implications for job selection and HR development can be derived from the present findings. It is interesting to note that a huge number of companies rely solely on measures of general intelligence in job selection processes (Boudreau et al., 2001). Based on the interpretation of the present findings, what can the organization do to establish and increase JS?

In particular, in future job selection processes, not only general intelligence should serve as a measure on which applicant selection is based. In addition to general intelligence, facets of intelligence should be included, and the fit between facets of intelligence and both complexity and requirements of the future job should be determined. By this, under- and over qualification could be avoided.

All in all, the results indicate that intelligence does not have a direct influence on JS and that JS is determined by other variables. One variable that clearly determines the establishment of JS is job complexity. In the present study, job complexity was positively related to JS. Regarding the organization, this finding implicates that the establishment of job complexity should be of particular importance, for instance through *job enrichment* that refers to increased autonomy. In other words, the employee's tendency to seek challenges should be met by giving greater responsibility and autonomy as well as timely feedback on performance. In addition, by means of increased variety, *job enlargement* would contribute to a larger job scope and employee satisfaction (Schneider et al., 1982).

In addition, HR development should put an emphasis on anticipation of changes of JS (Fried et al., 2001). Organizational changes may lead to changes in the level of job complexity and this may result in a mismatch between individual abilities and requirements of the job. For instance, the level of crystallized intelligence changes throughout the life span, and people might habituate to the complexity of the current job. As a result, at any time of their professional career, employees might get bored with previous challenges, overqualified and thus dissatisfied and may look out for a new job in order to find a greater challenge. This line of reasoning reveals the importance of a constant or even increasing level of job complexity since JS is only likely in case those individual abilities match the requirements of the job.

4.6 Limitations of the present study and future research

A number of limitations of the present study need to be addressed. First, the sample of the present study was relatively small, especially when the relationships were compared within forms of occupational training. This could have led to the absence of a direct impact of facets of intelligence on JS as reported by Ganzach (1998) who investigated the relationship in a huge sample (N = 5423). Lounsbury et al. (2004) found significant relationships between intelligence and JS in a sample size comparable to the present study (N = 136). However, he only examined two occupational groups, and thus there were more subjects in any occupational group when the relationships were examined within occupational groups. Finding out whether the effects of facets of intelligence on job complexity and JS are more pronounced in a larger sample with more power would be worthy of more investigation.

Second, in a related vein, the participants of the present study were homogenous with respect to age and were all trainees from one occupational setting. Future research should examine the relationship of individuals varying in age, occupational group and setting.

Third, it was not distinguished between facets of JS such as extrinsic or intrinsic JS. For this reason, future research should be directed towards a combination of the study of Ganzach (1998) who investigated the influence of intelligence on facets of JS and the present study in which the influence of facets of intelligence on JS was examined. It would be interesting to see whether facets of intelligence have differential effects on facets of JS, and whether job complexity has differential influences on facets of JS. In addition, the measure of JS used in the present study was designed for employees that hold their occupation for several years already. Future research should therefore investigate the question whether different results would be obtained if JS was measured by an instrument especially designed for the work situation of young trainees (differentiating between satisfaction with the vocational school and the company; Jungkunz, 1996). Furthermore, no one-item measure of JS was relied on in the present study, whereas all other studies used one-item measures. The finding that no relationship between intelligence and JS was found in the present study could be due to the fact that no one-item measure of JS was used.

Fourth, Stone, Stone and Gueutal (1990) point to the importance of interpreting the results of subjects differing in cognitive ability with caution. They report that participants with a low level of cognitive ability may produce less reliable data than those higher in cognitive ability since they might get frustrated. However, these negative consequences are in particular present with small-item measures. In the present study, a reliable measure of intelligence was used, and therefore, one may assume that the results are probably not distorted.

Finally, some analytical limitations are noteworthy. Since correlational method was used in order to investigate the connection between the concepts, the relationships between the variables but not the causal paths between the three concepts could be determined. In addition, the reliability of the measure of job complexity may be doubted since the reliability coefficient was relatively low. In order to increase confidence in the generalizability of the findings, the present study should be replicated with another measure of job complexity.

Besides the limitations of the present study that need to be overcome in future research, analysis and interpretation of the results shows that there is still a realm of possibilities left open for future research.

First, the present study could be extended to an investigation of the combined influence of personality traits and intelligence on JS. To the author's knowledge, only one study thus far examined the combined influence of personality traits and intelligence on career satisfaction as one aspect of JS (Lounsbury, 2004). No study could be located that examined the combined influence of personality traits and intelligence on JS.

Second, Ahmad (2003) suggests that a number of moderator variables are likely to influence the relationship between intelligence and JS. He investigated the moderating role of group size as an independent and objective measure of the work environment concerning the link between three measures of intelligence, pay satisfaction and JS. He obtained evidence for the moderating effect of group size, and reported a negative relationship between the concepts in smaller groups and a positive relationship in larger groups.

Finally, it would be interesting to examine whether the relationships between the three concepts would change over time. For this reason, longitudinal studies should further explore the influence of facets of intelligence on job complexity and JS.

5. Conclusion

Concluding, the results of the present study indicate that there is no direct relationship between intelligence and JS. Rather, it can be assumed that job complexity meditates the relationship between intelligence and JS. Moreover, evidence was obtained that facets of intelligence are worthy of investigation when examining the influence of intelligence on real-life criteria. In the present study, crystallized intelligence was the only facet of intelligence that was positively related to job complexity. Furthermore, the results of the present study suggest that job complexity has a major influence on JS, indicating that more complex jobs lead to a higher level of JS.

Overall, the present findings indicate that organizations should focus on the assessment of fit between various characteristics of the person such as intelligence and characteristics of the future job, including its complexity. The optimistic message is that the establishment of JS and its numerous positive consequences can actively be carried out by considering intelligence as a determinant of job complexity and job complexity as an antecedent of JS.

The Conger and Kanungo Model of Charismatic Leadership

Jens Rowold and Kathrin Heinitz

The chapter explores the Conger and Kanungo model of charismatic leadership in organizations. First, the theory of charismatic leadership is reviewed. Second, it is explained how Conger and Kanungo developed their model of charismatic leadership. Next, an instrument for the assessment of charismatic leadership is discussed. The Conger and Kanungo Scale (CKS) of charismatic leadership, its development, factor structure, and psychometric properties are presented. Third, empirical results of international research implementing the CKS are reviewed. Next, the model is compared to other approaches to charismatic (e.g., House and Shamir) and transformational (e.g., Bass) leadership. In addition, first results from validation studies that implemented a German translation of the CKS are presented. Finally, the pros and cons of Conger and Kanungo's approach are summarized and evaluated critically. Fields of future research are identified.

1. Theory of charismatic leadership

On a scientific level, charismatic leadership was first explored in the 1920s by German sociologist Max Weber. He emphasized that charismatic leaders address followers' emotional needs and their search for meaning and identity. Also, within Weber's theory of charismatic leadership, it was argued that charismatic leadership works best in times of change or crisis.

Beginning with House (1977), the last quarter of the 20th century saw a revival of charismatic leadership theory, as a group of theories alternatively labeled "new" or "neo-charismatic" leadership theories (Yukl, 1999; Yukl, 2002) evolved. Within transformational leadership theory, one main component of transformational leadership has been charismatic leadership (Bass, 1985). Several of Weber's original ideas found their way into these new leadership theories. Conger and Kanungo's Model of charismatic leadership was explicitly developed in accordance with Weber's theory (Conger & Kanungo, 1988; 1998). However, each new leadership theory had its own conceptualization, process model, and assessment instrument of leadership. Common to these theories was that they addressed the question how leaders can influence followers to make self-sacrifices for the good of the group. Additionally, these theories helped to explain the emotional and symbolic aspects of leadership.

Most of the theoretical literature focused primarily on transformational leadership (cf. below). For an overview, the reader is referred to chapters or books published elsewhere (Antonakis & House, 2002; Avolio & Yammarino, 2002a; Bass, 1998; 1999). However, other conceptualizations of "neo-charismatic" leadership theories might be valuable, but did get less amount of research attention in comparison to transformational leadership. The present chapter discusses the Conger and Kanungo (1998) theory of charismatic leadership and summarizes the theoretical and empirical literature. From the pros and cons of this approach to leadership it is demonstrated how this approach might contribute to our understanding of the leadership phenomenon. Hopefully, this chapter stimulates empirical research that implements the Conger and Kanungo approach to charismatic leadership.

2. Conger and Kanungo's approach to charismatic leadership

Nearly two decades ago, Conger and Kanungo developed their initial model of charismatic leadership (1987; Conger & Kanungo, 1988). In the decade that followed, important contributions were made leading to a revision of their theory (Conger & Kanungo, 1998). Recent research (e.g., Conger, Kanungo, & Menon, 2000) demonstrates that the theory of charismatic leadership - as articulated by Conger and Kanungo - is still alive and in use. In the following paragraphs, we provide with a brief overview of the most recent version of the theory (Conger & Kanungo, 1998).

The Conger and Kanungo theory of charismatic leadership describes leaders' behaviors in organizations. In contrast to many other "neo-charismatic" leadership theories, which focus on leaders' individual level of motivation and followers' outcome, Conger and Kanungo's model focuses on the organizational level. However, similar to other leadership theories, the Conger and Kanungo model describes the leadership phenomenon from a followers' perspective. Charismatic leadership is exerted by leaders and may be described as what roles leaders exhibit at work. That is to say, while other leadership theories focus on, for example, the task or social dimensions of leadership behaviors, the Conger and Kanungo theory was built on the dimension of charismatic leadership behaviors.

Conger and Kanungo (1988; 1998) postulate three temporarily distinct stages of charismatic leadership behaviors. First, leaders evaluate the status quo of their environment. That is, they look for opportunities to improve organizational processes. Leaders assess the resources and constraints of the work-related environment. This is one example for very active behaviors that distinguish charismatic from non-charismatic leaders. Following the evaluation, environmental resources such as technological innovations and constraints such as small budgets are used by charismatic leaders to reform established organizational products and processes. Thus, charismatic leaders often act as entrepreneurs. In addition to the assessment of the environment, followers' needs are carefully evaluated. This aspect of Conger and Kanungo's charismatic leadership theory echoes earlier theoretical developments that emphasized leaders' considerate or follower-centered behaviors (e.g., Stogdill, 1969). In sum, in stage 1, the leader knows what work-related processes might be improvable and what his/her followers need in order to achieve desired goals.

On the basis of information collected in stage 1, the respective leader is able to formulate an inspiring vision of the future in stage 2. Therein, specific environmental resources and constraints as well as followers' interests are accounted for. In addition, the vision may be described as an idealized goal. These kinds of goals are best characterized as highly desirable, based on commonly-shared values, and difficult to achieve. Also, the vision includes a desirable and attainable future state that is highly discrepant from the current status quo. Consequently, the leader communicates this vision in an inspiring way to followers, other organizational members, and outside the organization.

Finally, in stage 3, the leader aims at implementing the vision and motivating followers. Two leadership strategies are included into the Conger and Kanungo model of charismatic leadership for this final stage. First, leaders engage in unconventional behavior that demonstrates the importance of the articulated vision. For example, in order to demonstrate the importance of saving costs in his organization Chrysler CEO Lee A. Iacocca cut his own wages down to one dollar per year. Also, unconventional behavior conveys important goals that are part of the vision and demonstrates means of achieving these goals. In addition to unconventional behavior, the leader takes personal risk in order to motivate followers by personal example. Followers are more likely to believe in the leaders' vision if the leader engages in active, personal risks that demonstrate the importance of desired goals. For example, personal risks are potential financial loss or the potential loss of organizational power or positions. As a consequence of leaders' unconventional behavior and personal risk, the followers buy into the leaders' vision and develop trust and, ultimately, enhanced levels of motivation to achieve articulated goals.

Although Conger and Kanungo (1998) admit that in reality, leaders typically engage in all three stages simultaneously or engage in different stages for different goals at the same time, it is assumed that the three stage model describes the charismatic leadership process theoretically. Table 1 summarizes the stage model of charismatic leadership.

3. The Conger and Kanungo scales of charismatic leadership

From the theory outlined above, Conger and Kanungo developed an instrument to assess aspects of charismatic leadership. From their theory they hypothesized that charismatic leadership was defined as sensitivity to the environment and to member needs (stage 1, cf. above), strategic vision and articulation (stage 2), and personal risk and unconventional behavior (stage 3; cf. Table 1). This process of validating a measure of charismatic leadership was basically a two-step process. In step one, an initial version of the Conger and Kanungo Scale (CKS) of charismatic leadership was developed and tested in two independent studies (1992; Conger & Kanungo, 1994). Twenty-five items were constructed. Results of factor analyses revealed the presence of six factors. In addition to the five factors that were hypothesized by Conger and Kanungo (cf. Table 1), a sixth factor labeled "Does not maintain status quo" was identified.

In their subsequent revision of the instrument, items that showed high cross loadings or redundant item wording were eliminated. A new 20-items scale resulted that was implemented in stage two of the construction process. Several empirical studies (Conger et al., 2000; Conger, Kanungo, Menon, & Mathur, 1997) revealed that these new version of the CKS is a valid and reliable instrument for the five factors hypothesized by Conger and Kanungo (1998). Thus, for the remainder of this chapter, we refer to the five factors of the CKS as the standard model.

Table 1. **Stages of charismatic leadership and scales and sample items for the Conger and Kanungo (1998) scales (CKS) of charismatic leadership**

	Leader behavior				
Stage	Stage 1		Stage 2	Stage 3	
Scale	Sensitivity to the environment	Sensitivity to member needs	Strategic vision and articulation	Personal risk	Unconventional behavior
Items	4	3	7	3	3
Sample item	*"Recognizes the abilities and skills of other members in the organization."*	*"Influences others by developing mutual liking and respect."*	*"Provides inspiring strategic and organizational goals."*	*"Takes high personal risks for the sake of the organization."*	*"Uses non-traditional means to achieve organizational goals."*

4. Empirical research that implemented the CKS

In the following paragraph, empirical research is described that utilized the new version of the Conger and Kanungo Scales of charismatic leadership (CKS). We begin by presenting results for the factorial validity and reliability of the scales. After summarizing convergent, divergent, and criterion-related validity, we close by reviewing the literature concerning the process of charismatic leadership as assessed by the CKS.

4.1 Factorial validity and reliability

In their re-analysis of the Conger and Kanungo (1997) data, Conger and colleagues (1998) implemented confirmatory factor analyses to test the five-factor model of the CKS. The empirical results clearly support the five-factor model in comparison to an absolute null-model and a one-factor model of charismatic leadership. An additional study (Conger et al., 1998; study 1) tested the factorial validity of the CKS with a sample of N = 103 managers. Again, the five-factor model explained the data best.

Across studies, the five-factor model of charismatic leadership is also supported by the relatively low intercorrelations of the CKS-scales. In their summary of empirical results, Conger and Kanungo (1998) provide intercorrelations of the five CKS scales between r = .02 (p > .10) and r = .43 (p < .001). These results demonstrate that the scales of the CKS assess overlapping constructs only to a minor degree. In sum, confirmatory factor analyses and intercorrelation analyses provided evidence for a five-factor model of charismatic leadership. Despite the fact that subscales of CKS rely on only three to seven items, satisfactory levels of internal consistency estimates (Cronbach's alpha) have been reported in the literature across studies. Finally, empirical evidence supports the test-retest reliability of the five subscales of charismatic leadership (Conger & Kanungo, 1994).

4.2 Convergent and discriminant validity

In their initial empirical study, Conger and Kanungo (1992) found significant positive relationships between Bass' conceptualization of charisma (cf. below) and the CKS scales (.27 < r < .50). This supports the convergent validity of the CKS scales. These results were replicated by Conger and colleagues (1997; - .10 < r < .38; study 1). In study 3 of the Conger and colleagues (1997) paper, results of multi-trait multi-method analysis were interpreted as demonstrating divergent validity to Bass' (Bass, 1985) conception of charisma. However, the relatively high intercorrelation between the two conceptions of charisma (.51 < r < .72) show that the two conceptualizations are neither completely distinct nor overlapping.

In two independent studies, it was clearly demonstrated that in general, facets of charismatic leadership as assessed by the CKS are distinct from earlier approaches to leadership such as task-oriented (- .20 < r < .13) and people-oriented (.03 < r < .14) leadership (Conger & Kanungo, 1994; Conger et al., 1997). These studies also demonstrated convergent validity as task-oriented leadership was positively associated with the CKS subscale of sensitivity to the environment (.39 < r < .58) and people-oriented leadership correlated with sensitivity to members' needs (.68 < r < .75).

In order to further scrutinize convergent and discriminant validity, the CKS was implemented along with the Managerial Practice Survey (Yukl, 1988) in an empirical study (Conger et al., 1997; study 2). As expected, the results provided further evidence for the convergent and discriminant validity of the CKS. For example, strategic vision and articulation was positively associated with the MPS subscale of inspiring. As for discriminant validity, the CKS subscales of personal risk and unconventional behavior were not related to any of the MPS subscales.

In an interesting empirical study, Conger and colleagues explored whether the CKS can be utilized to distinguish charismatic versus non-charismatic politicians (Conger et al., 1997; study 2). With the exception of the unconventional behavior subscale, all CKS subscales successfully differentiated between the two types of politicians who had been classified as either charismatic or non-charismatic by experts.

4.3 Criterion-related validity

The first empirical evidence for criterion-related validity of the CKS was provided by Deluga (1995). Drawing on a sample from $N = 63$ leader-led dyads employed in a manufacturing firm, this study demonstrated that charismatic leadership was positively related to four aspects of organizational citizenship behaviors (i.e., conscientiousness, civic virtue, courtesy, and altruism). These relationships hold true while controlling for the influence of in-role performance.

In their recent study, Conger and colleagues (2000) showed that charismatic leadership (as assessed by the CKS) was related to several outcome criteria of the leadership process. Charismatic leadership showed significant relationships to followers' reverence, trust, and satisfaction, as well as to collective identity, group performance and empowerment. In sum, research provided support for the criteria-related validity of the CKS, as assessed by subjective indicators.

4.4 Process of charismatic leadership

Little empirical research exists that sheds light on the process of charismatic leadership. One open question is, for example, under what conditions charismatic leadership emerges. In an experimental study, Halverson, Murphy, and Riggio, (2004) explored the role of crisis in the emergence of charismatic leaders. Results showed that in stressful situations leaders were perceived as significantly more charismatic than leaders in the no-stress condition.

With regard to the study by Conger et al. (2000) mentioned above, it was found that reverence mediated the relationship between charismatic leadership and outcome variables (followers' trust and satisfaction). Moreover, collective identity and perceptions of group performance mediated the impact of charismatic leadership on empowerment. These results reveal details about the charismatic leadership process and have important implications for both researchers and practitioners.

5. Comparison to other approaches of charismatic leadership

5.1 Bass and Avolio's theory of transformational leadership

The idea that leadership behaviors can be categorized into either transformational or transactional has first been articulated by the political scientist James

MacGregor Burns (1978). Within transformational leadership, leaders emphasize development of higher motive, and arouse followers' motivation and positive emotions by creating and representing an inspiring vision of the future (Bass, 1997). In contrast, transactional leadership relies simply on a set of clearly defined exchanges between leader and follower.

Over the last twenty years, Bass and his colleagues (Bass, 1985; 1999) have made considerable effort to define and assess the aspects of transformational and transactional leadership. In order to develop what has been called "full range of leadership" behaviors, several aspects of transformational and transactional leadership were included in the standard instrument for measurement of transformational leadership, the Multifactor Leadership Questionnaire (MLQ-5X; Bass & Avolio, 2000). In its current form, the full range leadership theory represents nine leadership factors comprised of five transformational leadership factors, three transactional leadership factors, and one nonleadership or laissez-faire leadership factor (Antonakis, Avolio, & Sivasubramaniam, 2003; Avolio & Bass, 2004; Bass & Avolio, 2000; Rowold, 2005). What follows is a brief description of these factors.

5.1.1 Dimensions of transformational, transactional, and nonleadership behaviors

The first transformational scale is called *Inspirational Motivation*. Central to this subscale of transformational leadership is the articulation and representation of a vision. Consequently, being encouraged to view the future with a positive attitude, followers are motivated. *Idealized Influence-attributed* refers to the attribution of the leader's charisma. Because of the leader's positive attributes (e.g., perceived power, focusing on higher-order ideals, values), followers develop close emotional ties to their leader. Trust and confidence are likely to develop in the followers. *Idealized Influence-behavior* emphasizes a collective sense of mission and values, as well as acting upon these values. Next, *Intellectual Stimulation* includes challenging the assumptions of followers' beliefs, their analysis of problems, and solutions they generate to solve these problems. *Individualized Consideration* is defined as considering the followers' individual needs and developing their individual strengths.

As for the transactional leadership scales, *Contingent Reward* is a leadership behavior, where the leader focuses on clearly defined tasks, while providing followers with rewards (material or psychological) for the fulfillment of these tasks. In *Active Management-by-Exception*, the leader watches and actively searches for deviations from rules and standards in order to avoid these deviations; if necessary, corrective actions are taken. In contrast, in *Management-by-Exception Passive* intervention only occurs **after** errors have been detected or if standards have not been met. An even more passive approach is *Laissez-Faire*, which is basically defined as the absence of leadership. As such, laissez-faire is considered as a nonleadership behavior contrasting the more active forms of transformational and transactional leadership.

Several meta-analyses provide evidence for the criterion-related validity of transformational leadership (Dumdum, Lowe, & Avolio, 2002; Judge & Piccolo, 2004). The well-documented effect of transformational leadership on outcome criteria is one of the reasons why this leadership paradigm gains most of the current attention from scholars. For example, a literature research (PsycINFO; February 2006) for the terms "MLQ" and "transformational leadership" resulted in 67 and 583 hits, respectively. In contrast, the terms "Conger & Kanungo Scale" and "charismatic leadership" yielded 4 and 197 hits, respectively. These numbers might be interpreted as a relative high research activity in the field of transformational leadership, over and above charismatic leadership. Yukl (2002) compares these two leadership approaches by stating that:

> "... Attributed charisma and personal identification are more central to the charisma theory [...] whereas the essence of transformational leadership appears to be inspiring, developing, and empowering followers. [...] Thus, the essential influence processes for transformational leadership may not be entirely compatible with the essential influence process for charismatic leadership, which involves dependence on an extraordinary leader." (p. 260).

The differences between charismatic and transformational leadership has been further acknowledged by other researchers as well. For example, Barbuto (1997) provides an analysis of the two constructs. He describes charisma as a social process during which followers identify with the leader, whereas the transformational leader relies on inspiring followers to pursue organizational goals and transcendent their self-interests. Consequently, Barbuto (1997) advocates a theoretical and empirical distinction between charismatic and transformational leadership.

In both the theoretical and the empirical literature, the terms charismatic and transformational leadership are often used interchangeably. The instruments used to assess these constructs add to the confusion about the underlying meaning of transformational and charismatic leadership. As an example, the Multifactor Leadership Questionnaire (MLQ-5X; Bass & Avolio, 2000), which is used to assess transformational leadership, includes five subscales of transformational leadership. Of these five, three subscales were combined to one factor called charisma in earlier versions of the instrument (Bass, 1985). In turn, the empirical leadership literature uses the terms transformational and charismatic leadership inconsistently and interchangeably. In the following paragraphs, we compare and contrast the theories of charismatic and transformational leadership by discussing similarities and differences between the instruments that assess both constructs, namely the CKS and the MLQ.

5.1.2 Comparison of MLQ and CKS

As the theories underlying the MLQ and CKS both belong to what has been labeled "neo-charismatic" leadership theories (Antonakis & House, 2002), basic similarities between these two theories are discussed first.

Similarities. Fundamental to the theories from Bass (1985) and Conger and Kanungo (1998) is the representation and articulation of a vision. As a long-term attempt to change followers' attitudes, self-concepts (Shamir, House, & Arthur, 1993), and motivations, this vision is rooted in commonly-held ethics and values (Bass & Steidlmeier, 1999). The ethical foundation of a vision is fundamental to both Bass' and Conger and Kanungo's theories. Thus, they focus on socialized as opposed to personalized charisma (Howell & Avolio, 1992). Socialized charismatic leaders use their abilities to achieve benefits for all followers, not just for their own benefit.

A second similarity concerns the fact that both transformational and charismatic leaders are agents of change. In addition to the formulation of a vision, strong emotional ties between the leader and the led are a necessary condition in order to change their followers' belief systems and attitudes. Emotions such as pride and feelings such as trust are important for change processes. In addition, if the leader represents a trustworthy model and a code of conduct, transformation occurs more easily. As a consequence of the leaders' charismatic qualities and behaviors, followers identify with the leader. In turn, values and performance standards are more likely to be adapted by followers. Finally, as a third similarity, transformational and charismatic leaders foster performance beyond expectations (Avolio & Yammarino, 2002b).

These similarities between the theories proposed by Bass (1985) and by Conger and Kanungo (1998) highlight the fact that they share a basic assumption (cf. Antonakis & House, 2002). However, several important differences between these approaches to leadership assessment are clearly evident, as will be discussed in turn.

Differences. The main difference between the MLQ and CKS is that they are based on their own respective definition of charismatic/transformational leadership. As a consequence, these measures include different sets of leadership scales. Central to the theory of Bass (1985) is the distinction between transactional and transformational leadership. Over the last two decades, empirical research yielded in several subscales for the assessment of these two multi-faceted constructs (cf. above). In contrast to the MLQ, the CKS does not include scales for the assessment of transactional or nonleadership behavior.

While the MLQ assesses leadership behavior at a single point in time, the CKS views leadership as a process over time. Thus, one of the major differences between the two theories is their respective time frame. In order to assess genuine charismatic leadership behavior, Conger and Kanungo (1998; Conger et al., 2000) developed a model of charismatic leadership which focuses on three distinct stages of the leadership process (cf. Table 1).

Looking at these definitions of the contents of transformational (MLQ; cf. above) and charismatic (CKS) leadership, additional similarities can be noted. In both the MLQ scale intellectual stimulation and the CKS scale sensitivity to environment, the leader questions the status quo and seeks out new ways to solve problems. Furthermore, articulating a vision and inspiring followers are contents of the MLQ scale inspirational motivation as well as the CKS scale strategic vision and articulation. Thirdly, understanding and evaluating the needs of followers is a subject of both the MLQ individualized consideration and the CKS sensitivity to member needs scales. Looking at these similarities, the question arises as to what extent transformational and charismatic leadership influence subordinate performance differentially. Certain subscales, such as the CKS scales personal risk and unconventional behavior, seem to be unique. All in all, one can say from looking at the descriptions of the MLQ and CKS, that the two instruments do cover different but also similar facets of leadership behavior (cf. Antonakis & House, 2002).

5.1.3 Simultaneous impact of charismatic and transformational leadership on outcome criteria

The similarities and differences between charismatic (CKS) and transformational (MLQ) leadership might lead practitioners to the question which leadership style explains more variance in outcome criteria. For example, should management training be based on the charismatic or on the transformational leadership paradigm? Along the same line of thought, should manager selection be based on a certain theory of the leadership process?

In an empirical study, Rowold & Heinitz (2007) tested the rivaling influence of charismatic (CKS; Rowold, 2004a) and transformational (MLQ; Rowold, 2004b; 2005) leadership on several outcome criteria. Drawing on an organizational sample, it was found that the two constructs were highly convergent (.88 < r < .93). Both constructs explained unique variance in subjective criteria such as followers' satisfaction, over and above that of the respective other leadership style. However, only transformational leadership was significantly related to objective criteria (profit). These results underline the idea that the selection of theories that are to guide subsequent leader selection and development depend on the desired outcome criteria.

5.2 Other approaches to transformational leadership

Recent theoretical and empirical research aimed at developing additional instruments for the assessment of transformational leadership (Felfe, 2002; cf. Felfe, Tartler, & Liepmann, 2004). From a critique of the MLQ, Podsakoff and colleagues developed the Transformational Leadership Questionnaire (TLI), which was validated in several empirical studies (MacKenzie, Podsakoff, & Rich, 2004; Podsakoff, MacKenzie, Moorman, & Fetter, 1990; Podsakoff, MacKenzie, & Bommer, 1996). Although the TLI does not assess charismatic leadership explicitly, several subscales closely resemble constructs central to charismatic leadership, such as articulating a vision and providing an appropriate model. Additional research demonstrated high intercorrelations between transformational subscales of the TLI and the MLQ (Heinitz & Rowold, 2007).

Implementing a grounded theory approach, Alimo-Metcalfe and colleagues developed the Transformational Leadership Questionnaire (TLQ; Alban-Metcalfe & Alimo-Metcalfe, 2000; Alimo-Metcalfe & Alban-Metcalfe, 2001). According to these authors, transformational leadership includes a set of leaders' characteristics as well as leaders' behaviors. Altogether, nine subscales of the TLQ assess these characteristics and behaviors. Alimo-Metcalfe et al. (2001) explain the more differentiated and extended set of subscales of transformational leadership with culture- (United Kingdom) and context- (public services; health services) specific factors that guided their theoretical and empirical research. Comparing the TLQ with the Conger and Kanungo approach to charismatic leaderships reveals a certain degree of overlap between facets of transformational leadership (TLQ) and constructs that have been hypothesized to be central to charismatic leadership (CKS). For example, the TLQ-subscale vision could be easily assigned to the CKS subscale strategic vision and articulation (cf. Table 1). Nevertheless, while some aspects of transformational leadership, as assessed by TLI and TLQ, seem to be rooted in conceptualizations of charisma, these two instruments are valuable developments of transformational leadership theory.

5.3 House and Shamir's theory of charismatic leadership

One of the most elaborated theories of charismatic leadership is the theory that was developed by House and Shamir (House, 1977; Shamir et al., 1993). It postulates that leaders' behavior has an effect on subordinates' self-concepts. This process is mediated by motivational mechanisms. Charismatic leaders transform followers' self-concepts by increasing their self-esteem, self worth, and self-efficacy. As a consequence, followers identify with the leader on an individual and on a social level (Shamir et al., 1993).

While some of these theoretical ideas are in line with Conger and Kanungo's assumptions about the process of charismatic leadership, several differences should be noted. First, stage 1 of the Conger and Kanungo model of charismatic leadership (i.e., sensitivity to the environment and sensitivity to members needs) are not included in House and Shamir's approach. Second, while Conger and Kanungo proposed a stage model of charismatic leadership that focuses on leaders' behaviors and strategies, House and Shamir are interested in psychological variables (e.g., motivation, self-efficacy) of both the leader and the led that explain the working mechanisms of charismatic leadership. Only limited empirical support was found for the House and Shamir theory of charismatic leadership (Shamir, Zakay, Breinin, & Popper, 1998).

In their discussion of rivaling leadership theories, Conger and Kanungo (1998) conclude that all charismatic leadership theories include some form of empowerment strategies. Leaders utilize these empowerment strategies in order to accomplish goals and/or visions. In addition, the different theories overlap with respect to assumed influence processes. Charismatic leaders exert their influence over followers in order to change their self-concepts and core attitudes.

6. Psychometric properties of a German version of the Conger and Kanungo scales of charismatic leadership

Introduction and study goals The psychometric properties of the CKS have been evaluated in a number of empirical studies (cf. above). These studies support the validity and reliability of the CKS. However, for several reasons, it seems valuable to translate the CKS into additional languages and assess the respective psychometric properties. First, cross-cultural research relies on instruments that have been validated in several languages (Den Hartog, House, Hanges, & Ruiz-Quintanilla, 1999; Hunt & Peterson, 1997). Second, practitioners and researches from non-North American countries are interested in applying the concept of charismatic leadership and rely on validated instruments for the assessment of these constructs. Thus, an effort was made to translate the CKS into the German language in order to make the Conger and Kanungo approach to charismatic leadership available to both researchers and practitioners.

Method and translation The Conger and Kanungo Scales (CKS; Conger & Kanungo, 1998) were carefully translated from English to German by a professional and then back translated by an English native speaker, both experts in the field of organizational psychology (Behling & Law, 2000). As the comparison of both English versions of the CKS yielded virtually no differences, the German version was deemed appropriate for the purpose of this study. For each of the CKS items, participants rated the frequency of leaders' behavior on a 5-point rating scale (1 = *never*, 5 = *always*).

Sample and Procedure The study was conducted in a public transportation company in Germany. From a total of N = 298 supervisors in the company, 220 participants responded (i.e., response rate = 73.8%). The mean age of the participants was 40 years (SD = 7.1); 73% were male. All of the 220 supervisors worked in one of the companies' 45 hierarchically nested branches. At least two supervisors reported to their respective leader in these branches.

Results and Discussion For the assessment of the factorial validity, confirmatory factor analysis (CFA) is an appropriate method. CFA of the German version of the CKS was performed ($N = 220$) and yielded a $\chi^2_{220}= 482.28$ (p = .000). Comparison to the null model yielded a Tucker-Lewis index (TLI) of .975, a comparative fit index (CFI) of .980, and a RMSEA of .077. Thus, the empirical data showed a reasonable fit to the proposed five-factor model. Moreover, these results exceed the results reported by Conger et al. (1997).

As for reliability, Cronbach's alpha coefficients were .87 (strategic vision and articulation), .83 (sensitivity to the environment), .88 (sensitivity to member needs), .73 (personal risk), and .83 (unconventional behavior), respectively. The reliability of the combined measure of charismatic leadership is very good (α = .94).

In sum, these results seem to be a justification for the use of the German version of the CKS (Rowold, 2004a). However, additional research needs to provide evidence for a) convergent and divergent validity as well as b) criterion-related validity.

7. Discussion and implications for future research

In this final section, we review the theoretical and empirical literature briefly presented above from a wider perspective. Following this discussion, several implications for future research are presented. In sum, this section provides with a critical evaluation of the pros and cons of the Conger and Kanungo model of charismatic leadership.

Advantages of the Conger and Kanungo approach In their effort to develop a theory of charismatic leadership, Conger and Kanungo (1988; 1998) draw on earlier theory development by the German sociologist Max Weber. Over more than a decade, Conger and Kanungo carefully developed a process theory of charismatic leadership. Three stages of the charismatic leadership are described and propositions for research were developed. The Conger and Kanungo Scales of charismatic leadership provide researchers and practitioners with a tool for the assessment of five subscales of the tripartite charismatic leadership process. Empirical research demonstrated that these scales have adequate psychometric properties. In contrast to other approaches to charismatic and transformational leadership, the Conger and Kanungo model includes the subscales of personal risk and unconventional behavior. Several research studies demonstrated that these subscales are most distinct to other facets of charismatic or transformational leadership. Thus, discussions about a "full range of leadership behaviors" (Antonakis & House, 2002; Avolio & Bass, 2002) should turn their attention to the Conger and Kanungo model in order to arrive at a more complete set of leadership behaviors. In contrast, other subscales of the CKS demonstrated highly convergent validity of instruments of transformational leadership.

Considerable effort by different researchers resulted in strong support for the five-factor structure of the CKS. Thus, the model of charismatic leadership that was articulated by Conger and Kanungo (1998) relies on a valid tool for assessment.

Disadvantages of the Conger and Kanungo approach Despite the claim that their model of charismatic leadership describes a three-stage process, Conger and Kanungo did not provide evidence for this longitudinal sequence of leadership. Empirical research drawing upon observations or self-assessment should be able to demonstrate that for single projects, missions, or tasks, leaders follow the three-stage process as articulated by Conger and Kanungo. Because the sequence of facets of charismatic leadership is central to Conger and Kanungo's theory, empirical validation of this part of the theory is urgently needed.

In comparison to other leadership theories, the Conger and Kanungo model of charismatic leadership needs to be tested with a stronger emphasis on outcome criteria of charismatic leadership. While several meta-analyses demonstrate the criterion-related validity of transformational leadership, no such analyses have been conducted for charismatic leadership as assessed by CKS. Especially, objective indicators should be used. Indicators that could be used are branch-level performance on the individual (leader's) level and outcome criteria such as profit on the organizational level. In sum, including objective performance indicators in future research will complement subjective performance indicators such as followers' satisfaction that have been used in prior research.

Implications for future research In addition to the more urgent call for research that was articulated in the prior paragraph, the following points express ideas for future research that will lead to a more differentiated picture of the leadership process.

First, it seems desirable to compare and contrast Conger and Kanungo's approach to charismatic leadership with other conceptions of leadership. As each theory relies on a different approach to the assessment of its components, it would be interesting to learn more about the potential overlap of these theories. Therefore, research focusing on the convergent and divergent validity of rivaling charismatic leadership research will lead to a more complete picture of the scope of charismatic leadership behaviors (cf. Yukl, 1999). As a result, the concept of charismatic leadership in organizations will be clarified.

Second, it seems plausible to assume that contextual conditions moderate the relationship between charismatic leadership and outcome criteria such as followers' motivation and organizational profit. For example, Alimo Metcalfe and Alban-Metcalfe (Alban-Metcalfe & Alimo-Metcalfe, 2000; Alimo-Metcalfe & Alban-Metcalfe, 2001) were able to demonstrate that in the case of transformational leadership, facets of these constructs differ between profit (i.e., industries) and non-profit (i.e., government agencies) contexts. In the same line of thought, it might be speculated that charismatic leadership in different contexts might rely on different components in order to be effective.

Additional recent calls for research (Judge, 2005) emphasize the need for comparing leadership theories with each other. For example, to which degree is charismatic leadership and the "initiation structure and consideration" approach redundant? Does one leadership style mediate the effects of other styles on followers? It is interesting to observe that in the past decades, several streams of leadership research existed independently from each other. From both a practical and a theoretical point of view, it seems desirable to learn about the empirical overlap between these theories. While Rowold and Heinitz (2007) made a first attempt to compare and contrast charismatic and transformational leadership, these leadership styles should be compared to LMX (Graen & Uhl-Bien, 1995), consideration and initiating structure (Seltzer & Bass, 1990), and path-goal theory (House, 2004), for example.

An additional field for future research is training of charismatic leadership. While the recent study by Frese, Beimel, and Schoenborn (2003) demonstrates that several core aspects of charismatic leadership (e.g., rhetoric skills) are trainable, additional research is needed to demonstrate which facets of Conger and Kanungo's theory - or other theories of charismatic leadership - are trainable. This field of research is especially relevant for practitioners.

The here expressed ideas highlight the fact that many potential fields of investigation exist. In general, more research is needed that implements the Conger and Kanungo Scales of charismatic leadership and relates these scales to prerequisites, correlates, and outcomes of the charismatic leadership process.

Implicit Leadership Theories:
Theory, Research, and Application

Jan Schilling

1. The concept of implicit leadership theories

Since the pioneering study three decades ago by Eden and Leviatan (1975), a growing stream of leadership research is concerned with the study of implicit leadership theories (Schyns & Meindl, 2005). Eden and Leviatan (1975) – and in a replication study Adler and Weiss (1981) – were able to show that if people are asked to describe the leadership behaviour of an imaginary person, they produce behavioural ratings that are quite similar to those of real leader descriptions (i.e. an identical factor structure). The implication is that questionnaire-based descriptions of leadership behaviour might only partially capture actual behaviour. While the majority of leadership studies still focuses on behaviour and behavioural styles (Brown, Scott, & Lewis, 2004), the concept of implicit leadership theories (ILTs) now plays an important role in understanding the underlying processes that cause behaviour by influencing perceptions and evaluations in leader-member interactions. Implicit theories can be defined as complex cognitive structures containing the beliefs held by individuals or collectives about the traits and behaviour typical of leaders, the causes for these traits and behaviours as well as about their consequences. By means of such "naïve" models people try to explain and predict their own behaviour and that of others and derive their action strategies. In German literature (Laucken, 1974) a distinction is made between trait- and process-oriented implicit theories. With regard to ILTs this would mean to distinguish between implicit leader theories and implicit theories of leading. In this sense, people not only have ideas about prototypical leader traits but also cognitive maps (e.g. Fiol & Huff, 1992) on causal relations in the leadership process (i.e. scripts: Foti, 1983). Concluding, implicit leadership theories can be seen as important cognitive constructions of perceivers that help them make sense of social situations (House, 1997).

In the aftermath of Eden & Leviatan (1975) and the critical evaluation of the status of leadership as a scientific concept by Calder (1977) and Pfeffer (1977), Robert Lord and his associates (e.g. Lord, Foti & De Vader, 1984; Lord & Maher, 1991; Phillips & Lord, 1986) developed the theoretical foundation for the concept based on cognitive categorization theory (Rosch, 1978). The basic idea is that perceivers (e.g. followers) classify stimulus persons (e.g. their supervisors) by comparing them to prototypes of a category (e.g. effective leader). Maurer and Lord (1991) made clear that this leader categorization is not dependent on cognitive resources of the person. Lord and his colleagues (Lord, 1985; Lord et al., 1984; Lord, Foti & Phillips, 1982) point out that implicit leadership theories reflect a cognitive category or schema in human memory, hierarchically organized in three levels. The levels of leader categories are superordinate (leader vs. non-leader), basic (different types of leaders: business, religious, political), and subordinate (different person types of leaders). Prototypical leader characteristics with a high family similarity (i.e. typical for many different basic leader categories) are for instance "intelligent", "honest", "understanding", "verbally skilled", "determined", "decisive", and "dedicated". The presentation of prototypical leader behaviour also has a positive impact on the attributed responsibility of a leader for organizational success (Lord et al., 1984). Smith and Foti (1998) stress that prototypes involve patterns of traits: the pattern of high general self-efficacy, high dominance, and high intelligence is strongly associated with leadership emergence. Once someone is labelled as a leader, perceivers find it difficult to distinguish between observed and unobserved behaviour which is prototypical of leadership (Lord & Emrich, 2001). Besides these spontaneous recognition-based processes (i.e. recognizing individuals as leaders based on their fit with leadership prototypes), leadership perceptions are also formed by deliberate and controlled inferences (Lord & Maher, 1991). Effective or favourable leadership of an individual is inferred from favourable outcomes, resulting in higher ratings concerning the classical leadership dimensions of initiating structure and consideration. These ratings do not represent (in case even contradict) a leader's actual behaviour, but reveal more about the rater's implicit assumptions and concepts on leadership (e.g. Bryman, 1987; Larson, 1982; Mitchell, Larsen, & Green, 1977; Rush, Thomas, & Lord, 1977). This "performance cue effect" can be explained in terms of a simplified summary evaluation of leadership that intervenes between performance cues and behavioural ratings. Rush, Phillips, and Lord (1981) found impressive support for this explanation: by partialling to a one item general leadership rating, they eliminated the performance cue effect on the behavioural ratings. It is important to note that the effect is dependent on the perception that a leader's behaviour reflects personal qualities (internal attribution) rather than being situationally induced (external attribution). Following Konst, Vonk, and Van der Vlist (1999), Shultz (1994) and Singer (1990), this view is rather common among academics and practitioners: students and professionals (followers and leaders) place more importance on internal-dispositional determinants of effective leadership than on external-situational factors. Brown et al. (2004) state that the performance cue is a robust effect (a) which is equally potent, regardless whether the performance information is presented before or after viewing the leader, (b) influences ratings even in case of personal interaction with the group, and (c) affects global ratings of leadership more than ratings of specific behaviour. Nevertheless, this general tendency can be suppressed. Murphy and Jones (1993) show that inferred leadership based on performance only occurs, if subjects are instructed and/or manipulated to focus on the person (e.g. by different camera angles in a video presentation or different instructions: salience of leadership; Phillips & Lord, 1981). While leadership categorization theory originally conceptualized the leader category as rather stable and fixed, recent developments have put forth the idea of ILTs as flexible and fluid knowledge structures (Brown et al., 2004). Lord, Brown, Harvey, and Hall (2001) propose a connectionist network model which explains the existence of different images for different targets by introducing the idea of contextual constraints. Four types of constraints (values and norms of the societal culture; goals, affect, and norms of the leader; values and goals of the follower; affect and goals of the current task) as well as actual leader behaviour form the basis of leadership schemes. Perceivers simultaneously integrate a multitude of internal (e.g. identification with the own team; Hogg, 2001) and external sources of information (e.g. cultural values) to generate a contextually appropriate leader prototype.

Extending the view of implicit theories to the level of organizations, Meindl (e.g. Meindl, 1990, 1995; Meindl, Ehrlich, & Dukerich, 1985) points out that the concept of leadership has a prominent status in organizational sensemaking. Most people share the view that leadership is central for explaining organizational events and effectiveness. Meindl speaks of a romantic, larger-than-life conception that he terms "romance of leadership". Individual differences with regard to this personal disposition can be measured by the romance of leadership scale (RLS: Meindl & Ehrlich, 1988; for the German version: see Schyns, Meindl und Croon, 2004). Interestingly, high RLS scores go along with an internal locus of control orientation (Meindl, 1990). Therefore, a speculation by Pfeffer (1977, p. 109) concerning the causes of this romantic bias finds indirect support: it "may derive partially from the desire to believe in the effectiveness and importance of individual action, since individual action is more controllable than contextual variables". Also, high RLS scores are associated with the tendency to perceive more charisma in highly public leaders (Meindl, 1995). In a series of archival studies Meindl et al. (1985) found that the academic and popular interest in leadership seems to rise when social systems (i.e. enterprises or societies) face extreme highs or lows concerning their performance (e.g. productivity or employment rate). Their experimental evidence shows that leadership attributions for the explanation of organizational outcomes are also linked to extreme results (positive or negative). This cognitive relationship between extreme results and leadership inference seems to work both ways. Meindl and Ehrlich (1987) found that subjects evaluated the performance of a fictitious firm to be more positive when the case material pointed to leadership as the main cause for this performance (rather than other factors like governmental regulations, employees or market situation). This is especially astonishing as the actual performance data were the same for all experimental conditions.

2. Functions of implicit leadership theories

Implicit leadership theories can serve a variety of functions. Based on their conceptions, individuals make sense of experiences (diagnosis), explain (explanation), predict events and behaviour (prognosis), and derive action strategies (technology) (Schilling, 2001). Besides these rational functions, ILTs are also used to maintain one's self-esteem, to legitimate actions taken (self-presentation), and to preserve the impression of control in complex and ambiguous situations (Hewstone, 1983). For followers, these functions might imply

- to attribute success to themselves and failure to their leader. In case that they strongly identify with their leader, success might be attributed to their leader and failure to other causes like chance or inefficient organizational policies.
- to present their actions in ways they assume suits their bosses' expectations or preferences. Their implicit leadership theories will guide them especially in case the actual preferences and expectations of their leaders are rather unknown (e.g. in case they have a new leader).
- to see organizational events as caused by their leader's action rather than by impersonal forces like market situation or technological developments (Pfeffer, 1977).

In contrast, leaders will mainly attribute success to internal and failures to external factors, present their actions in ways they assume is appropriate for or typical of a ("good" or "effective") leader, and tend to emphasize their personal contribution to organizational success. Interestingly, the goals of maintaining self-esteem and the illusion of control at the same time conflict with each other in case of failure. While a leader does not want to be associated with negative events (externalizing blame), it is not always beneficial to deny one's accountability. This might encourage perceptions that the leader is not in control of the situation and – in the worst case – leads to the perception of a chronic deficiency in one's ability to effectively harness the potential control implied by one's position (Meindl, 1990). The so called "Teflon effect" describes the phenomenon when blame for bad events never sticks to a person (McElroy, 1991). To achieve this perception and at the same time maintain the illusion of control is therefore easier said than done. As these "irrational" functions of ILTs are often more important than having "realistic" conceptions of leadership, it is not surprising that implicit theories are difficult to change and resist empirical falsification.

3. Development and perseverance of implicit leadership theories

Generally, the following four processes form the basis for the generation and development of knowledge structures (Genser, 1978; Sarbin, Taft, and Bailey, 1960): direct experience (reinforcement and punishment), vicarious learning (behaviour modelling), instruction by authorities (instrumental compliance, personal identification, or internalization), and inferences based on existing implicit theories (deduction). In one of very few empirical studies concerning the development of ILTs, Keller (1999) found several instances where the perception of subjects concerning their own personality and the personalities of their parents predicted their ILTs. People who rated themselves higher on agreeableness, dedication, and extraversion scored higher on the ILT dimensions sensitivity, dedication, and charisma. If they described their parents (especially the father) as high in dedication and tyranny, the subjects showed high scores for these dimensions in their ILTs (i.e. dedication and tyranny were seen as prototypical traits of leaders). Therefore, individuals not only characterize ideal leaders as similar to themselves. Their idealized leadership images also mirror descriptions of parental traits. Matthews, Lord, and Walker (1990) tested the hypothesis that leadership perceptions would shift with increasing age from being based on specific exemplars (e.g. parents, teacher) or observable characteristics (i.e. actions, outcomes) to abstract prototypes. By analyzing children's statements regarding their conceptions of what it means to be a leader, they found support for this hypothesis. Relative to older children (i.e. 6th, 9th, 12th grades) younger children (i.e. first and third grades) base their leadership judgements more on specific actions, outcomes, and persons.

Nevertheless, implicit theories do not necessarily develop and differentiate over time. Anderson and Lindsay (1998) describe three classes of processes by which naïve or implicit theories can survive empirical disconfirmation:

1. Illusory correlations: This describes the case when people perceive a relationship between two variables when in fact there is none.

2. Data distortions: These are instances in which the perceiver mentally or behaviourally changes the data being used to assess the validity of the implicit theory.

3. Availability heuristic: Implicit theories directly and indirectly influence the availability of particular elements/arguments and thereby distort the judgment on the appropriateness of the implicit theory itself.

As these mechanisms have been mainly described and studied for naïve or implicit theories in general, it seems especially interesting to look at their implications for implicit leadership theories. Illusory correlations can be based on numerical distinctiveness, associative links, and self-generated data (Anderson & Lindsay, 1998). Numerical distinctiveness means that it is easier to remember undesirable behaviour of members of a minority because both types of information stand out due to their relative infrequency. For ILTs, this could mean that women (who are a minority in leadership positions) would be associated with negative behaviour or traits to a higher degree. This is especially true as leaders are typically associated with positive traits and behaviour (Lord et al., 1984). Chapman and Chapman (1969) were able to show that subjects' frequency estimates tend to be based on a priori associations rather than the actual number of stimulus presentations. Therefore, it can be assumed that being exposed to different leaders does not necessarily alter or differentiate implicit leadership theories (Epitropaki & Martin, 2004). Finally, it could be shown (Slusher & Anderson, 1987) that people tend to fill in missing information with stereotype congruent default values. By this means, they unconsciously confirm their own convictions as they show great difficulties distinguishing between facts and self-generated fiction. This is consistent with the finding of Lord and Emrich (2001) that perceivers cannot easily distinguish between observed and unobserved behaviour that is prototypical of leadership. Therefore, it seems likely that there is no need for a leader to show the full behaviour pattern (e.g. idealized influence, individual consideration, intellectual stimulation, inspirational motivation in the case of transformational leadership) constituent of a specific leadership style, so that showing certain salient behaviour (e.g. articulating a vision for one's organization) is sufficient to be rated as a (e.g. transformational) leader. The distortion of data can be a consequence of behavioural or mental operations. Snyder, Tanke, and Berscheid (1977) were able to show that people elicit expectation-congruent behaviour of their interaction partner with their own actions and thereby confirm their prior implicit theories.

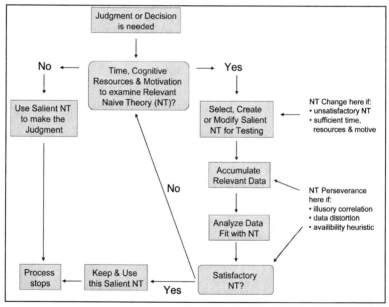

Figure 1. **The process of the development, perseverance, and change of implicit theories (Anderson & Lindsay, 1998)**

For the leadership context this means that leaders and followers are likely to provoke the expected behaviour of their counterpart based on their ILTs which become self-fulfilling prophecies, a phenomenon early described by McGregor (1960) in his conceptions of Theory X and Y. Mental operations which distort data include biased attributions that lead to memory intrusions, biases based on outcome knowledge, the devaluation of contradictory data, and biases in the perceived covariation strength of variables (Anderson & Lindsay, 1998). Finally, the high mental availability of confirming instances, supportive arguments, and causal scenarios related to one's implicit theories are also likely to prevent ILTs from being revised and changed on the basis of new and contradictory experiences. All of these mechanisms are particularly relevant in the context of performance evaluations either by leaders or by followers. A comprehensive overview of the process of activation, change and perseverance of implicit theories is presented in Figure 1.

First empirical support for the consistency of ILTs over time was presented by Epitropaki and Martin (2004) who tested for alpha (i.e. change in the strength of agreement concerning the prototypicality of leader traits), beta (i.e. change in the respondents' metric in the form of stretching or shrinking in the measurement scale), and gamma change (i.e. change in the definition of what a prototypical leader is like) in ILTs after a period of one year. Even a manager change did not influence the subjects' ILTs.

4. Structure and content of implicit leadership theories

One line of interest in the research on ILTs resulted in a critical questioning and testing of the validity of questionnaire research on leader behaviour (Eden & Leviatan, 1975; Phillips & Lord, 1986; Rush, Thomas & Lord, 1977; Adler & Weiss, 1981). It could be shown that behaviour ratings from followers (a common practice in leadership research) might be prone to biases based on implicit leadership theories. The other, more extensively studied line of research focuses on the structure and content of implicit leadership theories. With these and other results as a starting point, Offermann, Kennedy & Wirtz (1994) studied the content of ILTs in a very comprehensive approach. Different samples of students and employees generated and rated traits associated with (business) leaders, resulting in the eight dimensions of sensitivity, dedication, tyranny, charisma, attractiveness, masculinity, intelligence, and strength. Based on these foundations, considerable progress has been made concerning our knowledge on ILTs in the last decade. Martin & Epitropaki (2001) and Epitropaki & Martin (2004) continued and advanced the work of Offermann et al. (1994) by investigating their item pool and reducing the ILT-questionnaire to a 21-item scale with a slightly different factor structure: sensitivity, intelligence, dedication, dynamism, tyranny, and masculinity. Their findings also indicate a factorial invariance of ILTs across different groups of age, organizational position and time (see above), thus supporting the idea of the general leader category as a rather context-free schema. In another line of research, specific subtypes of the leader category have been investigated. Kenney and his colleagues (Kenney, Blascovich & Shaver, 1994; Kenney, Schwartz-Kenney & Blascovich, 1996) examined (in the sense of Lord's three-level model) the subordinate leader categories "new leaders" and "leaders worthy of influence". Gardner and Avolio (1998) introduce the "charismatic leader" as a subtype of the general leader prototype that is reserved for those leaders who engage in visionary behaviour. While research on content and structure of ILTs has gained some attention, only very few studies have examined the importance of implicit leadership theories for leadership processes. Engle and Lord (1997) found that ILT congruence between leaders and followers did not predict subordinate liking and leader-member exchange (LMX), while congruence of implicit performance theories (IPTs) did. Thus, high quality exchange forms around dyads that define good performance, but not necessarily good leadership similarly (Lord & Emrich, 2001). Nye and Forsyth (1991) report higher ratings of leader effectiveness (particularly of males) for leaders who matched the prototype of the perceivers whereas the attribution of responsibility to the leader is not influenced (Nye, 2002). Prototype-based biases concerning leader collegiality were only noted for female targets. The importance of a prototype-leader-match is also supported by a longitudinal study of Epitropaki and Martin (2005): the closer the fit between personal ILT and perceived manager's personality, the better the quality of LMX. Indirect effects on employee attitudes and well-being could also be confirmed.

As Brown et al. (2004) point out, compared to subordinate focused research the attention towards understanding leader's knowledge structures and content has been scant. Sims and Lorenzi (1992) present a qualitative study on prototypical traits of managers producing excellent or poor results. These lists include a wide variety of different personal attributes like personality traits (e.g. „introverted"), motives (e.g. „willing to take responsibility"), skills/abilities (e.g. „intelligent/knowledgeable") as well as leadership behaviour (e.g. „good at training and developing subordinates"). The high number of items that are part of the prototype and the anti-prototype of leadership brings up the question if the leader anti-prototype is really a distinct cognitive category or merely the mirror of the leader prototype. Similar to the open approach of Sims and Lorenzi, Bresnen (1995) presents an interview study with leaders from the construction industry concerning their implicit leadership theories. Despite all variety in their perceptions of leadership, the leaders draw heavily on the traditional leadership concepts of initiating structure, consideration, and participation. Participants place considerable emphasis on one key idea or image to develop their explanatory framework for leadership. The similarities between the leaders included the idea of different leadership styles that have to be applied with regard to the leader's situation (especially the kind of followers he or she has). In accordance with the studies of Konst et al. (1999) and Singer (1990), the behaviour of a leader is mainly internally attributed to individual characteristics like temperament, personality, natural ability, and experience. Bresnen stresses that the statements of his participants do not represent academic knowledge: „managers referred to exemplars and/or created their own vignettes to illustrate and catalogue the perceived benefits of certain ‚leader behavior'" (p. 505).

Schilling (2001) investigated the content and structure of personal conceptions on leadership of managers in a telecommunications company. Nonmetrical multidimensional scaling (nMDS) was used to analyze the coincidences of different leadership categories in the statements of the participants. The two-dimensional solution explains 55% of the variance (RSQ = .55) and received a

Kruskal-stress value of .27. The stress value is an indicator for the goodness of fit in multidimensional scaling. Following Fahrmeir, Hamerle & Tutz (1996), this result can be considered as a moderately successful scaling of the dissimilarity between the categories. The configuration of the categories concerning the first dimension shows a clear partition between task-related leadership behaviour on the left and follower-related behaviour on the right side. The second dimension differentiates between aspects of leadership that necessarily include participation (like „delegating", „developing & mentoring", „teambuilding & conflict management") or cooperation of followers („recognizing/criticizing", „consulting", „monitoring", „supporting", „clarifying roles & objectives") on the one hand and aspects that stress the leader as a rather autonomous actor on the other („planning & organizing", „problem solving", „motivating & inspiring", „rewarding/ punishing", „informing", „networking") (see Figure 2). These results complement those of Eden and Leviatan (1975) and Weiss and Adler (1981) in that respect as very similar dimensions of ILTs can be found by using a qualitative approach to analyze leadership conceptions.

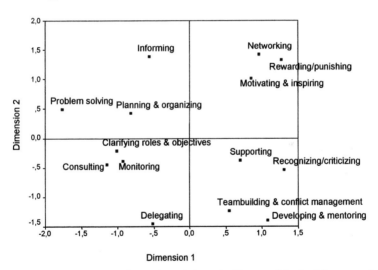

Figure 2. **Two-dimensional configuration of the coincidences of leadership categories (Schilling, 2001)**

While the studies of Sims and Lorenzi (1992), Bresnen (1995) and Schilling (2001) are descriptive in nature, Wofford and his colleagues (Wofford and Goodwin, 1994; Wofford, Goodwin, & Whittington, 1998) have undertaken the endeavour to link leader's cognitive structures and behaviour. Schemas and scripts were investigated by open-ended questions given to a sample of managers. The answers were analyzed for statements representing transformational and transactional leadership (Bass & Riggio, 2006). Leader behaviour was measured by MLQ ratings of the managers' subordinates.

The results show a clear relationship between managers' schemas and followers' ratings concerning transformational and transactional leadership respectively. Likewise, Lin and Shih (1997) find a positive correlation between leaders' ILTs (leader-based rather than contingency-based views of leadership) and followers' ratings of initiating structure. Different studies (Connelly, Gilbert, Zaccaro, Threfall, Marks, & Mumford, 2000; Day & Lord, 1992; Mumford, Marks, Connelly, Zaccaro, & Reiter-Palmon, 2000) find support for the notion that leaders with better and more broadly developed leadership schemas and scripts should perform more effectively than those with poor leader knowledge bases (Hoojiberg & Schneider, 2001). Thereby, the presented studies provide empirical support for the assumption that effective behaviour regulation is dependent on the accessibility of appropriate leadership scripts and schemas. This stresses the point that leaders' ILTs are not just personal opinions or attitudes with little importance for follower and leader behaviour, but form important sources for perception, evaluation, and action.

5. Context of implicit leadership theories

By introducing the idea of contextual constraints, Lord et al. (2001) reflect the growing amount of literature concerning the influence of environmental factors on the activation of ILTs. The different aspects of context described by Lord et al. (2001) will be used to describe the state of empirical research in this area.

National, professional and organizational culture: There has been some work on cultural differences und similarities in implicit leadership theories (e.g. Chong & Thomas, 1997; Gerstner & Day, 1994). In a groundbreaking international study (the GLOBE project) Den Hartog, House, Hanges, Ruiz-Quantanilla, Dorfman and associates (1999) studied the content of ILTs in 60 different countries. As the main result the authors show that managers from different countries had in part very similar ideas about leader attributes (contributing or inhibiting outstanding leadership). Several traits reflecting charismatic/ transformational leadership are thought to contribute to outstanding leadership across different cultures (e.g. motive arouser, foresight, encouraging, communicative, trustworthy, and dynamic). In an attempt to create a culture-specific scale for Chinese implicit leadership theories Ling, Chia, and Fang (2000) employed an open-ended approach to collect typical leader characteristics which were tested afterwards with a different sample of Chinese employees. Factor analysis yielded four factors of leadership that did not correspond with Western research (e.g. Offermann et al., 1994) and were interpreted as personal morality, goal efficiency, interpersonal competence, and versatility. The authors point to the problem, that cross-cultural research on ILTs has to be sensitive to specific societal cultures and is always in danger of misleadingly transferring culture-specific models and instruments. Konrad (2000) compared Eastern and Western European managers with regard to their ILTs. While the rank order of prototypical leadership characteristics is very similar for both samples, Western managers place greater value on inspirational leadership. Eastern managers expect outstanding leaders to be more administratively competent. Western managers are also "more convinced that being self-centred, autocratic, non-participative, and a face-saver would impede effective leadership" (p. 343). Likewise, professional or organizational cultures seem to influence the content of ILTs. Konrad and Kranjcek (1997) found differences between students and managers concerning their task vs. relationship orientation: to qualify as an outstanding leader, students place more importance on relationship, managers on task orientation. Pillai and Meindl (1998) discovered that followers perceive more charisma in their leaders when their work units are characterized by an organic structure and a collectivist corporate culture.

Characteristics of the leader An important source of leadership categorization stems from physical appearance. Cherulnik, Turns, and Wilderman (1990) found that student leaders receive higher ratings on attractiveness and facial maturity than nonleaders. Interestingly, the authors chose real student leaders and nonleaders (based on information from their yearbook) while the participants were not informed about the respective status of the different targets. Cherulnik (1995, p. 293) showed "that subjects that were judged more maturefaced and attractive also report greater confidence in their social skills and more extensive past experience as leaders". These results are in line with research on gender differences concerning leadership perceptions. People (male and female) with more masculine characteristics (i.e. appearance and clothes) receive higher ratings on leadership skills (Rennenkampff, Kühnen, & Sczesny, 2003). However, research on perception differences between male and female leaders consistently shows that people perceive a stronger overlap between characteristics of managers and men than between managers and women (Schyns & Meindl, 2005). This effect was termed the "think-manager-think-male" phenomenon (Schein, 1973) and was replicated for different cultures (Schein & Mueller, 1992; Schein, Mueller, Lituchy, & Liu, 1996). As more and more women are entering middle and top management positions, it can be speculated that the leader category is changing. Empirical support concerning this hypothesis is mixed. While Schein (2001) and Sczesny (2003) found evidence of a more androgynous view of leadership (especially held by female perceivers), Powell, Butterfield, and Parent (2002) come to the conclusion that the image of a successful leader is still close to the male stereotype.

Characteristics of the follower Not only the gender of the target person, but also that of the perceivers influences leadership perceptions. To describe leaders men use more instrumental, women more expressive traits (Graves and Powell, 1982). Also, women consistently attach more importance to all determinants of leadership: being an effective leader requires both appropriate personal traits (i.e. personality traits, intelligence, and competence) and a favourable working environment (i.e. subordinate control, organizational characteristics, and factors beyond control) (Singer, 1990). Shultz (1994) found that men with a rather negative view of women as managers rate male leaders' success as based on internal causes more than that of female leaders. On the contrary, women with a positive image of female managers rate female leaders' failure as based on external factors more than that of male leaders. In line with the results of Keller (1999) (see above), Felfe (2005) presents evidence for the influence of personality traits on people's romantic conceptions of leadership. While occupational self-efficacy, self-esteem, extraversion, conscientiousness, and dominance are positively related, neuroticism is negatively linked to romance of leadership. A positive correlation between need for leadership and romance of leadership exists for people with low self-esteem. The results indicate that leadership perceptions are formed on the basis of a similarity to the self-concept. Besides internal variables, social influences are assumed to influence ILTs. In his social contagion view, Meindl (1990, 1995) stresses the importance of group membership (between-group factor) and status within a group (within-group factor) as determinants of the dispersion of leadership constructions. Groups with high-density networks and high group cohesion should be more homogenous in their ILTs than groups with low-density networks and low cohesion. Deviant views of leadership within a group should be more likely for "followers who are at the sociometric fringes of the group" (Meindl, 1995, p. 337). First empirical support for these hypotheses was presented by Pastor (1998). Finally, Martin and Epitropaki (2001) found evidence that low organizational identification leads to systematic biases in the judgment of followers concerning their leader's actual behaviour based on their ideal leader prototype.

Current task and leadership behaviour Emrich (1999) found that people perceive more leader qualities when the group of the potential leader is a troubled one rather than a tranquil one. This complements the results on the performance cue effect in such a way that negative events in the group (in terms of negative results and/or negative social relations) damage the reputation of the incumbent leader (e.g. Pillai & Meindl, 1998), but may create a romanticized picture of the potential leader. These results are in line with other studies that point to the importance of crises to enhance perceivers' attributions of leadership to target persons (Brown et al., 2004). Enduring hardship in the sense of giving up something important (sacrificing) seems to be a behaviour that is likely to provoke perceptions of charisma and internal attributions of leader behaviour that result in greater influence on followers (Yorges, Weiss, & Strickland, 1999).

While the presented studies were mainly directed at context effects on the perception of followers and/or perceivers of leadership, there is also empirical evidence for context effects on leaders' scripts and schemas. The perceived ability and motivation of followers leads to the activation of different cognitive structures. Wofford, Joplin, & Comforth (1996) found that leaders apply more directive leadership scripts in case of leading a group with difficulties to fulfil an assigned task, especially when the group members were believed to be low in motivation and ability. As Goodwin, Wofford, & Boyd (2000) were able to show, transactional leadership scripts are dependent on low performance, while transformational leadership conceptions are activated by high performance information concerning one's followers. The results are in line with earlier studies by Neubauer (1982, 1986) who found different strategies of leaders for employees performing as expected and not as expected respectively. Followers performing as expected are granted with more freedom for own decisions, participation and responsibility, as well as a close, personal relationship. Followers performing below expectation are restrained to inferior tasks, excluded from personal contacts to the leader, and will be reminded of the power distance between leader and follower. The qualitative studies of Stewart (2002) and Elke, Neumann, and Schuld (1990) stress the importance of the respective managerial position and branch in which the leader is working for the activation of different leadership conceptions. Following Stewart (2002), IT managers are more focused on developing teams which are skilled and work autonomously, while business executives stress the importance of articulating a vision for their followers. Elke et al. (1990) report a higher tendency of leaders in technologically innovative branches to refer to task-related than to follower-related problems when asked about leadership. While managers from classical branches attribute poor performance to stable traits, managers from innovative branches rather refer to a lack of knowledge and learning.

6. Implications of implicit leadership theories in different fields of practice

In this final section the implications of the presented theory and research for different fields of application will be discussed (employee surveys, personnel selection, performance evaluation, leadership training and development). Many employee surveys in organizations include ratings on leadership. The research on ILTs has shown impressively that the ratings in such questionnaires do not necessarily represent the leader's actual behaviour, but might be biased by implicit assumptions on leadership (e.g. Bryman, 1987; Larson, 1982; Mitchell, Larsen, & Green, 1977; Rush, Thomas, & Lord, 1977). Rush and Russell (1988) demonstrate that there is a tendency for individuals with similar prototypes of leadership to describe leader behaviour of their (different) supervisors in a similar fashion. It could also be shown that reliability (i.e. internal consistency) and behavioural accuracy are inversely related (i.e. if a specific behaviour was shown or not shown by a target person) (Phillips & Lord, 1982). Therefore, Phillips and Lord (1986) are highly sceptical of the appropriateness in defining accuracy by reliability (i.e. internal consistency) or replicated factor structure. They distinguish behavioural from classification accuracy which refers to the ability of a measure to adequately classify or categorize a person. The question at hand concerns the level of accuracy necessary for organizational practise. While certain purposes (e.g. assessing the effects of behavioural training for leaders) necessitate behaviour-level accuracy, Phillips and Lord (1986, p.35) state that classification accuracy may suffice "for identifying leadership problems, assessing subordinates' reactions to their superiors, allocating rewards for leadership, or identifying potential leaders". With respect to the use of leadership ratings in organizations, this statement is in some respect problematic. The screening of general leadership quality can be an important tool in human resource management. It might be helpful to get a rough impression of followers' opinions on the general quality of leadership (e.g. effective/ineffective) and thereby identify departments or groups with leadership problems. However, in many cases employees' ratings are used as part of 360° feedback systems (Schyns & Meindl, 2005). By definition, constructive feedback should be behaviourally accurate to inform the leader about his strengths and weaknesses in regard to the interaction with his followers. For reasons of personnel selection, the rough classification of leader vs. non-leader might also suffice for a first screening of potential leaders. Nevertheless, the typical use of assessment centres (the predominant approach for identifying leader potential) implies feedback for the candidates so that they can develop their leadership behaviour. Also, it has been stressed that "segmenting the environment into leader/nonleader categories, which emphasize traitlike personal qualities while underemphasizing situational factors may lead to erroneous selection decisions" (Lord, Foti, & Phillips, 1982, p. 117). This might result in a tendency to fill leader positions rather with leaders without knowledge of the specific branch than with branch experts without leadership experience: a rather common practice especially for higher level positions in politics and business. Therefore, classification-level accuracy of leadership measurement might result in suboptimal leadership succession practices. In the same sense, rewards for leadership are often coupled with guidelines for concrete leader behaviour. In performance evaluations, superiors have to rate their subordinate leaders with regard to their achievement on these behavioural guidelines. If the measurement is not able to distinguish between different kinds of leadership behaviour, the rewards will be distributed based on general perceptions of leadership without achieving the implementation of a specific leadership culture. Therefore, it seems necessary to develop ideas on how to improve leadership measurement in applied settings. Different suggestions have been made concerning this matter:

- Subordinates, raters in assessment centres and supervisors of leaders could be trained to minimize biases (Schyns & Meindl, 2005) by teaching them the nature and operation of implicit theories (Larson, 1982) and using confirmatory and disconformatory strategies (i.e. look for leader behaviour inconsistent with salient features and overall classification). However, Baltes & Parker (2000) found that performance cue effects are difficult to eliminate by means of conventional rater training. With regard to performance appraisals, raters could also be instructed to use external storage media (e.g. diaries) (Lord, 1985).
- The questionnaires should be changed so that raters are required to provide more specific behavioural information (Larson, 1982) or using in-

structions that lead to script- rather than person-based schema activation (Foti, 1983; Lord, 1985).

– Finally, one could try to statistically correct for the tendency to integrate information of actual behaviour and personal ILTs into a unified whole by partialling out a global leadership rating or a measure of rater leniency (Phillips & Lord, 1986). This should be done with caution as correcting for rater biases may remove true behavioural variance as well as error variance (Lord, 1985).

Besides training raters, research on ILTs also has implications for leadership training and development. Epitropaki and Martin (2005) underline the importance of increasing leaders' awareness of their subordinates' ILTs to get a clearer understanding of the expectations of their followers concerning leadership. Therefore, survey results on ILTs could be used in formal training arrangements as a starting point to discuss leadership behaviour and effectiveness. The findings of Eden and his colleagues (Eden, Geller, Gewirtz, Gordon-Terner, Inbar, Liberman, Pass, Salomon-Segev & Shalit, 2000) concerning the impact of the "Pygmalion leader training" should also be noted. They could show that supervisors' beliefs concerning the leadership potential of subordinate leaders dramatically influenced followers' performance. Together with the results of Wofford and colleagues as well as of Neubauer (see above) on the behavioural impact of different scripts and schemas, it becomes obvious that leader training might greatly profit from the development and implementation of new training methods concerned with the change or activation of productive leader schemas and scripts. The magnitude of changes in ILTs that can be achieved by training should be regarded with caution. Anderson and Lindsay (1998) have convincingly argued that different processes work to preserve personal belief systems. A third line of implications for leader training and development should be mentioned which is concerned with the training of impression management. Leary (1989) points to the importance of public images for effectively exercising leadership. Being perceived as an effective leader or a leader worthy of influence (Kenney, Schwartz-Kenney & Blascovich, 1996) will effect the amount of influence one can exercise (Lord, 1985; Yorges, Weiss, & Strickland, 1999). One important aspect in this regard concerns implicit reasoning on control and responsibility for positive and negative events. The described "Teflon effect" (Meindl, 1990) implies that leaders are not blamed for failure, but – in the best case – made responsible for success. Based on examples from political leadership, McElroy (1991) develops different strategies (proactive and reactive) to manage this attribution process of perceivers. However, there is also some empirical evidence for effective attribution management. Tiedens (2000) was able to show that overt emotional impressions influence perceivers' sensemaking for a negative event. While showing anger leads to more external attributions of an event and therefore a more favourable view on the leader, sadness is associated with internal factors and thereby personal responsibility for failure. It might be criticized that training leaders in such tactics of impression management (e.g.

Turnley & Bolino, 2001) will result in manipulative approaches to present one-self as a competent leader (in the worst case without actual groundwork) to achieve personal benefits (e.g. promotion). This must not necessarily be the case as leaders are also in the role of being a spokesman for their group or department. Therefore, it is important for them to convey an appropriate public image for the benefit of themselves *and* their followers.

Leadership Training and Coaching

Jens Radstaak and Jens Rowold

The terms "leadership training", "leadership development" or "management training" have been used interchangeably in both scientific (Yukl, 2002) and practitioner (Noe & Colquitt, 2002) literature. All of them have one purpose in common: Supporting individuals to perform effectively in managerial roles (Baldwin & Padgett, 1993). The importance of training in organizations has increased over the past decades. Rapid changes in the environment of organizations such as the global economy, the increasing pace of technological development and fierce competitions produce new challenges for leaders (Kahn, 1990). Thus, offering effective leadership trainings that help leaders to enhance their skills and adapt to changing environments and both external and internal conditions is an important business for training professionals.

The term "coaching" embraces at least as many concepts and approaches as the term "leadership training" (Kampa-Kokesch & Anderson, 2001; Rauen, 2003). Coaching was regarded as a development oriented leadership style in the 70s, whereas leaders were considered as coaches for their employees in the 80s (Thomas, 1998).Thereafter, coaching gained an increasing acceptance and was used in different settings of leadership development. Today, it can be divided into team and individual coaching (Lippmann, 2005). Typical for most forms of coaching is the one-on-one setting of the coaching intervention. Usually, the coach is an external agent who helps individual leaders with their specific, work-related problems. However, one recent trend is that issues such as e.g. work-life balance are also the content of organizational coaching interventions. In contrast to training interventions, the content of the individual coaching sessions is typically not fixed until the first session. In general, training programs are designed to address the needs of groups of people while coaching sessions address needs of individual persons (Graham, Wedman, & Garvin-Kester, 1994).

In addition to managerial coaching, there are many other forms of coaching, for example, in educational settings such as schools or in the field of sports (Hudson, Miller, Salzberg & Morgan, 1994). In sum, coaching and training are important interventions in organizations that improve the performance of an individual or a team.

1. Different approaches to leadership training

Leadership trainings can be viewed from different perspectives. We first turn our attention to different target groups of leadership training. Next, elements of effective trainings are reviewed. Third, main theories of leadership as well as their respective approaches to leadership training are summarized.

Target Group Most leadership trainings are designed in order to improve skills of lower- and middle-level managers (Rothwell & Kazanas, 1994). In contrast, other trainings aim at the qualification of participants for a higher position (Rosenstiel, Nerdinger, Spieß & Stengel, 1989). Some leadership trainings were especially designed for women (Domsch & Regnet, 1990). In sum, the variety of managerial trainings has increased over the last twenty years.

Elements of effective training Due to many different leadership approaches, a huge amount of methods and designs of leadership trainings were established (Noe & Colquitt, 2002). Yukl (2002) demonstrated seven factors that support the learning process in successful training programs.

First, before starting the training, participants should have clear learning objectives. They should be informed about the purpose of the training and the expectations concerning behavior, skills and knowledge. Optimally, this information is provided by supervisors.

Second, the training content should be clear and meaningful. On the one hand, it should build on participants' prior knowledge. The under- or overestimation of trainees' knowledge leads to less effective learning results. On the other hand, the training content should focus only on important issues and should be well structured. Illustrating summaries and learning goals during the training adds to its effectiveness.

Third, a well designed sequence of training contents is at least as important as the content itself. Prior to practical exercises, the underlying theoretical concepts of these exercises should be introduced. Complex material should be separated into subunits in order to maintain the interest of the participants. Repeated practice as well as intermissions help avoiding fatigue during the training sessions.

Fourth, the appliance of different training methods instead of only one method (e.g. lecturing) arouses interest in the trainees and thus helps them to focus on the content. As a result, the use of several methods ensures a higher level of learning transfer - provided that the methods are appropriate for the respective training conditions and settings. For example, a brain storming exercise in a heterogeneous class would be inappropriate if some participants were too shy to open up to the group.

Fifth, one rule of thumb says that an opportunity for active practice should always be given. Theoretical knowledge should be complemented by practical implementation, because new information will be processed deeper if practical exercises are accomplished. If special skills are trained or behavior is practiced under training circumstances it is more likely that the new information will be implemented in job situations.

Sixth, feedback to training participants also represents an important part of effective training. In different situations, feedback from different sources should be implemented. First, the trainer should reflect the participant's performance and suggest improvements. Second, the other participants should comment the respective behavior. Additionally, the possibility of self-criticism should be given. These different sources of feedback are included into '360-degree feedback' which can be considered as very effective (Luthans & Peterson, 2003).

Finally, the transfer of the training content back to the workplace describes the most important part of a training program. The main goal of an effective training should be the remembrance of the learned information and the implementation of the training content in real life working situations. Follow-up activities such as post-training meetings in smaller groups support a successful transfer as well as a training diary with clear, timed instructions.

Different leadership theories and their trainings A short overview of the most common leadership training approaches and their underlying theories will now be presented.

Yukl and Van Fleet (1992) summarized five different leadership trainings that were based on their own respective leadership theory. The classification of these theories followed the five main approaches to leadership: the "traits and skills", the "behavioral", the "power and influence", the "situational" and the "transformational and charismatic" approach (cf. Yukl, 2002).

The "traits and skills" approach tries to explain leadership behavior as a function of constructs like intelligence or personality traits. In addition, motives are also taken into account (e. g., self-regulation). Thus, trainings based on these theories aim at improving personality traits that are related to managerial effectiveness.

The behavioral approach analyses how executives deal with their tasks at work. The "work-activity-research" (Luthans, Hodgetts & Rosenkrantz, 1988) tries to identify managerial competencies that are critical to success. Behavioral trainings like the training of interpersonal competencies (e.g. communication), time management, team development and performance appraisal are typical examples of this approach.

The "power and influence" approach focuses on the leader-member exchange (Graen & Uhl-Bien, 1995). It describes the quality of the dyadic leader-led relationship. Empirical research underlines that this relationship predicts important organizational outcomes such as job satisfaction and performance (Gerstner & Day, 1997). Trainings based on the "power and influence" approach aim at improving the relationship between the leader and his/her subordinate with the help of behavioral elements.

The situational approach emphasizes the importance of contextual factors that influence leadership processes. Basic situational variables are a) work complexity (e.g. high vs. low complexity), b) type of organization (e.g. public vs. private organizations) and c) the characteristics of the followers (e.g. homogenous vs. heterogeneous skill levels). The contingency theory of leadership (Fiedler, 1967) assumes that leader behaviors have to fit into the respective situation in order to be effective. Thus, a desired leadership style can only be defined as a function of situational variables. Another important leadership model of the situational approach is the normative decision model (Vroom & Yetton, 1973). It suggests that the effectiveness of a decision procedure depends on the respective situation. The quality of a decision and the decision acceptance by the subordinates is regarded as a function of the way the leader comes to a decision in a respective situation. Vroom and Yetton developed decision trainings in order to improve individuals' leadership skills.

The fifth approach to leadership is the transformational (Bass, 1985) or charismatic (Conger & Kanungo, 1988) theory of leadership. Some theorists treat these two types of leadership as essentially equivalent, whereas other theorists view them as distinct but overlapping approaches (Yukl, 2002; cf. chapter X, this volume; Rowold & Heinitz, 2006). We first describe charismatic leadership before we move on to transformational leadership.

Weber's work (1972) strongly influenced the concept of charisma. According to his theory, charismatic leaders are most effective in times of social crisis. Some potential leader emerges with a radical vision that offers a solution to the crisis. Followers believe in the leader's vision and, consequently, become attracted to the leader. Therefore, the leader experiences success that makes the vision appear attainable and the followers finally perceive the leader as extraordinary. Recent research by Conger and Kanungo (1998) applied some of Weber's ideas to today's organizations and developed a new version of this theory in order to describe charismatic leadership in organizations.

Like in charismatic leadership, transformational leadership relies on the formulation and articulation of a vision. However, over the last 25 years, theory of transformational leadership was expanded and contrasted with transactional leadership (Bass, 1985). While transactional leaders rely on a straightforward clearly defined exchange relationship (i.e., contingent reward), transformational leaders utilize several behaviors that motivate followers to perform beyond expectations.

Transformational leadership is one component of the "full range leadership theory" (FRLT) developed by Avolio and Bass (1994). In sum, the FRLT consists of three categories of leadership styles: transformational leadership, transactional leadership and laissez-faire or nonleadership. Table 1 shows nine factors that form the basis for the three types of leadership described within the FRLT.

"Within transformational leadership, the followers feel trust, admiration, loyalty, and respect toward the leader, and they are motivated to do more than they are originally expected to do." (Yukl, 2002 p. 253). Many research studies have been conducted in the field of transformational leadership (Yammarino & Bass, 1990; Yammarino & Bass, 1990; Seltzer & Bass, 1990; Podsakoff, MacKenzie & Bommer, 1996). Meta-analysis provided evidence for the effectiveness and utility of transformational leadership (Judge & Piccolo, 2004; Dumdum, Lowe & Avolio, 2002). For example, it was demonstrated that transformational leadership was positively related to job performance, over and above the influence of transactional and nonleadership. While we know a great deal about the relationship between transformational leadership and outcome criteria, there have been very few investigations on the training of transformational leadership.

Table 1. **The nine leadership factors of the full range leadership theory (Bass & Avolio, 1999)**

Leadership style	Definition
Laissez-faire	Indicates the absence of leadership, or the avoidance of intervention.
Transactional Leadership	
Management by Exception – Passive	Maintains the status quo. Generally, the modes of reinforcement are correction, criticism, negative feedback, and negative contingent reinforcement, rather than the positive reinforcement used with Constructive Transactional leadership.
Management by Exception – Active	Generally associated with an active monitoring for mistakes that arise or could arise.
Contingent Reward	Involves a leader-led interaction that emphasizes an exchange of what is expected by the leader for what is desired by the follower. May also involve a clarification of roles and responsibilities.
Transformational Leadership	
Idealized Influence	The leader is viewed as a respected role model, is authentic, trustworthy and highly credible.
Inspirational Motivation	An inspirationally motivating leader provides meaning and simplifies complex ideas and problems.
Intellectual Stimulation	Encourages followers to question their old way of doing things, work procedures and procedures or to break with the past.
Individualized Consideration	Followers are treated differently but equitably on a one-to-one basis. Emphasis is on developing people to higher levels of potential.

2. Training transformational leadership

Although several approaches to transformational leadership training exist, empirical research evaluating the effectiveness of these trainings is rare. Table 2 lists and summarizes the empirical studies that have been conducted.

Table 2. **Transformational and charismatic leadership training evaluation studies**

Evaluation study	Sample and training methods
Frese, Beimel, & Schoenborn (2003): Action training for charismatic leadership: Two evaluations of studies of a commercial training module on inspirational communication of a vision	Sample: 47 midlevel managers Improving communication skills in managers Methods: two day training including role play of a speech, mental modeling, feedback
Dvir, Eden, Avolio, & Shamir (2002): Impact of transformational leadership on follower development and performance: A field experiment	Sample: 320 Israel army leaders Methods: three day leadership training including goal setting, role play, group discussions, simulations, presentations, video cases and peer and trainer feedback
Barling, Weber, & Kelloway (1996): Effects of transformational leadership training on attitudinal and financial outcome	Sample: 20 bank managers Methods: one day group-based training program including, goal setting, role play plus individual booster sessions
Towler (2003) Effects of charismatic influence training on attitudes, behavior, and performance	Sample: 48 business school students Methods: 2,5 hrs training including behavioral modeling, role play with feedback and instruction on charismatic communication styles

These empirical studies provided evidence for the notion that training in transformational and charismatic leadership yields enhanced leadership skills or behaviors and, ultimately, enhanced levels of performance. However, given the complexity of the training process and the variety of potential training methods and potential groups of trainees, more research is needed.

Bruce Avolio, one of the most active researcher in the field of transformational leadership, utilized the above described full range leadership theory for the development of a leadership training. This training is well documented (Bass & Avolio, 2005) and has been applied in many organizations worldwide for more than twenty years (Avolio, 1999).

Prior to the training, trainees participate in an internet-based 360°-feedback which results in a detailed description of their individual leadership behaviors strengths and weaknesses. Within the training, training elements like role play, peer feedback, goal setting and behavior modeling are utilized to overcome trainees' individual weaknesses.

Given the strong relationship between transformational leadership and performance, empirical studies that evaluate leadership training as described by Bass and Avolio (2000) in different cultural contexts seem desirable. However, a necessary precondition to these non-north American studies is the translation of training manuals and materials. In order to meet scientific standards of evaluation, our efforts yielded a German translation of both manual and materials such as the 360°-Feedback system. In the present, we offer full range leadership trainings to organizations and evaluate these trainings. Moreover, in order to further enhance the effect of these trainings, we combine these trainings with team coaching. Before we describe the specific coaching method that was combined with the full range leadership training, we provide with a brief introduction to coaching methods in leadership development.

3. Coaching as a leadership development tool

Lippmann (2005) distinguishes between team and individual coaching. At first, we will describe individual coaching before we will concentrate on team coaching in chapter 5.

Leaders who receive coaching are often on a higher organizational level. The last 15 years saw a rapid increase in the popularity of the method of coaching (Hall, Seibert & Hollenbeck, 1999). The main purpose of such an individual "executive coaching" (Hall et al., 1999) is to communicate certain skills or to give advice concerning special situations or problems. Also, the coach comments and discusses behavior with the coachee. Of course, strict confidentiality is a necessary precondition to each coaching. The length of a coaching period varies from several days to a few years. Typically, the coach is an external agent such as a former executive, human resource expert, or consultant.

What are the advantages of executive coaching in comparison to formal trainings? The major advantage of coaching is the individual attention: The one-to-one relationship between coach and coachee allows for intense work and for a detailed assessment of the coachee's individual situation (Hillmann, Schwandt & Bartz, 1990). In contrast, in a formal training one trainer has to divide his/ her attention in order to teach - or provide help to - several persons. Within an individual coaching, the coach can easily adapt his/her method and by doing so, meet the needs and individual concerns of the participant. Additionally, high confidentiality allows for deep-level problem analysis and solving (Laske, 1999; Kilburg, 2001). The main disadvantage of coaching interventions is obvious: Individual coaching is always combined with very high expenses.

4. Team coaching

As a way to overcome the disadvantages of individual coaching, team coaching was developed. Team coaching can be defined as "direct interaction with a team intended to help members make coordinated and task-appropriate use of their collective resources in accomplishing the team's work" (Hackmann & Wageman, 2005). Hackman (2005) identified four different approaches of team coaching. First, within eclectic interventions, activities and methods are utilized that derive from no particular theoretical perspective. A coach tries to help a team to perform better - which is comparable with the work of a management consultant. These models are often found in practitioner literature (e.g., Fischer, 1993). Second, the concept of process consultations has been developed by Schein (1969). According to his theory, interpersonal relationships are essential for effective task performance. Only if the members of the group analyze and improve these relationships, they will have the chance of performing well.

Third, within behavioral models of team coaching, feedback and support are the main tasks for the coach who should encourage the team to learn new and effective team behavior. For example, Komaki (1998) proposed operant conditioning to modify the team behavior.

Finally, within developmental coaching, the timing of coaching is the most important factor. Only at certain group development stages interventions are regarded as useful. For example, team building is fostered in times where several new members join a team.

5. The Peer-based Team Coaching

In contrast to the four approaches mentioned above, the "Peer-based Team Coaching" (PTC) involves a coach who is not offering final solutions to the team, but moderates the team coaching and helps the team members to find solutions on their own. Team members are viewed as experts and are encouraged to use the potential of the group to find solutions. Each team member is coached by the respective other team members. This process is guided and moderated by an experienced PTC-coach. Within the coaching process, each team member's role (e.g., writing protocol, coach) is defined clearly. Individual themes for personal development are developed by the group. Each member of the coaching group receives a developmental theme, which is formulated positively and future orientated (e.g., "I will write my own script for my journey into the future"). Each coaching session lasts between 1 and 1 ½ hours. Afterwards, the leader applies the developmental theme in his/her daily work routines. In future PTCs, the leader will reflect his development and receives additional help from team members. This concept ensures sustainability, fosters leaders' long-term development and supports the transfer of new insights and skills into the work context (Olivero, Bane & Kopelman, 1997).

In contrast to other coaching methods, empirical research has been conducted that support the effectiveness of the PTC. In a sample of middle-level executives in a Swiss company, PTC helped coachees to achieve their work-related goals (Rowold, in press). Moreover, coachees' performance improved continually within the study temporal frame of 18 months.

6. Combination of leadership training and coaching

In this section, we will describe our efforts to combing full range leadership training with peer-based team coaching. In general, the idea is to provide leaders first with the full range leadership training, where leaders learn about their strengths and weaknesses, and where first steps for improvement are taken. Second, in the months after the training, trainees meet in groups of six on a regular basis. In these groups, the method of peer-based team coaching is implemented to develop participants' strengths and to further reduce individual weaknesses that have been identified by the 360° feedback prior to the training intervention. For example, if one leader has potential for enhancing his/her Intellectual Stimulation (cf. Table 1), he/she can choose to focus on the respective leadership behaviors in the coaching.

In sum, the combination of leadership training and coaching includes several elements or methods that have been identified as effective leadership development methods (Van der Sluis-den Dikken & Hoeksema, 2001; Woodall, 2005): 360°-Feedback (Van Velsor, Leslie & Fleenor, 2001), peer feedback (Luthans & Peterson, 2003), role play (Prideux & Ford, 1987), behavior modeling (Robertson, 1990), goal setting (Locke & Latham, 2002), coaching or "booster" sessions (Smither, London, Flautt, Vargas & Kucine, 2002). In prior research, the isolated effect of each of these methods has been evaluated. In contrast, the combined effect of these methods has not been evaluated yet. It is our hope that the described combination yields advancements within the field of leadership development.

Health Management in the Context of Personnel and Organizational Development

Kathrin Heinitz and Detlev Liepmann

Setting up a basis for health management within organizations seems quite difficult. The reasons for this are not just to be found in the breadth of the research and application fields, but can also quite equally be found in the framework given, which is being discussed publicly and questioned again and again (Schwarzer, 1997). The political and economic discourse increasingly impedes the focus on that what is important. Empirically challenging research concepts, for instance within the framework of appropriate long-term studies, as well as difficulties when it comes to an optimum program evaluation or process monitoring strengthen this view as long as one takes the more scientific side of it into account (Rossi, Freeman, Lipsey, 1999; Schulz & Koch, 2002).

If one, as a first step, attempts to make the problem at hand more transparent, then one can see that an optimal implementation of health programs and intervention measures – that in the end target long-term changes and are supposed to be integrated into the specific organizational development processes – must take three levels of social structures into account. Here, one can include the individual level, the group (in the broader sense) and, finally, the organization as a whole. In addition, there is the embedding in situational prerequisites that, in turn, map the interaction process "organization-environment" and quite clearly show what the chances and what the risks are. Apart from psychological and sociological aspects, questions pertaining to the learning organization are addressed herewith (among others). If one understands the matter as being a medium to long-term process, then the phases of problem identification, the introduction of promotional measures, training and the generalization of specific abilities as well as maintaining change have to be taken into account and all of this on an equal basis.

Individual and organizational approaches are primarily different when looking at their general frameworks. At the organizational level one can see the foundations of health programs in the implementation of methods of health education, health circles, work organization or work provision. When it comes to individual approaches, however, psychological principles such as behavior training, behavior modification, special knowledge or concepts of a change in attitude as well as approaches to stabilize and generalize relevant behavior areas are in the foreground. In addition, taking into account aspects of "management" (in the broader sense), then competencies are necessary that allow for the point of intersection between features of intervention measures, the individual will to change as well as organizational, political and economic approaches.

Operational health management is increasingly being seen as an integrative component of organizational development measures. The classic concepts of organizational development such as participation, longevity and continual feed-back are also reflected in health management. If one takes concrete concepts such as health circles that depict themselves as comprehensive participatory and process models, then differentiated analysis and diagnosis steps as well as sub-sequent measures and their evaluation are also elementary building blocks. In-creasingly, standards arise with regard to quality management or total quality management (TQM) (Badura & Ritter, 1998; Liepmann & Felfe, 1996); that means that also here health management can be interpreted as being a momen-tary instant of an open system. Health audits, health controlling or a systematic review of the health status supplement the management process. Furthermore, it should be taken into consideration in how far an optimal realization is inevitably reflected in a corresponding corporate culture, whereby, among others, informa-tion policy, participation, cooperative leadership structures and commitment are the trademarks of a respective organization (Bamberg, Ducki & Metz, 1998; Liepmann & Felfe, 1997, 2002; Resch 2003).

The framework of health management can often be seen in the wish for a long-term cost reduction. In many cases the proposed strategies and processes are quite similar. Thereby, time and again, the question at the fore is in how far, for example, workplace-related measures are suitable in order to optimize thera-peutic and preventive strategies. The conceptualizations vary to a large degree according to their dependence on the individual organization and the specific workplaces. For example, administrative organizations report other focal points and approaches than production organizations do. On the one hand, measures are planned and executed by the management, on the other hand by employee bodies or in cooperation between the two. Furthermore, it can be stated that a far-reaching bandwidth with regard to the voluntariness is required (Nathan, 1984; Wilbur, Hartwell & Piserchia, 1986).

As can easily be shown, a change in attitude by the management towards the use of health programs in the last few years can be observed (Liepmann & Felfe, 1997). However, it must also be underlined that in many cases the complexity of health management in the framework of personnel and organizational develop-ment measures is underestimated. The complexity does not just result from the matter at hand, but is primarily marked by the process-oriented character of health measures in organizations. Therefore, apart from an "assessment phase" and an "intervention phase", the entire evaluation process should be looked at closely. At this point in time we will primarily focus on the assessment phase.

1. Assessment phase

The assessment phase within the process of health management should, in the first instance, be viewed under the aspect of a deficit or needs analysis. There-fore, strategies should be installed that allow for target-performance compari-sons and make perspectives for an individual and organization-suitable imple-mentation possible.

A systematic confrontation with health management concepts whilst taking into account theoretical, methodical and application-oriented foundations is becoming more and more important. Operational health promotion as a facet of personnel and organizational development (in a broader sense) was discussed for quite a long time as a topic area that was to be pragmatically worked on in accordance with current requirements (Ducki, 1998; Friczewski, Jenewein, Lieneke, Schiwon-Spies & Westermayer, 1989; Westermayer & Bähr, 1994). The reconcilement of scientifically founded insights that have resulted from, amongst others, basic principles-oriented views on learning and development psychology, pedagogic psychology and didactic approaches or methodical orientation of evaluation research was missing for quite a long time. This may, on the one hand, have to do with the fact that much of the time practical needs and scientific cognition research did not develop simultaneously. On the other hand, the thought of a complex model that is applied in the sense of a "metatheory" is quite hard to realize. It seems all the more necessary then to approach the matter in a manner that defines the central purpose of a theoretically and methodologically oriented health management and prepares this for practical implementation. As basic strategic considerations the following aspects can be taken into account:

- Operational health promotion and health management must be formulated as strategic targets of the company.
- Requirement analyses that record and take into account the needs at the individual, organizational and social level must be executed by company-external as well as in-house cooperation partners.
- The need for health promotion intervention measures must be ascertained both quantitatively and qualitatively; this affects the already mentioned three levels.
- Surveys of action possibilities and necessities should be continuously installed and executed in-house under the directive of an optimal fit.
- Transparency is to be established in that internal as well as external pointers are to be taken into account on all hierarchical levels.
- Evaluation concepts are to be provided that have to be indispensable components, both in the sense of process monitoring as well as a summative strategy.
- The transfer (effect) (as long as external measures outweigh the others) from the learning location to the operational location must not only be guaranteed, but must also be checked after different time intervals have passed.
- In extreme examples and due to limited resources, the costs of measures for health promotion should be calculated in the framework of "profit centre thinking".

- The cooperation with external institutions must be guaranteed for the entire process.

If a modeling is not possible within the theoretical area, then at least on the implementation level a high level of professionalism must be ensured. With this, amongst others, at least the already mentioned cornerstones of a needs and deficit analysis, a congruous internal marketing, success or quality control and transfer should be looked at more closely.

Another possibility of categorizing operational health promotion is phase models that map health promotion as a development process (Ducki, 1998; Mittag & Jerusalem, 1997). We are, in the end, dealing with an "institutionalization phase" that is characterized by the fact that operational health promotion must be supplemented by a corresponding health management. The second part, the differentiation phase, often already provides a service orientation that is planned by full-time staff in larger organizations and resorts to internal as well as external experts. The integration phase, being the third part, is characterized by the fact that there is a high level of self-initiative. The management task is therefore seen as being mainly process monitoring and to advise those affected (participants, employees, personnel etc.).

Therefore, contrary to service orientation one can definitely speak of demand orientation here. Just in this section, though, the necessity of needs and deficit analyses comes to light. With this, in the end, two aims are being pursued. On the one hand it is necessary to convey a quite exact picture of the current situation. At what level of awareness are the employees or where can deficits be found and communicated in a direct and open form, which can, in turn, be reduced by intervention measures? On the other hand, needs and deficit analyses are future-oriented. They adjust themselves to the future requirements that ensue in the workplace needs (in a much narrower sense), social interaction patterns (horizontal and vertical) but also in salutogenic target definitions. Analyses must therefore go beyond documenting the current status; i.e. they must also illustrate target requirements that allow for a connection between the individual as well as organizational level and, at the same time, provide the necessary intervention strategies.

The on the practical side still hesitant discourse on health management concepts is based not just on the theoretical deficits that were discussed at the start. The methodological shortcomings can, at the same time, not be overseen. Here the organizational setting is often ignored; as an example one can mention taking into account the specific organizational structure. The current discussion on organizational-specific analyses, for example also in the area of small and medium-sized companies, clearly shows the necessity of looking at individual companies much more, and accordingly, to provide instruments as well as modifying these if necessary. Structuring help for operational health management can depict action-theoretical workflows that, amongst others, view the systematic process of an economic planning of health promotion as the indispensable prerequisite for an optimal cost-benefit relation. According to Gluminski and Stangel-Meseke (1993), who discuss theoretical action workflows in the framework of operational further education concepts, the process of health management within the framework of needs and deficit analyses can be shown along these lines. One can differentiate several phases as follows: (a) target explication, (b) target-related actual and projection analysis, (c) a survey of the employee willingness, (d) target vs. current state comparison, (e) solution strategies. Thereby five assumptions (economical, organizational, methodical, psychological and social) are formulated that must be fulfilled in order to comply with the theoretical sequence of events.

2. Early education systems as a component of deficit analyses

An interesting introduction that underscores the necessity of needs and deficit analyses in the area of health management is the concept of early education systems. Herewith an instrument is being addressed that was originally assigned to a future-oriented personnel development. In this framework the time gain is the central factor of the optimization process in which the depiction of the current situation assumes an important position.

In the face of permanent discontinuities in the organization context, but also within their direct area of influence, the aspect of time has continually gained in relevance. At the core we are dealing with the necessity of an ever higher organizational adjustment speed with regard to the changes in its direct or indirect environment. Here the insight that a system can only survive if its adjustment speed is equal to or greater than the change speed of its environment is quite trivial. For organizations this viewpoint is becoming more and more a strategic survival question. The services that are to be rendered, however, can only be fixed against the background of individual resources. Optimal reactions require a minimum of subjective stress sense.

One possibility of reacting optimally to changes, and at the same time also instigating or influencing modifications, is the on-time recognition of chances and dangers as an instrument of a future-oriented health management with the help of strategies that are in line with this and build upon it. Such strategies are capable of decidedly enlarging the time period between recognizing a latent chance or danger and its acute occurrence. This presupposes, though, that the organization members (on all hierarchical levels) have certain abilities, skills, aims and resources at their disposal. Thereby gaining time becomes a strategic company objective and the provision of appropriate resources becomes a central task of health management in the framework of personnel and organizational development.

Traditionally, analyses and prognoses make up the information basis within these processes. Therefore, needs and deficit analyses are an important facet in the framework of health management measures. Admittedly it should be noted that the prognostic value of such analyses is often overrated. It is evident that the prognosis accuracy and the validity increases as long as the prognosis time period is short. The more influence factors that are known that prove to be stable with regard to time and clearly pass operationally defined criteria, the higher the prognosis value is as well as the success probability of programs being implemented. Thereby it goes without saying that a comprehensive empirical basis for model depiction must be at hand that allows for a variety of segmentations that manifest themselves in both socio-demographic as well as individual characteristic traits (in the narrowest sense).

The realization possibilities are, in all cases, likely to contain a number of different problems. Only in a few cases will they both deliver satisfactory information. Thereby one has to take into account that these prerequisites cannot be discussed independently of one another, but rather they influence one another and work in a strengthening and interactive manner. A high level of dependence will emanate from each individual setting. The specific organizational features should definitely and paramountly be taken into account for each and every case when setting up the instrument, the implementation phase as well as the evaluation.

In the face of these problems the (future-oriented) significance of analyses and the accuracy of prognoses have been drastically reduced. It seems to be more and more questionable to infer things from past and current events with enough validity and relevance in order to predict future occurrences. If one views early education in this relationship, then one should not rely on the hope that more exact prognoses on potential developments can be given. It is much more likely that latent, already existing - but with the conventional information gaining instrument not (yet) recognizable - developments can be clearly shown quite early on. One can also add innovative aspects with regard to winning time and flexibility as well as an adequate analysis of the organization with the possible consequences of latent developments being taken into account.

The debate (Krystek & Müller-Stewens, 1990) provides us with the strategic early education. It represents a renunciation of familiar paradigms and is also not characterized by the prospect of short-term "successes". If one looks at the *Process of strategic early education*, then one can describe in simple terms the following process steps:

– Locating/registering "weak signals"
  Locating "weak signals" can occur using the help of basis activities within strategic early education. Firstly with a "360 degree radar" with which, in principle, "weak signals" are being searched for, everywhere and all the time. This activity can be understood to be a type of "scanning", i.e. a screening and rasterizing of the environment around the person, the work area or the department. If, using the identification of a "weak signal", signs of a relevant occurrence for the person, the working group or the department are received, then, secondly, we are dealing with trying to find additional information – that means extending the information structure of

the process. Such an activity can be defined as "monitoring", a deep, long-term and focused observing of the event that one thinks one has identified.

- Analysis of registered "weak signals"
  The task of the analysis is to point out possible dissemination and behavioral patterns of the registered signals. Questions on the generalization possibilities onto the different task areas, groups of individuals, hierarchy levels - that means the horizontal and vertical diffusion of the organization - are hereby the focus of attention. Furthermore, in this phase we are dealing with the analysis of causes as well as the prognosis of effects of the analyzed events.
- Evaluating the relevance of "weak signals"
  The subject matter of this phase is an inter-subjective, traceable categorization of the relevance of the information based on the cause/effect analysis that has already taken place. Thereby, activities that are geared individually should be taken into account, e.g. the portrayal of different stadiums of individual concern or the necessity for reaction strategies.

3. Health management and quality assurance

If one analyses the stark increase of health programs and health consultancy in organizations (see, for example, Cataldo & Coates, 1986; Fielding, 1982; Jacobs & Chovil, 1983; Manuso, 1983, Macdonald & Wells, 1994), then especially with a business-oriented view the question is posed in how far these should not be classified as being part of strategic management. Here, without a doubt, what should be taken into account is the aspect of personnel development.

Apart from education, training and further education concepts, the highest priority when it comes to the discussion should be put on programs that, amongst other things, serve to maintain and improve the health-related aspects. Safeguarding a qualified employee workforce must be made the focal point. Therefore health programs are becoming an integral component of the prerequisites for effective personnel development planning as well as health management. However, with this we are leaving the field of "classic" personnel development that can be situated per definition between "personnel development as job training" (traditional personnel management) on the one hand and the "planned development of the personnel" on the other hand (Fielding, 1979; Warner & Murt, 1985).

If one looks at the actual goals being pursued (increasing the competitiveness, flexibility, motivation and integration, the safeguarding of a qualified employee workforce and taking into account individual and educational as well as political demands) by the organization and the organization's members, then health programs, as indicated above, should definitely be attributed to safeguarding a qualified employee workforce, this being the view of the management. On the other hand, taking into consideration individual demands as a goal formulation is more in line with the employees' view on the matter. Questions on reducing pressure, increasing the social safety level, realizing equal opportunities etc. are sub-targets that can be partially aimed for through health programs. All in all, though, it should be taken into account that employee and organizational targets are only compatible under certain preconditions. As a rule individual goals can only be taken into consideration as far as these do not conflict with management goals.

A not to be underestimated factor are the considerations on quality management of health programs. Definitions of quality are traditionally shaped by a business-oriented background (Sethi, Caro, & Schuler, 1987; Staehle, 1999). Therefore, apart from a product-related view (quality is measurable) one should differentiate between an application-related (quality is the fulfillment of customer wishes), a process-related (quality comes about due to reliable work) and a cost-benefit-related (quality is a certain service at an acceptable price) one. In the last few years a socioscientific ("humane") point of view has been increasingly discussed as well. Quality is becoming a social value in the sense of an overall strategy.

The question as to a quality control system and the way it functions does not seem to be answerable when looking at it for the first time. This, among other things, has to do with the fact that the term system in this relationship refers to numerous aspects and their interrelations. Thereby not even all of the possible interrelations have been realized. This can best be documented if one, on the one hand, asks if and in which magnitude health management has already been established as a central goal or even idea within companies. On the other hand, within the theoretical discussion a number of scientific and professional fields claim priority when it comes to this area. This is shown clearly in the variety of perspectives and practical orientation. However, it should be noted that more and more integrative views are coming to the fore that in the end articulate themselves as "metatheoretical deliberations" (in the literal sense). Connected to this is also a change in the organizational targets so that in the end the question as to safeguarding as well as controlling quality within the area of operational or company-related health support and promotion can be answered much "easier".

Under the concept and thoughts on evaluation, three rough orientation directions with regard to the quality assurance of operational health promotion can be pinpointed. There is a consensus that there has to be a differentiation between an output, input and process-oriented (evaluation) variant. Thereby the output evaluation is the strategy that is used most often that at the same time also delivers the least knowledge and scientific progress potential in most cases. The procedures used deliver information on a certain operational condition in that they, for example, deliver cross-section statements on the self-evaluation of those affected, on assessments etc. Quality assurance is only possible to a limited scope as numerous aspects, amongst others the individual conditions or requirements of the participants or the specific setting (in the literal sense), are not necessarily taken into account. Here in the end the input-oriented orientation begins. The starting point is the inclusion of individual resources as well as the assessing and then comparing the commitment and the resources that the participants have at their disposal on the one hand and the requirements of the measures taken in dependence of the stipulated targets on the other hand. Process-oriented strategies go beyond the interlinkage of input and output-oriented evaluations; at the same time they take these on board. In addition, they emphasize a continuous recording of the entire situation as a focal point and thereby open up the possibility of registering the changes taking place. Thereby a system of permanent quality control and assurance is given which is not necessarily directly connected or oriented towards the individual measure being taken; instead the entire framework of health management is being included.

Process-oriented strategies do not only serve the purpose of quality assurance, but at the same time they are tools for a permanent improvement of quality. A rough illustration can be seen in Figure 1 (Liepmann & Felfe, 1996).

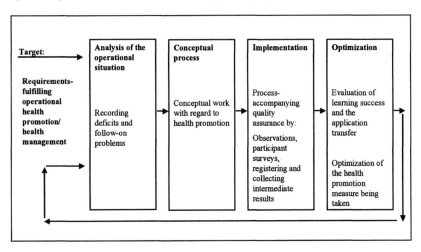

Figure 1: **Regulatory loop: Quality assurance of operational health promotion (according to Liepmann & Felfe, 1996).**

The concept of quality control or assurance that is being discussed the most at the moment has entered the debate under the label of "Total Quality Management (TQM)" (Frehr 1994a; 1994b; Kersten, 1994). Thereby three aspects are emphasized time and time again: (a) the increase in quality, (b) a reduction in costs and (c) a shortening of the time required or being used. If one wants to summarize this one can say that a comprehensive quality management will be realized when quality targets are formulated within the framework of "customer orientation" that in turn are laid down for the organization in order to implement these in a continuous and consequent quality management. If one transfers the basic thoughts of this concept onto operational health management, then quality management and quality assurance are realized (amongst other things) through the process of continuity. If one understands comprehensive quality management and quality assurance to be a dynamic system, then – with this – permanent modifications and improvements are necessary on all of the sub-fields in order to reach an efficiency optimization for the company or authority and its employees.

Assuming that the "satisfied customer" (i.e. the organizational member) is the strived for target of a comprehensive health management, then the analysis of the desires, requirements and expectations of the members of the organization is compellingly necessary (see above). The product "health" is clearly defined; it is essential to decrease health risks and to use as well as increase the chances of maintaining and promoting health. The recommendations of the World Health Organization (WHO; Ottawa Charta, 1993) already made it clear that health promotion is designed not only to reduce health dangers and risks, but also to allow for and promote the strengthening of health within the work context. Health is not only defined as the absence of sickness. It should moreover be understood as being a design concept whose aim it is to ensure physical, psychic and social well-being. The search for health promotional conditions and resources (Antonovsky, 1987) is the subject matter here. On the side of the employees this means that questions as to the individual competence development play a central role (Bamberg, Ducki & Metz, 1998).

If one on the other hand looks at effective health management under the aspect of quality thinking and sees in individual contentment an indicator for having reached the target, then – amongst others – comprehensiveness, faultlessness, understandability, concepts of transfer, modification possibilities or keeping to time-related framework conditions are definitely necessary for the concepts being realized.

On the operative level all possibilities of an interactive information exchange should be used. Health cycles, quality cycles, project work, improvement teams etc. that can be drawn up both vertically as well as horizontally constitute possible forms of an optimization process.

Occupational Health Program Evaluation: Combinations of Individual and Organizational Interventions and the Role of Process Quality

Nicole Wundke and Jörg Felfe

According to the European Agency for Safety and Health at Work every third employee in Europe experiences work-related stress and 28 % of employees report having health problems due to work stress. This indicates that stress has become one of the most important health risks in the workplace in Europe (European Agency for Safety and Health at Work, 2000). The identification of relevant psychosocial workplace characteristics (as opposed to physical aspects of the working environment) and their health effects were subject to scientific attention since the mid-twentieth century (Barling & Griffiths, 2003). European occupational health and safety legislation took the growing importance of psychosocial health risks at work into account by introducing the Framework Directive on Safety and Health of Employees at Work in 1989 (compare Bamberg, Ducki & Metz, 1998; Cox, Griffiths & Rial-Gonzalez, 2000). The requirements of this directive have been translated into national legislative frameworks of the European Union member states by 1992. This created a supportive background for the further development of occupational stress prevention and stress management interventions (Geurts & Gründemann, 1999).

Evaluation research on the effectiveness of stress management interventions started in the early 1970's and was mainly focused on inidividual-oriented stress management training (Murphy, 1996). The number of evaluation studies on organizational-oriented stress management interventions is still very small and many questions such as the moderating role of process variables are not yet answered (Bunce, 1997). In addition several authors (e.g. Mohr & Semmer, 2002, Aust & Ducki 2004) stress the importance to combine individual-oriented and organizational-oriented stress management interventions. So far studies evaluating those combined approaches are hardly available.

The study presented in this chapter aims at contributing to the extension of knowledge in this research field by evaluating an occupational stress management intervention, which combines individual and organizational oriented activities. Particularly the role of process variables and their relation to intervention effectiveness is taken into account as this is of key importance for a further development of evaluation reseach in the field of occupational stress management.

1. Theoretical models for workplace stress management

Stress is defined as the individual experience of an intensively disagreeable tension arising from the threat of a situation, which is extremely aversive, will subjectively occur soon or has already occurred and will possibly persist for a subjectively long time (Greif, 1991). This situation is perceived to be not completely manageable and therefore the avoidance of this situation seems to be important. Also Zapf & Semmer (2004) define stress as a disagreable state of arousal arising from the fear of not being able to manage a situation suffiently. German literature on occupational stress mainly refers to the transactional stress model (compare e.g. Lazarus, 1966; Lazarus & Launier, 1981) and the action regulation theory (Hacker, 1978; Volpert, 1987b; Oesterreich, 1981). The transactional stress model emphasizes cognitive and emotional processes of an individual when confronted with external stressors. The elaboration and achievement of goals and the regulation of action – especially work related action - are subject to the action regulation theory (Oesterreich, 1998). Based on these two theories Semmer (1984) developed a classification of external factors that disturb action regulation and lead most likely to the stress process as postulated by Lazarus. These external factors are defined as stressors (Greif, 1991). Zapf & Semmer (2004) support a similar definition of stressors and explicitly distinguish stress as an internal state from stressors as external factors leading most likely to stress. External factors which support the action regulation and provide the possibility to deal effectively with stressors have also been conceptualized within the scope of action regulation theory and are called external resources (Ducki, 1998b, 2000). This conceptualisation of external stressors and resources is very similar to the Job Demand-Control(-Support) (JDCS)-model (Karasek, 1979; Johnson & Hall, 1988; Johnson, Hall & Theorell, 1989), which is one of the most important models of stress sources (conceptualized as psychological job demands) and resources in the workplace. The main advantage of Semmer's (1984) conceptualisation of external stressors (i.e. regulation problems) is its theoretical derivation from the action regulation theory. According to Zapf & Semmer (2004) the experience of stress is characterised by emotional and physiological processes accompanied by changes in information processing and action regulation. These processes can also be summarized as short-term stress reactions (Zapf & Semmer, 2004).

Lazarus' assumption that personal characteristics are influencing the stress process raised the question for personal variables which enable an individual to deal effectively with stressful situations and to stay healthy. Such variables are referred to as internal resources and are conceptualized as general characteristics which co-determine more proximal coping behaviours (Semmer, 2003a). Because of their health promoting effect these variables are also conceptualized as positive health indicators (Ducki, 1998b).

Figure 1 illustrates how the above mentioned concepts and theories can be intregrated to build a comprehensive and functional theoretical basis for organizational and individual stress management interventions. Work-related stressors (Semmer, 1984) and work-related external resources are described in more detail in the following.

The action regulation theory provides a basis for a theoretically derived taxonomy of stressors by analysing the impact of working conditions on the action regulation process. Regulation problems refer to working conditions that disturb the regulation process of actions and may lead to negative health effects, whereas regulation requirements correspond to task characteristics that support the action regulation process and have positive health effects (Oesterreich, 1999).

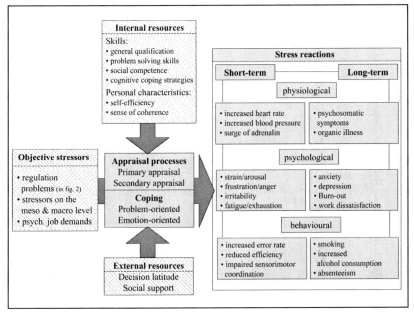

Figure 1. **Stressors, appraisal process and stress reactions (compare Zapf & Dormann, 2001)**

Legend: ▨ Transactional stress model   ▨ Resource concepts
           ▨ Action regulation theory and JDCS-Model

Task characteristics and working conditions that disturb the action regulation process are defined as regulation problems respectively stressors. With reference to the transactional stress model Greif (1991) defines stressors as hypothetical factors which are most likely to initiate the experience of stress. Leitner et al. (1987) and Semmer (1984) differentiate regulation problems into three groups: regulation obstacles, regulation uncertainties and overtaxing regulations (Frese & Zapf, 1994). Figure 2 illustrates this classification.

Regulation obstacles negatively affect an intact action and cause additional effort in order to reach the defined goal (Semmer, 1984). They can consist of *regulation difficulties* and *interruptions*. Regulation difficulties are related to a special task or operation. The execution of the task is still possible but more difficult. For example information difficulties occur if necessary information is not available, ambiguous, incomplete or incorrect. The additional effort in such cases consists of inquiries to receive the necessary information. Interruptions can be caused by persons, by technical and organizational problems. The additional effort in such cases can consist of starting again to think about the interrupted task or starting activities to solve technical and organizational problems (Frese & Zapf, 1994; Oesterreich, 1998).

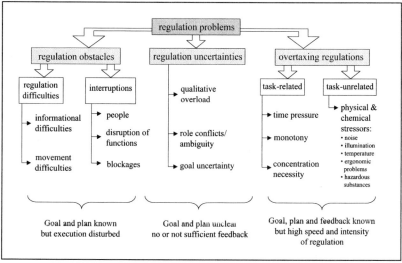

***Figure 2.* Classification of regulation problems**

Note: The content of this figure is taken from Frese & Zapf (1994) and Leitner (1999). The relation of the different regulation problems to the action regulation process has been added according to the text of Frese & Zapf (1994).

Regulation difficulties are often small but regular and unpredictable problems, also called „daily hassles". It is the overall sum of these daily hassles and the resulting additional effort which can cause psychological strain if no additional resources (e.g. more time) are provided to compensate the additional effort (Oesterreich, 1998).

The second group of regulation problems are **regulation uncertainties**. This means that the goal of an action and/or the concrete action program is unclear. Regulation uncertainties can emerge from a lack of action competence or a lack of feedback concerning the action result (qualitative overload). It can also result from role conflict or role ambiguity. Goal uncertainty may arise from conflicting and unclear work instructions (Frese & Zapf, 1994; Antoni & Bungard, 1989).

Overtaxing regulations refer to extreme speed and intensity of the action process. For instance time pressure requires a high working speed which does not allow for adaptation to normal individual performance variations (Frese & Zapf, 1994; Oesterreich, 1998). Monotonous tasks belong as well to the group of overtaxing regulation (Leitner, 1999). The disagreeable feeling of monotony arises from repeated and uniform tasks, which do not require planning and decision activities but full concentration. Beside this group of task-related overtaxing regulations Leitner (1999) defines unpleasant physical and chemical working conditions (i.e. noise, high temperature, ergonomic appositions) as a task-unrelated group of overtaxing regulations.

Regulation problems are often classified as work-related stressors, which are differentiated from the group of social stressors in the working place. Social stressors consist of a lack of social support, social conflicts and restrictive leadership behavior of supervisors (Ducki, 2000).

The above presented classification of stressors refers to the level of concrete tasks and working conditions at a special workplace. Semmer (1997) defines this level as the "micro level". By introducing the "meso level" and the "macro level" of workplace stressors he also takes into consideration stressors on other levels of an organization and its environment such as poor working organization between different departments, unfavourable working times, intransparent organizational information policy and bad social atmosphere (Ducki, 2000).

The two central **regulation requirements** in the working place are **decision latitude** and social support. Decision latitude means to have an impact on one's activities in the working place and on the working conditions such as the sequence, the time frame and the content of a task (Frese & Zapf, 1994). It is related to the following aspects which support the basic human need to influence and shape the environment according to own goals in a self-determined way: (1) *hierarchical and sequential completeness of the work task* (goal-generating, planning, executing and controlling), (2) *possibility for learning and personal development*, (3) *task variety*, (4) *purpose and meaning*. By supporting all these aspects decision latitude leads to positive health effects such as job satisfaction, pride and enjoyment causing a positive self-perception and self-confidence (Ducki, 2000; Oesterreich, 1998).

The Job Demand-Control(-Support) (JDCS) model (Karasek, 1979; Johnson & Hall, 1988; Johnson, Hall & Theorell, 1989), as one of the most influential models of stress sources in the workplace (van der Doef & Maes, 1999) "describes the joint, interactive effects of the three basic characteristics of the work organization: job demands, job control and workplace social support" (Buunk, De Jonge, Ybema, De Wolff, 1998, page 154). High levels of stress are experienced in "high strain jobs" (high demands combined with low job control). High demands, low job control and low social support ("iso-strain job") lead to the most severe stress reactions. Job control and social support can buffer the negative health effects of high demands. These assumptions of the Job Demand-Control(-Support) (JDCS) model have been supported in several studies (Van der Doef & Maes, 1999). Furthermore high-strain jobs have been shown to be a risk factor for cardiovascular disease (Theorell & Karasek, 1996).

Numerous studies (e.g. Leitner, 1993; Semmer & Frese, 1991; Semmer, Zapf & Greif, 1996) have shown the effect of regulation problems and requirements on stress-related health complaints. Whereas regulation problems have a negative impact on health, regulation requirements affect health in a positive way. As shown by Leitner (1993, 1999) regulation problems lead to psychosomatic symptoms (r = .40), irritability (r = .36), depression (r = .28) and severe illness (r = .23). Regulation requirements (decision latitude and social support) are moderating factors in this relationship. They reduce the negative health effect of regulation problems (Frese & Semmer, 1991).

According to Semmer et al. (1996) correlations between work-related stressors and strain are typically between r = .20 and r = .30. Additional support for the stressor-strain relationship has been provided by longitudinal studies confirming the causal relationship between work-related stressors and impaired psychological well-being (e.g. Parkes, Mendham & Rabenau, 1994; Marmot et al., 1999; De Jonge et al., 2001). In conclusion one can say that the relationship between work-related stressors and negative health outcomes is now quite well established (Semmer, 2003a).

2. Stress management interventions

Stress management is one of the most popular methods within the scope of work-site health promotion activities, which often include also non-stress-related issues such as nutritional counseling, smoking cessation and fitness programs (Busch, 1998; Ivancevich, Matteson, Freedman & Phillips, 1990). Ivancevich et al. (1990) define workplace stress management interventions as "... any activity, program or opportunity initiated by an organization, which focuses on reducing the presence of work-related stressors or on assisting individuals to minimize the negative outcomes of exposure to these stressors." With reference to the theoretical framework outlined before stress management interventions can target three different points in the stress process: the objective stressors respectively regulation problems and social stressors, the individual cognitive appraisal of stressful situations and the way of coping with stress responses (Ivancevich et al., 1990). In addition, with respect to a positive understanding of health, stress management interventions should also address external and internal resources (Bamberg, Ducki & Metz, 1998). A common classification of intervention types is the distinction between interventions on the organizational level and on the individual level (e.g. Bamberg & Metz, 1998; Busch, 1998). Design and redesign of working places, working conditions and organizational structures with the goal to reduce work-related stressors and enhance external resources are subject to interventions on the organizational level whereas inter-

ventions on the individual level focus mainly on enhancement of personal resources by improving cognitive-emotional processes and coping skills.

On the **organizational level** stressor reduction and resources enhancement
activities are distinguished. Stressor reduction activities aim at maintaining and
stabilizing health and consist mainly of improving working conditions. They are
not adequate for enhancing health promotive resources such as self-confidence
and pleasure of work. Such positive health effects can only be generated by resources enhancement activities such as redesign of the working task to achieve
appropriate decision latitude as well as hierarchical and sequential task completeness (Bamberg & Metz, 1998). Health circles as an analysis- and intervention instrument have become a popular method within the scope of stress management actions on the organizational level (Westermayer, 1998; Liepmann &
Felfe, 1997). The development of the health circle concept started when the
German occupational safety legislation set higher value on the prevention than
on the cure of work-related illness in the early seventies. The principle of health
circles is that a group of employees works on the identification of workplace
stressors, the analysis of their causation and the development of suggestions for
solutions (Westermayer, 1998; Zapf & Dormann, 2001).

The improvement of personal resources, cognitive-emotional processes and
coping skills is the goal of stress management interventions on the **individual
level**. The principal method on this level is stress management training using
cognitive-behavioral techniques. Problem-oriented trainings focus mainly on
skills which are necessary to deal with the concrete problem leading to the
stressful situation. They include for instance problem solving skills training (e.g.
Kämmerer, 1983), goal oriented action training (e.g. Preiser, 1989), communication and social competence training, assertiveness training and time management
training (e.g. Mackenzie, 1991). Emotion-oriented stress management trainings
aim at the perception of a stressful situation and at the regulation of stress reactions. Trainings based on the rational-emotive therapy by Ellis (1977) concentrate on promoting a realistic perception and evaluation of external stressors,
whereas several relaxation techniques such as autogenic training (Schulz, 1932),
progressive muscle relaxation (Jacobson, 1996) and meditation target at physical
and mental arousal reduction.

Most stress management interventions in practice refer to the individual
level. Stress management trainings are the most often employed stress management interventions. Because organizational-oriented interventions are difficult to
implement and are often disruptive to production schedules they have tended to
be less acceptable to management (Busch, 1998; Murphy, 1995). However the
proliferation of the health circle method during the last years gave rise to the use
of organizational-oriented interventions within the scope of workplace health
promotion (Mohr & Semmer, 2002).

Moreover, several authors (Mohr & Semmer, 2002; Zapf & Dormann, 2001;
Semmer, 2003b; Bamberg & Metz, 1998; Murphy, 1995) stress the importance
of combining individual and organizational interventions. Numerous studies

within the scope of general stress research show that occupational stress is related to objective workplace features (Leitner, 1993; Semmer & Frese, 1991; Semmer, Zapf & Greif, 1996) as well as to personal characteristics (Semmer, 2003a; Parkes, 1994). This suggests that occupational stress management interventions have to consider both aspects – the organization and the individual – in order to be effective. Bunce (1997) requested to improve the theoretical background of stress management intervention research and suggested a model to describe impact mechanisms of individual-oriented stress management interventions. With reference to this model, Lazarus' transactional stress theory (Lazarus, 1966; Lazarus & Launier, 1981) and empirical results from occupational stress research the following theoretical model on the effectiveness of combined stress management interventions is suggested.

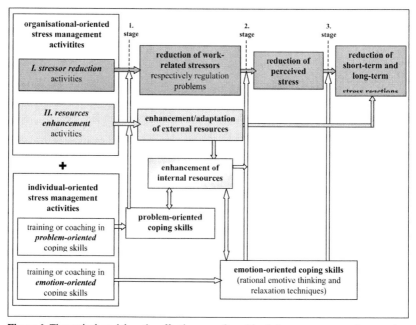

Figure 3. Theoretical model on the effectiveness of combined stress management interventions

▬▬▬▷ Impact mechanism of stressor reduction activities

▭▭▭▷ Impact mechanism of resources enhancement activities

▭▭▭▷ Support mechanisms of individual-oriented stress management activities

As shown in figure 3 the two types of organizational-oriented activities – stressor reduction (type I) and resources enhancement (type II) - are supposed to influence the stress process via different mechanisms (compare Bamberg & Metz, 1998; Ducki, 2000). **Stressor reduction activities** are expected to reduce different types of work related stressors respectively regulation problems. This objective reduction of work related stress sources should lead to a decrease in subjectively perceived stress and consequently result in reduced short-term and long-term stress reactions. **Resources enhancement activities** should lead to an adjustment of external resources such as decision latitude and social support. An optimal match between these workplace features and individual skills and needs is supposed to influence the stress process in two ways. Firstly, it reduces negative short-term and long-term reactions to stress sources in the workplace (buffering effect) (Frese & Semmer, 1991). Secondly, it leads to increased internal resources (Ducki, 2000), which are assumed to reduce subjectively perceived stress by positively affecting the stress process in the stage of secondary appraisal according to Lazarus (1966). Bamberg & Metz (1998) stress that this positive effect of resources enhancement activities can only be reached if they are combined with training or coaching providing suitable skills (e.g. self-management skills) to use the enhanced external resources successfully.

With regard to the organizational stressor recuction activities **individual-oriented stress management activities** – training or coaching in problem-oriented and emotion-oriented coping skills - are expected to support and stabilise the stressor reduction process during three stages (compare Bamberg & Metz, 1998; Mohr & Semmer, 2002). Training or coaching in problem-oriented coping skills should improve the program participant's skills to reduce stress sources in a proactive way (stage 1). Training or coaching in rational-emotive thinking enhances the ability to perceive and interpret external situations more realistically and to avoid overestimation of stress sources during primary appraisal (compare Ellis, 1977; Lazarus, 1966). Therefore it is assumed to facilitate the reduction of subjectively perceived stress (compare Busch, 1996) (stage 2). Training in relaxation techniques provides the participants with the ability to deal better with their stress reaction and should thus support the stressor reduction process at stage 3. The successful use of these coping skills is supposed to enhance internal resources (Bunce, 1997) which are supposed to facilitate a positive evaluation of personal stress management abilities during secondary appraisal resulting again in the reduction of perceived stress (Lazarus, 1966; Lazarus & Launier, 1981). This mechanism is supposed to support the organizational stressor reduction process additionally in stage 2.

Further developments of the health circle approach involve combinations of organizational-oriented and individual-oriented interventions. In addition to project work aiming on the improvement of the organizational environment, education and training components are integrated. Such approaches are called "integrated circle-, workshop- and training conceptions" (Westermayer, 1995; Ducki, Jenewein & Knoblich, 1998; Riese, 1998).

3. Effectiveness of stress management interventions

3.1 Individual-oriented stress management interventions

During the recent years two metaanalyses dealing with the effectiveness of stress management trainings have been conducted. Bamberg and Busch (1996) analysed studies evaluating congnitive-behavioural stress management trainings published from 1983 until 1993 and van der Klink, Blonk, Schene & van Dijk (2001) covered studies evaluating several types of individual-oriented interventions from 1977 until 1996. Busch and Bamberg found a small but significant overall effect of $d = .34$. The largest effects are achieved for outcome variables on the individual level ($d = .41$) with psychological and psychosomatic stress symptoms showing the largest effect ($d = .42$). A smaller but still significant effect size has been found for variables belonging to the individual-organizational interface ($d = .27$). The effect size for variables on the organizational level was nonsignificant. Thus, Busch and Bamberg conclude that cognitive-behavioral stress management trainings show a good effectiveness for individual-oriented outcome variables and reduced effectiveness for variables on the individual-organizational interface. With regard to organizational-oriented variables (e.g. absenteeism or job performance) the evaluated trainings seem to have no effect.

Van der Klink et al. (2001) included 48 studies in their metaanalysis. They draw the conclusion that individual-oriented stress management interventions are generally effective. The overall effect size of these interventions amount to a significant effect of $d = .44$. The analysis of differential effects of the different intervention types revealed that cognitive-behavioral trainings are more effective ($d = .68$) than relaxation trainings ($d = .35$) and slightly more effective than multimodal programs ($d = .51$). Differential effects could also be observed with respect to outcome variables. Cognitive-behavioral approaches had the strongest effects on variables relating to quality of work life, psychological resources, health complaints and anxiety. Multimodal programs led to a similar pattern of effects but appeared to be less effective in enhancing psychological resources. Training in relaxation techniques seems to be less effective for the former outcome variables but is the only approach leading to significant effects on physiological outcome measures. None of the analysed individual-oriented stress management interventions was effective in reducing absenteeism rates.

The significant effect of cognitive-behavioral trainings shows high variability across the included studies. This indicates the significance of moderating variables. Exploratory analysis detected three possible moderating variables: number of sessions (inverse and significant correlation between number of sessions and effect sizes of $r = -.27$ indicating that shorter cognitive-behavioral trainings are more effective), baseline level of stress and occupational status. With regard to the evaluated time period most of the studies including individual-oriented interventions only assessed short-term effects (mean interval between pre-intervention and post-intervention assessment of 9 weeks). Despite 20 studies realized some kind of long-term follow-up assessment no one of these assessments could be considered in the metaanalysis due to a lack of methodological rigor.

From the results the authors of the reviewed studies conclude that stress management interventions on the individual level are generally effective (Murphy, 1996; Bamberg & Busch, 1996; van der Klink et al., 2001). It is important to note that these positive results refer to a short time period. Both metaanalyses included only studies covering a time period of two to three months after training. Altogether, individual-oriented stress management interventions are effective with respect to outcome variables on the individual level for a short period. Concerning the long term effects no conclusions can be drawn from literature (Mohr & Semmer, 2002).

3.2 Organizational-oriented stress management interventions

In comparison to individual-oriented interventions the number of studies evaluating the effectiveness of organizational-oriented interventions is rather small (Mohr & Semmer, 2002; Ivancevich et al., 1990). Van der Klink et al. (2001) included five studies that evaluated organizational-oriented interventions in their metaanalysis. Results show that these interventions lead to a small and nonsignificant effect except for psychological responses and resources. Due to this lack of organizational-oriented intervention studies in stress research no firm conclusion about their effectiveness could be drawn. Semmer (2003b) solved this problem by paying attention to studies stemming from other research traditions which include indicators of well-being, stress and health. He classifies the different organizational-oriented stress management interventions according to three intervention targets: task characteristics, working conditions and social aspects such as improvement of role clarity and social support.

Studies concerning the improvement of **task characteristics** (e.g. decision latitude, variety and skill use) are mostly rooted in the motivational research tradition and are mainly based on Hackman and Oldham's Job Characteristics Model (Hackman & Oldham, 1980). Semmer found 15 studies including measures of psychological, physical and psychosomatic health, well-being, strain and absenteeism. Five of the six studies assessing proximal outcome variables achieve their proximal goal to improve the targeted task characteristics. The results indicate that increases in decision latitude, variety and skill use have a positive effect on mental health and job satisfaction as most of the studies assessing these variables report positive results. Also variables on the organizational level such as absenteeism rates, productivity and turnover seem to be positively affected by interventions targeting on task characteristics. Semmer states that beneficial effects do not occur for every variable in every case. Some studies report null findings for well-being and health complaints and in some cases even negative effects.

Studies evaluating the effects of reduced sources of stress and improved **working conditions** such as ergonomic improvements, usability of computer programs, reduction of work load and flexible working time report improvements with regard to perception of working conditions, mental health, physical parameters, job satisfaction as well as absenteeism. All studies measuring these variables report positive results. Some null findings occur with regard to psychosomatic and physiological health complaints due to differential effectiveness of the interventions with respect to different variables.

Studies targeting **social aspects** deal with interventions aiming at clarification of roles, goals and expectations and the reduction of interpersonal conflicts, hence the improvement of social relationships and social support. The concepts and methods for such interventions originate from organizational development approaches and leadership training and have not been strongly linked to stress research. Nevertheless some studies assessed effects on stress and health related variables. The results indicate that social interventions have the potential to affect stress and health related variables positively. In all studies assessing proximal outcomes of social interventions the proximal goals – an improvement of role ambiguity and social support – could be achieved. For more distant strain and health related variables most of the studies report positive effects but null findings occur as well. The effects of social interventions on absenteeism rates are inconsistent. Both studies assessing turnover report positive results.

It is remarkable that interventions with multiple targets lead to rather inconsistent results (except for absenteeism rates) in comparison to interventions with only one intervention target (Semmer, 2003). Semmer states that negative effects occurred mainly in studies reporting poor implementation of the intervention. Possibly interventions searching to improve several aspects of the working situation in parallel suffer losses in process quality which could lead to a reduction of intervention effects. Actually, **process quality and program implementation** seem to be more important within the scope of organizational-oriented interventions than during individual-oriented interventions, as the former are stronger related to the complex organizational context. For the same reason not only the implementation of an organizational-oriented stress management intervention itself is more difficult but also its methodologically sound evaluation.

The conclusion that Semmer (2003b) draws from his review is rather positive. The majority of variables were positively affected (75% of the proximal variables, 70% of variables related to mental health and well-being, 59% of strain-related variables and health complaints, 86% of job satisfaction measures, 86% of absenteeism rates and 80% of turnover measures). Consequently Semmer (2003b, p. 340) states: "Altogether, the studies reported convey the impression that work-related interventions do have potential for positive effects". Despite most of the outcome variables have been positively affected this conclusion is formulated cautiously because not all of the reported results reached a significant level and some studies did not use a control group. The most consistent and significant results emerged for job satisfaction and absenteeism.

3.3 Combined interventions (Health circles)

The number of evaluation studies regarding the health circle strategy is limited as well. The most extensive study has been published by Sochert (1999) and is therefore summarized in the following as a key reference of evaluation studies on health circles. Sochert evaluated 41 health circle projects which have been realized in 16 companies since 1995. Six months after finishing the health circle work the process variables and effect variables were assessed using a reliable and valid questionnaire which has been developed especially for the evaluation of health circle projects.

The questionnaire assesses the achievement of the three main **process goals** of health circles – identification of relevant work-related stressors, elaboration of suggestions for the reduction of these stressors and realization of these suggestions. In addition process variables relating to the composition of the health circle group, meeting frequency, meeting duration, meeting atmosphere, participation and information are included in the questionnaire. The results show that the health circle projects achieved the three main process goals to a large extent. On average 36 work-related stressors per health circle group have been identified. These stressors have been rated by 95% of the circle members (N = 386) to be the most important ones. Each health circle elaborated on average 50 suggestions to improve the working situation. These suggestions have been rated by 90% of the circle members to be sufficient and for 81% these suggestions were the most important in their department. Six months after the health circle work was finished 60% of the suggestions have been realized. The finding that 58% of these realized suggestions have been rated to improve the working situation to a large extent indicates that the most important suggestions have been tackled at first.

With regard to the **process variables** the results support the basic conception of health circles. Most of the circle members (90% of the work safety experts, 84% of the supervisors, 67% of the employees) rated the circle composition to be adequate. With respect to the meeting atmosphere and moderation 70% of the participating employees saw satisfying possibilities to participate actively in the discussions and elaboration of suggestions for improvement. Most of the health circle members (92% of the supervisors, 83% of the work safety experts, 64% of the employees) rated the meeting atmosphere to be open and agreeable.

After the health circle projects positive **effects** on the working situation, work-related health complaints and work satisfaction have been reported by the health circle members as well as by employees of the intervention area. An improvement of the working situation has been reported by 50 – 75% of the respondents. The strongest improvements emerged for social support at the working place, working material and decision latitude. For these aspects of the working situation 50 – 55% of the respondents reported strong or partial improvements.

With respect to health complaints 44% of the respondents reported strong and partial reductions especially of skeletal and muscle complaints, psychosomatic health complaints and cardiac and circulatory troubles. Correlational analyses confirmed that these improvements of health complaints are strongly related to the improved working situation (r = .33 to r = .53; p < .01). A strong or partial enhancement of work satisfaction reported 62% of the respondents. For this variable correlational analyses showed significant (p < .01) relations to improvements of the working situation as well, with the highest correlational coefficients for social support (r = .56) especially from supervisors (r = .52) and decision latitude (r = .55) (Sochert, 1999).

An extensive review that has recently been presented by Aust and Ducki (2004) including 11 studies evaluating 81 health circles realized in different industrial sectors and hospitals reports similar positive results. However, due to difficulties to implement experimental studies in a complex organizational context most studies (including the above described study by Sochert, 1999) employed retrospective pre-post-intervention comparisons without or nonequivalent control groups. Therefore caution is advised when interpreting these results. Aust and Ducki (2004) could include three studies that used at least nonrandomized control groups but no pretest-posttest design, as well. In addition Aust and Ducki (2004) criticize that most of the reviewed studies did not apply statistical analysis and reported only descriptive results. Despite this lack of methodological rigor the authors draw the conclusion that "health circles are an effective tool for the improvement of physical and psychosocial working conditions and have a favorable effect on workers' health, well-being, and sickness absence" (Aust and Ducki, 2004, p. 258). Also Slesina (2001) draws a positive conclusion from his overview on the effects of health circle projects as most of studies report positive results (Slesina, 2001).

Other intervention concepts that combine organizational-oriented and individual-oriented activities have hardly been evaluated until now. One evaluation has already been realized in the 80ies by Jones et al. (1988). The intervention involved a survey feedback process combined with videocassette training modules providing general information about work-related stress and teaching coping skills (especially relaxation techniques). Individual counseling within the scope of an employee assistance program was the third component of this intervention. It was implemented in general care hospitals and comparisons between the 8-month period before the program started and the 7-month period after the program showed a significant (p < .03) reduction of monthly medication errors over time from M = 10.25 prior to the program to M = 5.14 after the program. A significant difference between the intervention and the control group (p < .05) after the intervention has been reported as well.

A similar more recent study has been realized by Munz, Kohler and Greenberg (2001). A combination of a survey feedback process with self-management training that provided the participants with several stress management techniques such as cognitive restructuring, breathing techniques, self-suggestion and relaxation techniques has been implemented in a telecommunications company. Outcome variables involved the individual level (perceived stress, emotional well being, depressiveness) as well as the organizational level (productivity, absenteeism). As a result the treatment group reported significant ($p < .05$) improvements on all three individual level outcome measures in comparison to the control group after the interventions. Concerning the organizational outcome variables the treatment group showed 23% improvement of productivity versus only 17% in the control group and 24% of reduced absenteeism versus only 7% in the control group.

Semmer (2003b) included in his review about organizational-oriented stress management interventions six studies, which integrated some kind of individual training (e.g. stress management training or leadership training), thus representing a combined intervention. Most of these studies (5) report positive effects on absenteeism. The two studies assessing work characteristics and conditions, found improvements on these variables. Outcome measures on the individual level (physiological health, well-being, emotional stress) were positively affected as well in three studies, but two studies reported no change concerning these variables (Semmer, 2003b).

These findings support the assumption that interventions which combined organizational-oriented and individual-oriented components are more effective in the sense that they affect organizational as well as individual outcome variables. But more research on this topic is needed to allow firmer conclusions about the advantages of combined stress management interventions (van der Klink et al., 2001).

3.4 Moderating and mediating variables

Bunce (1997) identified three types of variables possibly moderating or mediating the effectiveness of occupational stress management interventions: personal characteristics of the intervention participants, organizational variables and process variables of the intervention itself. With regard to the role of **personal characteristics** of the intervention participants Bunce (1997) states a considerable lack of research. Especially the role of internal resources such as self-efficacy and sense of coherence have not yet been investigated. The only variable on the side of intervention participants that has been included in some studies is the initial type and severity of the stress reaction. Van der Klink et al. (2001) included four studies in their metaanalysis, which selected intervention participants with high baseline stress levels (remedial interventions). The results show larger effects for remedial ($d = .59$) versus preventive stress management interventions (44 studies, $d = .32$). Similarly, Murphy (1996) reports in his review that 79 % of preventive interventions versus 94 % of curative interventions showed positive effects. These results can be interpreted in two ways. Firstly, stress management interventions are more effective for employees with high stress levels. Secondly, these results emerge from the employment of rather clinical measuring instruments, which are not sensitive enough to detect the rather sub clinical levels of stress of the normal working population and their improvement (Murphy, 1996).

The impact of **organizational** culture and climate has recently been investigated by Saksvik, Nytro, Gensen & Mikkelsen (2002). In a qualitative process evaluation of seven different individual and organizational stress management interventions in 44 sub-units of larger organizations they identified the following key factors which affected the implementation of the interventions: (1) general motivation and attitudes towards intervention projects – often the motivation seems to be decreased in the form of "project fatigue" due to numerous previous interventions, which were enthusiastically introduced but not completed, (2) organizational culture and readiness to change – an atmosphere of mutual blame for responsibility between employees and managers has been found to be detrimental in contrary to a climate of co-operation, common interests and commitment to continuous improvements, (3) concealed informational attitudes and behavior during the intervention – in most of the concerned work units "passive sabotage" of the implementation process has been observed in the form of unwillingness of a few employees and managers to participate, (4) competing projects and reorganization – competing projects and organizational changes such as budget cuts, shifts in management personnel, quality and employee evaluations were found to reduce the commitment to the stress management interventions whereas major reorganizations seem to have a more direct influence on the intervention effectiveness due to an increase of general job insecurity.

In recent research two types of **process variables** have been recognized – process quality and achievement of process goals (i.e. program implementation) (Bunce & West, 1996; Sochert, 1999; Saksvik et al., 2002). Bunce (1997) refers to process quality as non-specific factors of an intervention such as safety, warmth and alliance with the trainer or moderator during group sessions (i.e. meeting atmosphere). Achievement of process goals includes according to Bunce (1997) variables relating to significant insights and changed perceptions of oneself, others and working procedures as a direct result of the group sessions. Evaluation studies (e.g. Drazen, Nevid, Pace & O'Brien, 1982; Sallis, Trevorrow, Johnson, Hovell & Kaplan, 1987; Murphy, 1983; quoted according to Bunce, 1997) which controlled for placebo effects by including a placebo control group (education about stress without special training) found no significant between-group differences between education and treatment conditions indicating some influence of non-specific process variables on the effectiveness of stress management interventions. This assumption is supported by Bunce & West (1996), who directly measured variables related to session comfort and safety as well as to significant insights into oneself, others and working procedures. When controlling for these variables the significant intervention effect became non-significant.

Within the scope of process evaluations of health circles information and participation of employees have been shown to be of key importance for the process quality and successful implementation of organizational stress management interventions (Sochert, 1999).

3.5 Conclusion

Several reviews and metaanalyses about the effectiveness of individual-oriented stress management interventions showed that stress management trainings are effective mainly with regard to outcome variables on the individual level such as perception of stress in the workplace, psychological and physiological stress reactions. Cognitive behavioral training in combination with relaxation exercises has been found to be most effective. However the reported effects are mainly related to short-term periods and the long-term effects of stress management trainings have hardly been investigated (Mohr & Semmer, 2002).

The number of studies evaluating organizational-oriented and combined stress management interventions is rather small. By paying attention to studies from other research traditions including indicators of well-being, stress and health Semmer (2003b) could present a first review. In addition a comprehensive evaluation of health circle projects in several companies (Sochert, 1999) has been summarized. Results support the assumption that organizational-oriented interventions lead to the expected positive effects. Most of the reviewed studies report an improvement of working tasks and working conditions. Effects on job satisfaction and absenteeism are most consistent and significant, but outcome variables on the individual level (mental health, psychosomatic and physiological health complaints) are positively affected as well. However, not all studies show significant effects and some of them do not provide sufficient scientific rigor or report inconsistent results. Insufficient process quality and program implementation seem to be the main reason for inconsistent and non-significant effects (Semmer, 2003b). Thus results of organizational-oriented and combined stress management interventions still have to be interpreted with caution and more research is necessary to draw firmer conclusions. For further research it seems to be of key importance to pay more attention to process quality and program implementation as moderators and mediators of the intervention outcome.

4. Research question and hypotheses

The presented study focuses on the evaluation of the program effectiveness of an occupational stress management program and its relationship to program implementation and process quality. With this focus the study contributes to further research on the effectiveness of combined stress management interventions and gives consideration to the need for more insights into the moderating role of process variables. The program is realized in the Belgian subsidiary of a large industrial science company and is conceptualized as a combined intervention integrating organizational-oriented as well as individual-oriented stress management activities. The program goal is to reduce work-related stress and its negative short-term and long-term consequences. A pretest-posttest and control group design is applied to answer the following research questions:

1. Does the stress management program reduce work-related stressors, subjectively perceived stress and its short-term and long-term consequences?
2. Does the stress management program lead to an enhancement of external and internal resources?
3. How do process variables (process quality and achievement of process goals) influence the effectiveness?

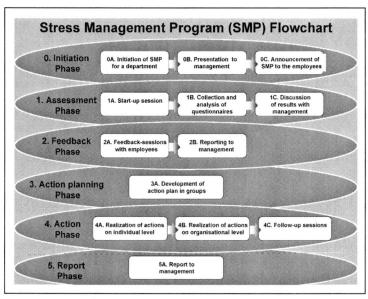

Figure 4. **The concept of the evaluated stress management program**

The stress management program consists of a survey-feedback process which is very similar to the health circle approach. As shown in figure 4 the program comprises several phases including a participative analysis of relevant sources of stress, elaboration of action plans and realization of suitable organizational-oriented and individual-oriented stress management activities.

The presented stress management activities are expected to reduce the severity of short-term and long-term stress reactions and to enhance pleasure of work by influencing working conditions, workplace characteristics (organizational-oriented actions) and individual coping skills (individual-oriented actions). These effects are expected to be related to the degree of program implementation and to process quality.

The following hypotheses will be tested:

H_1: In the intervention group *work-related stressors, perceived stress, irritation, psychic exhaustion and psychosomatic symptoms* will be reduced at time 2 in comparison to the control group.

H_2: In the intervention group *decision latitude, social support* and pleasure of work will be increased at time 2 in comparison to the control group.

H_3: The higher the session comfort, participation and information the better is the program effectiveness.

H_4: The better the process goals are achieved the better is the program effectiveness.

5. Method

5.1 Design and procedure

For testing the hypotheses H1 and H2 a pretest-posttest design with a non-equivalent control group is applied. Two independent variables are generated: participation in the stress management program and time of measurement. The first data collection has been realized in May 2003 before the program started. The post-test has been realized in May 2004. The stress management program has been started in three departments: one laboratory department, one production department and one administrative department. In each department only one working group, which asked for the realization of the program beforehand, participated in the program. These three working groups represent thus the intervention group of the evaluation study. Working groups of the same department that did not participate in the program served as control group of the evaluation study. Due to this situation it was not possible to randomly assign the involved employees to the two conditions (participation/no participation). As the employees in the control group belong to the same departments, have similar working tasks and are confronted with similar working situations, it has been assumed that the control group would provide a minimum degree of equivalence with the intervention group. A spill-over of the treatment effect, which could be possible in this situation, was largely prevented by the fact that the intervention and control group in every department were separate groups (separated by location or working time) so that an extension of the intervention effect through exchange of information about the stress management program during everyday work was limited.

The evaluation questionnaire has been distributed in total to 222 employees working in the three involved departments. The intervention group (104 employees) completed the questionnaire during the start-up session. During the same time period the questionnaire has been distributed by e-mail or as hard-copy to the control group (118 employees). Respondents were asked to return the completed questionnaire to the medical department. The response rate at time 1 was 67,1 %. The second data collection took place two months after the intervention group reached the action phase of the program, one year after the pre-test (response rate was 47.3%). Due to considerable fluctuation in the laboratory and administrative department a drop-out rate of 53.7% reduced the matched sample to $N = 69$. After excluding 13 respondents from data because of extremely positive or negative events in their private life during the course of the study, a final sample of $N = 56$ with $N_{intervention} = 29$ and $N_{control} = 27$ resulted.

5.2 Sample

The final sample consists of 25 females (44.6 %) and 29 males (51.8 %). Their age ranged from under 25 to over 55 with 69.6 % of respondents being between 25 and 44 years old. Most of the respondents are married (60.7 %), 32.2 % are single or cohabiting and only 5.4 % are divorced. At time 1 the respondents have been on average for 14.9 years in the work force ($SD = 8.9$ years, range: 0.8 – 30.0 years) and have been working on average 9.9 years for the organization ($SD = 8.1$ years, range: 0.2 – 29.5). Most of the respondents (76.8 %) are employees without management responsibility. Respondents in management positions (19.6 %) mainly belong to lower and middle management. No significant differences between respondents (responded at time 1 and 2) and drop-outs (non-responders at time 2) concerning the assessed demographic variables were found. Pre-intervention levels in the dependent variables were not significantly different in these two groups except for the level of psychological job demands. Drop-outs reported significantly higher psychological demands at time 1 than respondents ($t = 3.21$, p = .002).

5.3 Measures

The Job Content Questionnaire (JCQ, Karasek, 1985), which is based on the Job Demand-Control(-Support) model (Karasek, 1979; Johnson & Hall, 1988; Johnson, Hall & Theorell, 1989), has been used to measure **work-related stressors and external resources**. External resources are assessed by the two scales decision latitude and social support. Work-related stressors are measured with the scale psychological demands/workload. It refers to several sources of stress such as workload, role ambiguity, time pressure, concentration necessity, interruptions and organizational problems, which have been conceptualized more detailed in the concept of regulation problems (Leitner et al., 1987; Semmer, 1984). In this study internal consistency coefficients between $\alpha = .78$ and .93 have been found.

For the assessment of **subjectively perceived stress** the Perceived Stress Scale (PSS, Cohen, Kamarck & Mermelstein, 1983) was used. Test-retest reliability over six weeks amounts to $r = .55$. A coefficient α reliability of $\alpha = .85$ has been found in this study as well.

For the assessment of **irritation** the Irritation-Scale (Mohr, 1986) was used. In this study an internal reliability coefficient of $\alpha = .88$ has been found.

For the measurement of **psychosomatic symptoms, psychological exhaustion and pleasure of work** three scales of the measuring instrument for Diagnosis of Health-Promoting Work (DigA, Ducki, 2000) have been applied.

For these three scales internal reliability coefficients of $\alpha = .80$ (psychosomatic complaints), $\alpha = .74$ (psychic exhaustion) and $\alpha = .87$ (pleasure of work) have been found.

The BKK (German health insurance institution Betriebskrankenkasse) questionnaire for the evaluation of health circles (Sochert, 1999) has been used as a basis to elaborate a process questionnaire assessing **program implementation and process quality**. Program implementation is assessed by items asking for achievement of the three process goals (identification of important work-related stressors, elaboration of clear action plans and realization of stress management actions). Items concerning meeting atmosphere, moderation quality and participation/information are used to assess process quality. For the scales the following internal consistency coefficients have been found: identification of stress sources $\alpha = .67$, elaboration of action plans $\alpha = .73$, realization of actions $\alpha = .92$, session comfort including meeting atmosphere and moderation quality $\alpha = .73$ and participation/information $\alpha = .85$

All items are rated on a 5 point Likert scale. The BKK questionnaire also uses dichotomous items, Mohr's (1986) irritation scale uses a 7 point Likert scale.

5.4 Results

Preliminary analyses Equivalence of the intervention group and control group has been verified using t-tests and chi-square tests. The following variables have been assessed: age, sex, family status, occupational status, number of children, duration of being in the workforce, duration of working for the company and duration of working in the current position as well as the motivation to participate in the stress management program. No significant differences between the two groups were detected concerning these variables.

Program effectiveness A two-factorial ANOVA with repeated measures on one factor has been applied to test hypotheses H1 and H2. Due to the stress management intervention a decrease of work-related stressors (i.e. psychological job demands), perceived stress, irritation, psychic exhaustion and psychosomatic symptoms in the intervention group compared to the control group has been expected (H1). This should lead to a significant time x group interaction effect per outcome variable. Table 1 shows the results for these outcome variables.

Table 1. **Means and standard deviations of intervention and control group before and after the intervention for work-related stressors, perceived stress, irritation, psychic exhaustion and psychosomatic symptoms**

outcome variable	Intervention Group				Control Group			
	N	pre-test	post-test	$\Delta *^1$	N	pre-test	post-test	$\Delta *^1$
work-related stressors	29	2.41	2.26	-	26	2.38	2.14	-
		(.56)	(.58)	.15		(.57)	(.57)	.24
perceived stress	29	1.71	1.69	-.02	27	1.57	1.51	-.06
		(.53)	(.52)			(.57)	(.60)	
irritation	29	2.61	2.66	.05	26	2.80	2.83	.03
		(1.09)	(1.26)			(.98)	(1.08)	
psychic exhaustion	29	1.59	1.82	.23	27	1.91	1.83	-.08
		(.88)	(.88)			(.83)	(.64)	
psychosomatic com-plaints	29	1.13	.97	-.16	27	.97	1.02	.05
		(.53)	(.48)			(.45)	(.51)	

Notes. *[1] $\Delta \wedge$ change over time $\wedge$ difference post-test – pre-test (negative values indicate reduction)

A significant decrease of work-related stressors over time can be observed in both, the intervention group and control group (main effect time, $F = 8.56$, $p < .01$) but the time x group interaction effect reveals no significant difference in change over time between the treatment group and control group. With regard to perceived stress and irritation the results show marginal and non-significant changes. For psychic exhaustion results show a pattern of change which does not correspond to the hypothesis as the intervention group shows in comparison to the control group a slight non-significant increase over time. Concerning psychosomatic symptoms results show a pattern of change which corresponds to the hypothesis. Respondents in the intervention group reported a decrease in psychosomatic complaints ($\Delta = -.16$) whereas the control group remained relatively stable ($\Delta = .05$). This difference in change over time between the two groups is significant with $F = 3.29$ ($p < .04$, $Eta^2 = .06$). *In conclusion hypothesis H1 is supported with respect to psychosomatic complaints.*

In hypothesis H2 it has been expected that the enhancement of external resources (decision latitude and social support) combined with individual-oriented stress management activities during the course of the program leads to an enhancement of pleasure of work in the intervention group in comparison to the control group. Again this should be indicated by a significant time x group interaction effect. Table 2 shows the results for decision latitude, social support and pleasure of work.

Table 2. **Means and standard deviations of intervention and control group for decision latitude, social support and pleasure of work**

outcome variable	Intervention Group				Control Group			
	N	pre-test	post-test	$\Delta*^1$	N	pre-test	post-test	$\Delta*^1$
decision latitude	29	2.51	2.26	-.25	26	2.70	2.56	-.14
		(.62)	(.59)			(.49)	(.63)	
social support	29	2.50	2.19	-.31	26	2.90	2.60	-.30
		(.79)	(.63)			(.42)	(.58)	
pleasure of work	29	2.72	2.54	-.18	27	2.96	2.86	-.10
		(.66)	(.80)			(.61)	(.60)	

Notes. *[1] Δ $\wedge$ change over time $\wedge$ difference post-test – pre-test (negative values indicate reduction)

Unexpectedly a significant decrease of decision latitude and social support over time (main effect time) can be observed in both, the intervention group and control group. The effect sizes of $Eta^2 = .21$ (for social support) and $Eta^2 = .13$ (for decision latitude) are small. There is no significant difference in change over time between the treatment group and control group. Concerning pleasure of work results show a slight significant ($F = 3.35$, $p < .03$) decrease over time in both groups as well. There are no significant differences in change over time between the intervention group and the control group *On the whole hypothesis H2 is not supported by the data.*

Process variables: program implementation and process quality Most of the program participants reported to have attended two group sessions. Means and standard deviations for the assessed process variables are shown in table 3.

With a mean of $M = 2.25$ the first process goal – **identification of important stress sources** – has been partly achieved. According to the participants the survey results reflected by and large the situation in the departments ($M = 2.31$) and important stress sources have partly been discussed during the group sessions ($M = 2.19$). Table 3 shows that the second process goal – **elaboration of clear action plans** - has not been achieved to a satisfactory extent. Possibilities to reduce the stress sources ($M = 2.00$) seem to have been less discussed than relevant stress sources. Action plans have hardly been elaborated ($M = 1.68$).

Table 3. **Means and standard deviations of the process variables**

process variables		M	SD
program implementation (achievement of process goals)	Identification of stress sources (2 items)	2.25	(.86)
	Elaboration of action plans (2 items)	1.83	(.87)
	Realization of organizational actions (10 items)	1.29	(.59)
process quality	session comfort (7 items)	2.75	(.61)
	participation/information (6 items)	1.90	(.73)

Notes. N = 29, 0 = strongly disagree to 4 = strongly agree

Organizational stress management actions have rudimentarily taken place ($M = 1.29$). Participants did not agree with the statements concerning activities in the different action fields. Concerning the improvement of ergonomic workplace features an average of $M = 1.00$ resulted, statements concerning the improvement of working organization and organizational information processes were answered with an average of $M = 1.54$ and $M = 1.46$. These were the action fields with the highest ratings. The majority of all program participants (92%) did not take advantage of the offer for **stress management training** or coaching. Participants in all departments reported on average that they did not gain knowledge about stress ($M = 1.36$) and effective coping strategies ($M = 1.28$).

Session comfort (including meeting atmosphere and moderation quality) received good ratings ($M = 2.75$). Respondents agreed with the statements that the moderator has good competences and experience to guide such group sessions ($M = 3.04$), that he guided the discussions in a neutral and balanced way ($M = 3.13$) and that he reacted adequately to comments and suggestions ($M = 3.00$). On average respondents in the three departments were satisfied with the moderation of the group sessions ($M = 3.00$). The general meeting atmosphere including the agreement on communication rules, the compliance with these rules and the possibility to bring in own suggestions and opinions has been rated with an average of $M = 2.44$.

Participation and information received low ratings (M = 1.90). Program participants reported insufficient information on realized actions during the program (M = 1.28). On average respondents reported that a participative elaboration of clear action plans has not taken place (M = 1.68). When asked for their general satisfaction with the result of the group sessions respondents partly agreed. Respondents stated that more such group sessions should have taken place to discuss solutions for stress sources in their work environment more effectively. The **overall result** of the program has been evaluated by most of the participants to be partly positive, partly negative. Free comments reveal that especially the initiation of an open discussion about stress and the identification of stress sources have been appreciated by 59% of the participants giving positive comments (n = 12). The group sessions have been considered by 25% of these participants to be a good first step in a positive direction. In addition the official recognition of stress in the workplace and the feedback from an experienced person have been mentioned as positive aspects. Suggestions for program improvements have been given by 10 participants. 9 of these 10 participants suggested realization of more concrete actions in a shorter time and more regular progress follow-up . In addition respectful cooperation between employees and supervisors, the company's willingness to provide necessary financial resources and the overall approach to stress in the workplace, which should be "more global" have been reported as critical aspects of the program.

Relationship between process variables and program effectiveness It has been expected that two types of process variables – process quality and program implementation (achievement of process goals) - have an influence on the intervention outcome. This should result in a significant correlation between these process variables and change over time in the different outcome variables. For negative indicators (work-related stressors, perceived stress, irritation, psychic exhaustion and psychosomatic symptoms) this correlation should be negative – the better process quality and goal achievement the more decrease in negative stress symptoms can be expected. Analogously for positive indicators (decision latitude, social support and pleasure of work) this correlation should be positive – the better process quality and goal achievement are, the more positive indicators should increase. Results concerning hypotheses H_3 and H_4 are shown in table 4. It is important to note that the small sample size of $N = 29$ (intervention group) does not provide sufficient statistical power to detect a medium effect of $r = .30$ (compare Cohen, 1988).

Table 4 shows no significant correlations between **session comfort** and program effectiveness with regard to the different outcome variables. A significant negative correlation has been found between **participation/information** and change in psychic exhaustion ($r = -.33, p < .05$). This indicates that a high score in participation is significantly related to a decrease in psychic exhaustion. Other outcome variables have not been found to be significantly related to participation/information. *Thus, hypothesis H_3 is partly supported with respect to participation/information and change in psychic exhaustion.*

With regard to program implementation results (table 4) show that the achievement of the first process goal **(identification of important stress**

sources) is significantly correlated with a decrease in psychosomatic symptoms ($r = .38$, $p < .05$). The achievement of the second process goal (**elaboration of clear action plans**) is not significantly related to any outcome variable. However, correlations of $r = -.29$ ($p < .07$) with psychosomatic symptoms and $r = .32$ ($p < .06$) with pleasure of work are marginally significant. Thus, these correlations may indicate that the elaboration of clear action plans is related to a reduction in psychosomatic symptoms and to an enhancement of pleasure of work. The achievement of the third process goal (**realization of stress management actions**) is significantly related to a decrease in perceived stress ($r = -.52$, $p < .01$) and psychic exhaustion ($r = -.37$, $p < .05$) and to an increase in social support – especially supervisor support ($r = .35$, $p = .04$) and pleasure of work ($r = .37$, $p < .05$). In addition the marginally significant correlations with psychological job demands ($r = -.31$, $p < .06$) and decision latitude ($r = .29$, $p < .08$) imply a relationship between concrete stress management actions and a reduction of psychological job demands and an enhancement of decision latitude. *In conclusion hypothesis H_4 is partly supported.*

Table 4. **Correlations between process variables and intervention outcome**

	process variables				
	process quality		**process goals**		
change over time[1] in	Participation/ Information	Session Comfort	Identification of stress sources	Elaboration of action plans	Organizational actions
Psych. Job Demands	-.05	.08	.21	-.05	*-.31*[2]
Decision Latitude	-.02	.10	-.19	-.03	*.29*[2]
Social Support	.20	.17	-.17	.13	**.35***
Perceived stress	-.17	-.15	.23	-.09	**-.52****
Irritation	-.02	.06	-.13	.03	.03
Psychic Exhaustion	**-.33***	-.20	-.04	-.25	**-.37***
Psychosomatic Symptoms	-.23	.01	**-.38***	*-.29*[2]	-.14
Pleasure of Work	.26	.06	-.23	*.32*[2]	**.37***

Notes: N = 29
** correlation is significant at the 0.01 level (1-tailed)
* correlation is significant at the 0.05 level (1-tailed)
[1] change over time ∧ difference post-test – pre-test (negative values indicate reduction)
[2] marginal significant correlations (due to insufficient statistical power)

Analyses of the **correlations between the process variables** themselves revealed that participation is significantly related to the achievement of the second ($r = .90$, $p < .01$) and the third process goal ($r = .54$, $p < .01$). The correlation between participation and the achievement of the first process goal is, possibly due to a lack in statistical power, only marginally significant ($r = .35$, $p < .08$). For session comfort a marginally significant correlation with the achievement of the first process goal ($r = .34$, $p < .09$) has been found as well and session comfort is significantly related to participation ($r = .46$, $p < .05$). Furthermore the elaboration of clear action plans is significantly ($r = .56$, $p < .01$) correlated to the realization of stress management actions.

Summary of results With regard to **program effectiveness** one significant time x group interaction-effect has been found: after the program psychosomatic complaints have been reduced in the intervention group in comparison to the control group. In the intervention group as well as in the control group significant changes over time (main effect) in the expected direction (reduction) have been found for work-related stressors. For decision latitude, social support and pleasure of work a main effect has been found as well but in a direction opposed to the expectation. Scores on these three variables have been reduced after the program in the intervention group as well as in the control group.

With regard to **moderating process variables** a significant negative correlation between participation/information and change in psychic exhaustion over time has been found. This indicates that high participation and information during the intervention is related to a reduction of psychic exhaustion. For session comfort no significant correlations with change in the different outcome variables have been found. Concerning program implementation results show that the better relevant stress sources are identified the more psychosomatic symptoms are reduced. Marginally significant correlations indicate that the elaboration of clear action plans is related to a reduction in psychosomatic symptoms and to an enhancement of pleasure of work. Finally, the realization of concrete stress management actions is significantly related to change in several outcome variables. Additional explorative analyses revealed significant intercorrelations between the process variables.

6. Discussion

The aim of this study was to investigate if the presented stress management program is effective in reducing work-related stressors, perceived stress and its short-term and long-term consequences and in enhancing external and internal resources.

6.1 Program effectiveness

With regard to **program effectiveness** results show that the program led to a slight reduction of psychosomatic symptoms whereas other distal variables have not been significantly affected. This result is rather surprising as it is not in line with findings within the scope of general stress research indicating that psychosomatic symptoms represent medium-term consequences of short-term stress reactions such as irritation and psychic exhaustion (Leitner, 1999; Mohr et al., 2003). Thus, the reduction of irritation and psychic exhaustion should be a precondition for reduced psychosomatic symptoms. Two explanations are possible. Firstly, measurement problems could have led to distorted results. It could be supposed that physical symptoms are better observable or remarkable for the respondents than psychic short-term stress reactions. This could cause inexact measurement of the latter. Assuming that in an organizational context respondents are more reluctant to report psychic stress symptoms than physical symptoms, the occupational context could have led to inexact measurement of psychic variables as well.

Secondly, this program outcome could be explained by different degrees of process goal achievement. Results show that a reduction in psychosomatic symptoms is significantly related to the successful identification of important stress sources. Results show as well that indeed this first process goal has been slightly better achieved than the two other process goals and thus possibly led to the significant reduction of psychosomatic symptoms in the intervention group. The same argument can be applied to explain the lack of positive effects on perceived stress and psychic exhaustion. Results show that a reduction on these two outcome variables is significantly related to the achievement of the third process goal – realization of stress management actions, which has only been attained to a minor degree. Moreover, change in psychic exhaustion has been found to be negatively related to participation/information, which has only been realized to a minor degree as well. These impact mechanisms, however, can only be cautiously assumed as process variables have not been assessed in real time during the process but during the post-test of the outcome variables. Thus the results do not allow for a causal interpretation of the relationship between process variables and change in outcome variables. The same restriction has to be applied to all interpretations of this paragraph.

With regard to work-related stressors, decision latitude and social support no significant time x group interaction effect has been found, indicating that the program had no effect on these variables. The reduction of work-related stressors over time in the intervention group as well as in the control group (main effect over time) implies that stressors decreased independently from the intervention due to changed organizational circumstances within the whole department or even the whole company. However, independence between the control group and the intervention group could not be fully guaranteed in this study as supervisors responsible for both groups were involved in the program as well. Thus, it is possible that the control group has unintentionally been affected by stress management activities. Consequently, the main effect over time may also be interpreted as a spill-over of program effects from the intervention group to the control group. When we look at decision latitude and social support a significant reduction over time, which is opposed to the expectations, has to be stated. As the reduction took place in the intervention group as well as in the control group, it is most possibly founded on general changes within the organization (e.g. general restructuring processes).

With respect to pleasure of work – no significant interaction-effects have been found, indicating that the program had no effect on this variable. Insufficient resources enhancement activities (e.g. redesign of working tasks and content), which are considered to address external and internal resources could be a possible reason for this finding. The small but significant reduction of pleasure of work over time has possibly been caused by general organizational circumstances as both groups – intervention and control group – are concerned.

6.2 The role of process variables

In the first instance the **achievement of process goals**, especially the realization of stress management actions, seems to be much more important for program effectiveness than process quality. Changes in perceived stress, psychic exhaustion and social support are significantly related to the degree of realized actions (achievement of 3rd process goal) indicating that the more concrete organizational stress management actions are realized the more are perceived stress and psychic exhaustion reduced and the more social support is increased. The same conclusion may possibly be drawn for psychological job demands (i.e. work-related stressors) and decision latitude.

The first process goal – identification of relevant stress sources – seems to be of special importance for the reduction of psychosomatic symptoms. It is possible that the reflection and discussion of stress sources with colleagues during the group sessions is perceived as a kind of social support, which has already been found by Frese and Semmer (1991) to provide a buffering effect with regard to negative health consequences of external stressors and perceived stress. Consequently, it may be supposed that the first phase of the program (assessment phase) already provides the potential to reduce negative health consequences such as psychosomatic symptoms as it probably acts as a form of social support. However, the reduction of stress sources and the experience of stress can only be achieved by realizing concrete stress management actions.

The second process goal – elaboration of clear action plans – seems to be less important with respect to the intervention outcome as no significant correlations have been found. However, the lack of statistical power may be the reason for the insignificance of correlations especially concerning psychosomatic symptoms and pleasure of work. Results suggest that elaborating clear action plans is important for a reduction of psychosomatic symptoms and an enhancement of pleasure of work. Moreover, the strong relation between the two process goals elaboration of action plans (2nd goal) and realization of stress management actions (3rd goal) stresses the importance of the second process goal within the stress management process and shows that without planning realization is difficult.

Process quality (i.e. high scores in participation and session comfort) has been expected to have a positive effect on the intervention outcome. Results show that this is the case for participation/information with regard to psychic exhaustion. The significant negative correlation indicates that the more participative the stress management process is, the more reduction in psychic exhaustion can be expected. This corresponds to the earlier described findings of Sochert (1999). However, it is important to note that this result does not allow for a causal interpretation of the relationship between participation and reduction in psychic exhaustion as process variables have not been measured in real time during the process but during the post-measurement of the outcome variables. Thus, it is also possible that program participants who reported a reduction in psychic exhaustion tended to give positively biased ratings of participation. With respect to other outcome variables the degree of realized participation seems to be less important. The results for session comfort indicate that this process variable has no direct influence on program effectiveness.

This could provoke the conclusion that achievement of process goals is more important for program effectiveness than process quality. But looking at the intercorrelations between the process variables it becomes clear that probably the process quality variables participation/information and session comfort determine the degree to which process goals are achieved (moderation of the intervention effect) while the latter act as a precondition for positive intervention effects (mediation of the intervention effect). This corresponds to Bunce's (1997) assumption of moderated mediation. Based on the presented results it could be assumed that session comfort supports the identification of relevant stress sources and active participation of employees in the group discussions. This participation seems to be of key importance to elaborate good action plans, which are in turn precondition for the realization of stress management actions.

6.3 Limitations

Methodological barriers imposed by the organizational setting caused several threats to the internal validity of this evaluation study. Firstly, the equivalence between intervention group and control group could not be completely guaranteed. Despite the assessment and control of demographic variables, which may be related to indicators of the intervention outcome uncontrolled selection with respect to other unknown but important variables could have occurred. Secondly, complete independence between intervention group and control group could not be guaranteed as supervisors responsible for both groups were involved in the program as well. This caused difficulties when interpreting main effects over time. It remains unclear if effects that occurred in both groups over time resulted from general organizational changes which are unrelated to the intervention or represent program effects that spilled over into the control group.

Thirdly, a high drop-out rate between the two times of measurement had to be stated. Results show that respondents (responding at time 1 and 2) reported at time 1 significantly less work-related stressors than drop-outs. Thus, the results mainly reflect program effects on participants starting with a rather low stress level. This may have generated a floor effect in terms of a rather small possibility for further reduction of initially low scores.

6.4 Conclusion

In conclusion the evaluated program provides a high potential to reach effectiveness if emphasis is put on good program implementation and process quality. The following improvements seem to be of special importance to increase program effectiveness:

(1) A basic screening of work-related stressors prior to the program seems to be important to identify departments which will benefit most from the program. It is suggested to apply detailed work analysis instruments that refer to the earlier introduced classification of work-related stressors. (2) Detailed conceptualization and structuring of the action planning phase is recommended to assure regular follow-up and realization of stress management actions. It is suggested to use the health circle method according to Friczewski (1994) as a basis, as this method facilitates employee participation, efficient action planning and integration of individual-oriented stress management activities in form of education and training. (3) In addition to improvements of the intervention process itself a better integration of the program into the overall organization is strongly recommended. (4) General program resources need to be provided in order to enable a just-in-time realization of stress management activities (especially external training and coaching services) and to avoid long periods of program delay.

For further research it seems to be of high importance to pay more attention to process variables in order to gain knowledge about the effects of differences in intervention processes and contextual circumstances (Bunce, 1997; Nytro et al. 2000; Saksvik et al., 2002). This should allow identifying process variables representing important preconditions for intervention effectiveness regardless of the concrete intervention methods. First attempts in this direction have been undertaken by Bunce & West (1996), Sochert (1999) and Saksvik et al. (2002). This study tried to pursue this line of research. The importance of employee participation that has already been reported by Sochert (1999) could be supported. The important role of process goal achievement as defined by Sochert (1999) has been supported as well. In addition the results indicate differential functionality of these process goals with respect to the intervention outcome. Hopefully these interesting results encourage further research in this direction.

Backgrounds of Absenteeism

Dirk Hanebuth

1. What is absenteeism?

The meaning of absence from work depends upon the motivation attributed to this behavior, its timing, the frequency of its occurrence, and the social setting in which it occurs (Johns & Nicholson, 1990, p. 134; Rosse & Miller, 1984, p. 194). Nicholson even describes absence as a potential "flight from the work-place" (Nicholson, 1977, p. 241), and draws on the adverse and probably harmful influence of work on employees' health. In the following, I will first present an epidemiological perspective of the problem and provide a rationale for an extended model of sickness absenteeism and other forms of absenteeism. The first question to bediscussed is the relevance of absenteeism. This can be answered by recent incidence rates: A large epidemiological study from the European Foundation for the Improvement of Living and Working Conditions has contributed to the understanding of the relative weight of physical and mental health indicators across the EU member countries for working populations (Paoli & Merllié, 2001, p. 35). Of the 21,703 workers interviewed in face-to-face interviews in the year 2000, only 54% thought they would be able or willing to do the same job when 60 years old, 60% said their work does influence their health, 33% reported backache, 28% reported stress, 23% overall fatigue, and 9% reported absences due to work-related health problems. What does that imply? — First, absenteeism (in this case, absenteeism due to sickness) seems to be a considerable phenomenon in working populations. Second, the report does not explicitly reflect one of the important elements of the above-mentioned definition of the meaning of absence: the motivational aspect. The next sections extend the absence definitions step-by-step.

1.1 Phenomenology

Absenteeism has been regarded as visible behavior that comes in "pre-packed", discrete and objectively measurable units. Nevertheless, the real measurement problems for researchers do not occur at that phenomenological level. It is less important to ask how absenteeism can be measured than to query what the phenomenon is that we are measuring. The following section expatiates the most important aspects of absenteeism measurement. At the phenomenological level, coworkers are absent when they are not present at their designated workplaces. Thus, Johns congruously describes absenteeism as a "hard" criterion variable (Johns, 1978, p. 431). Reasons for this observable absence encompass a wide spectrum ranging from simple, short-term absences, such as to "take a cup of coffee in the office-kitchen", or "copy some documents in the copy room", to serious long-term absences such as sickness absences related to surgery. More-over, absence only comes into consideration if the absent employee should be present at work, which might be true for the coffee example, is not true for the copy example, and certainly not true for the surgery example. To avoid misun-derstandings, important conceptual differentiation regarding the notion "absen-teeism" must be considered: The minimum requirement for being able to define absenteeism is the existence of an explicit contract of employment, including formalities concerning working schedules and tolerated variations (Audas et al. even use the theoretical background of „malfeasance" to incorporate "both labor demands and supply side influences" in their absenteeism analysis (Audas & Goddard, 2001, p. 405)). Second, this privity of contract must include the duty to be present at specified times (for an anecdotal counter-example see Hulin, 1984, p. 393). This duty of attendance can be defined in various ways. For ex-ample, working times can be determined as working days per week/month (e.g. 40 hours/week - 5 days/week schedules) or by working hours per day in fixed intervals (such as shift-work models). A further differentiation concerns the de-grees of freedom for the employees to plan their working times independently. Workweek schedules differ immensely in respect of their degrees of freedom. Some schedules permit starting work between 8 a.m. and 9 a.m. with a subse-quent 8-hour working day. Others are more flexible and allow employees to vary the length of the working day, provided the total scheduled working time per week is guaranteed (flextime models). In contrast to that, most shift models in industrial assembly production dictate the beginning and the end of working shifts exactly.Summarizing these issues, non-attendance at the designated work-place is not always equal to absenteeism. This "first look" at the criterion re-veals that the strictly phenomenological "interpretation" of absenteeism is insuf-ficient. The next section elaborates on the context-dependency of current ab-sence definitions.

1.2 Absence definitions as a function of company reality

Company records on absenteeism differ systematically. A closer look reveals that employers in industry set specific absence definitions according to labor laws and production demands. Individual definitions partly depend on the spe-cific type of work organization. Some production processes demand simultane-ous presence of all members of the underlying process (e.g. car manufacturers with assembly lines). Here, non-attendance of employees can seriously disturb the entire assembly line. Companies therefore establish suitable "backup-solutions": In many production lines there are employees called "jumpers". These workers are well-skilled, they know the complete production process, and they can temporarily substitute any worker in the case of necessary short term absences (from minutes to hours) (also see Baltes, Briggs, Huff, Wright, & Neuman, 1999, p. 498). By contrast, flexible group-work production processes have an inherent propensity to buffer the absence of an employee. The tolerable buffering period depends on the clock time of the underlying production process (e.g. small series, as in handcraft watch manufacturing in Switzerland). In many cases it will even be possible for the absent employee to rework the time lost. Consequently, the differences in absence definition between companies and branches seem to be plausible. Finally, it should be mentioned that in Germany absence periods from one to three days do not require a medical certificate. Absence periods of more than three days must be certified by a physician. Regrettably, the absence data of the company do not include the reasons for absence. The following section discusses motivational aspects of absenteeism.

1.3 The multidimensionality of absence

The voluntary-involuntary distinction One of the most important theoretical contributions to research on absenteeism was the framework from Steers and Rodes. Many studies in the 80s and 90s referred to their concept of voluntary (as a placeholder for attendance motivation), and involuntary absenteeism (as a placeholder for the ability to come to work) (Steers & Rhodes, 1978). Researchers have linked various types of operationalization with voluntary and involuntary absences according to the theoretical concept. This methodology has been persistently criticized, especially the dichotomous approach of relating absence indicators to voluntary and involuntary absenteeism (Hammer & Landau, 1981). The most outstanding operationalization is the „attitudinal index" (voluntary one-day absences) (Chadwick-Jones, Brown, Nicholson, & Sheppard, 1971).

Criterion contamination There is evidence for the insufficiency of this simplification. Though it has been noted that there seems to be no reliable way to measure "voluntary absenteeism" (Nicholson, 1977, p. 240), it may be justified to cluster voluntary and involuntary reasons on a theoretical level only. Beyond this dichotomy, there may be reasons that encompass both elements, and this is considered in Steel's proposition of "misclassified and/or gray-area cases" (Steel, 2003, p. 247). The following example illustrates the problem: Assuming an employee has a painful headache (e.g. a migraine) and the physician's recommendation is to stay at home, with medical certification. From the employee's point of view it may be possible to go to work in spite of the reduced working capacity (for example, because the work on that day will not require much mental effort). How could the absence decision by this employee be classified at this moment? When the employee suffering from the migraine decides to stay at home for a day, but returns to work afterwards, the absence period may contribute to the "voluntary class" (see above). This criterion contamination cannot be explained by the theoretical framework mentioned above (for further critique see Brooke & Price, 1989, p. 574).

Time lost index and frequency index An early meaningful differentiation in absence measurement was proposed by Fox in the form of the time lost index and the frequency index (Fox & Scott, 1943). From that time on, most studies about absenteeism used at least one of these indices as criterion variables (or finer variants thereof). For a long time, the link between time lost and frequency indices on one side and the above-mentioned clusters of reasons on the other were unquestioned. Johns resumes the discussion about the varying predictability of these two absence measures by discussing three corresponding meta-analyses on the relationship between job satisfaction and absenteeism (Hackett & Guion, 1985; Scott & Taylor, 1985). He draws two conclusions: First, the frequency index shows a predominant sensitivity for short-term voluntary processes, and the time lost index a predominant sensitivity for random and bias-producing events, like accidents and illness (illness seemed to be the "most usual objective reason for absence" (also see Herzberg, Mausner, Peterson, & Capwell, 1957)). Second, firms are more interested in time lost indices (with sanctions for employees exceeding defined levels of absence) than in frequency patterns (Johns, 1991). Does this imply that employees may "voluntarily" avoid exceeding the "critical level of sanction"? The minimum requirement for such a notion is that employees are aware of their absences. New studies about the use of self-reported absenteeism data show surprising differences between the days when workers were obviously absent (company records) and the days when workers believed they were absent (Haccoun & Jeanrie, 1995; Jacobson et al., 1996; Johns, 1994). Consequently, a reliable "data basis" for this voluntary employee behavior to avoid sanctions seems to be lacking.

The relation between legal requirements, short-term absence and motives Another aspect concerns the guidelines for medical certification of absence spells. If employees do not have to provide a medical certificate for absence spells below n days, while longer absence periods require a physician's certificate, it can be hypothesized that absence spells below n days may be exploited for personal reasons ("an extra short-holiday"). In other words, the lack of certification alleviates or even provokes the misuse of short-term absences for personal, non-sickness-related motives. This hypothesis implies that short-term absence spells can be predominantly attributed to "voluntary absenteeism" and long-term absence periods predominantly to health-related sickness leave and involuntary absenteeism (Atkin & Goodman, 1984; Chadwick-Jones et al., 1971; Clegg, 1983; Steel, Shane, & Kennedy, 1990). These „certification-borders" vary between countries. In contrast to Germany, Belgian employers demand a certificate for each day of absence.

The attitudinal index As mentioned before, the most prominent support for the voluntary argument was introduced by Chadwick-Jones and coworkers, with the "attitudinal index" reflecting the number of one- day absences, such as "blue Mondays" or "blue Fridays" (Chadwick-Jones et al., 1971), also labeled as "strategic absenteeism on Mondays and Fridays" (Johns, 2003, p. 164). What would that imply for an analysis of absences? — For the employee with migraine who decides to stay at home for a day, but returns to work afterwards, the absence period would contribute to the "voluntary class". Classifications like this would be misattributed because the person had a true medical reason. The problem is aggravated by two-day absences (no medical certification needed in Germany): Landy and coworkers report equal probabilities of illness and subsequent two-day-sickness absences for employees and argue that these are "genuine physical-illness patterns" (Landy, Vasey, & Smith, 1984, p. 123). Other studies give further examples of the contamination of reasons for short spells: In the exploratory study with 280 employees from Nicholson et al., "self report data show that minor ailments are the most frequently occurring potential absence-inducing events, and by far the most frequent cause of absence" (Nicholson & Payne, 1987).

"Monday" absenteeism In spite of these interpretative restrictions, employers and managers potentially attribute one- day absences on Mondays to the "strategic absenteeism" class. Indeed, this conclusion can be justified: Methodological considerations from Searle examined the probability of accumulated one-day absences. He observed that many certificates of medical incapacity to work were issued at the start of the working week. Searle interprets these findings as an indicator that the "patient rather than the doctor decides when absence will start" (Searle, 1989, p. 353). On the other hand, results from a simulation study failed to support this argumentation, but instead identified a methodical artifact as the reason for these absences, characterized as sick- leave abuse. High absence probabilities on Mondays can be the result of the aggregation of illness that began on Saturday, Sunday or Monday: For each of these absence periods, Monday is the first day the absence will be objectively noticed (Pocock, 1974). Notwithstanding all critics, the concept of Steers and Rhodes was so influential that many popular meta-analyses used the voluntary-involuntary argument with time lost and frequency indices as criterion variables (Steel, 2003, p. 244). One plausible reasoning was the inverse relation between job satisfaction and frequency indices of short lengths. Despite that, many researchers failed to confirm this hypothesis. Some authors even reported finding the opposite of the expected relationships between job satisfaction and predicted absence indices. In an often cited meta-analysis, frequency and job satisfaction was correlated with $r = -.16$, whereas the correlation with the time lost index was $r = -.24$ (Farrell & Stamm, 1988).

Critique of the attitudinal index Subsequent to the meta-analysis of Farrell and Stamm, a fruitful methodological discussion emerged. The most insistent critics are Brooke and Hammer. Brooke summarizes five difficulties in testing the Steers and Rhodes model of absenteeism that may have led to misinterpretations of the original model (Brooke, 1986): The questionable construct validity and operationalization of "attendance motivation", "attendance pressure" and "ability to attend", the lack of a clear definition of outcome variables, a mixture of theoretical concepts and operationalized variables on different levels of the model (without testing their explanatory power), the lack of variables such as drug abuse, and finally the labeling of the reasons for sickness absence as involuntary. Hammer et al. concluded at the beginning of the 80s: "Despite considerable research, absenteeism cannot be predicted with high or even moderate accuracy. Part of the blame for inconsistent and low validity coefficients has been placed on an inadequate theoretical foundation (Steers & Rhodes, 1978). Additional reasons for the disjointed research findings revolve around problems in criterion measurement." (Hammer & Landau, 1981, p. 574).

An extension of the voluntary-involuntary distinction One representative study that uses latent constructs instead of clearly operationalized, manifest variables is the theoretical approach from Nicholson. He even extends the Steers and Rhodes dimension of "attendance motivation" with a new dimension of avoidability, the so- called "A-B continuum", characterizing absence-inducing events in respect of their avoidability. He assumes that the inter-person variance of the impact of these events is due to the moderating effect of motivation and defines absence not "in terms of whether the absentee has or has not actually made a decision about attendance or non-attendance, but in terms of whether he could have" (Nicholson, 1977, p. 242). The scale end of type-B absenteeism describes an absence event under complete control of the employee (e.g. to savor the remaining time of a medically certified sickness absence interval in spite of early recovery), whereas a type-A absence is completely externally controlled (e.g. a strike with lock-out).

Semantic issues A further differentiation in absenteeism criteriology is a semantic one: Since the Steers and Rhodes model, "attendance" has been discussed as a possible dependent variable. For empirical research, absenteeism can be assumed to be the logical and semantic reverse of attendance, indicating the same phenomenon (Nicholson, 1977, p. 241). Further differentiations do not contribute to a better understanding of absence patterns, as long as the company records do not encompass detailed reasons for absences. Twenty years after the critical discussion on the Steers and Rhodes model, Steel notes that: "Methodological studies have informed and strengthened the empirical absence literature by fostering a process of definition refinement. Better operational definitions have led, in turn, to the development of more sensitive criterion variables and to the improved predictability of outcome measures." (Steel, 2003, p 244).

2. Theoretical approaches to absenteeism

Absenteeism has been described as a multicausal and complex phenomenon (Johns & Nicholson, 1990; Nicholson, 1993). The finding that there is a weak relationship between job satisfaction and numerous forms of absenteeism sparked the development of new theories on absenteeism (Farrell & Stamm,

1988; Hackett & Guion, 1985; Nicholson, Brown, & Chadwick-Jones, 1976; Scott & Taylor, 1985). Three examples are given below, illustrating the range of empirical absenteeism research. Each of the underlying studies used a specific form of absenteeism as criterion. Furthermore, the predictors are linked with different theoretical backgrounds. Example 1 illustrates the "voluntary" part of absence behavior and stands for the cognitive approaches. This study is a typical example of the "voluntary-involuntary absenteeism phase" in research during the 70s and 80s. Smith examined the attendance of 3,010 managerial employees on the day following an unexpected and severe snow storm in Chicago. At this managerial level, occasional absenteeism for one day did not lead to negative consequences, such as financial penalties, for the employees (Smith, 1977). The company administered the organizational survey shortly before the introduction of attendance registration. Therefore, the examination of the relationship between work attitudes and work attendance on this specific day in a natural field setting was enabled. Smith assumed a decision-making process and tested Herman's hypothesis that work attitudes are predictive of either type of work-related behavior, as long as such behavior is under the control of the individual workers (Herman, 1973). The results confirmed the underlying hypothesis of a significant positive correlation between job satisfaction and job attendance on this specific day, but no significant correlation on a randomly chosen day (Smith, 1977). Example 2 shows the range of "sickness absences" across the European Union (EU) and suggests that there are various influences on the national level. The study reflects absenteeism as a baseline health indicator. The study compared the sickness absence frequencies in the 15 countries which constituted the European Union up to May 2004, when 10 further states acceded. The reported age- adjusted percentages of employees that were absent for at least one day in the year 2000 varied between 6.7 % in Greece and 24 % in Finland (Gimeno, Benavides, Benach, & Amick, 2004, p. 868). Here, only accidents at work, health problems caused by the work, or other health problems were included in the analysis. The descriptive study reflects different contexts on a national level within the European market. Social insurance systems, wage continuation in the case of sickness, and labor laws still differ remarkably between the European countries. Assuming there is a country- independent base rate of sickness absences (i.e. assuming that the probabilities of Finnish and Greek employees getting sick are nearly equal), the differences can only be explained by third variables. Example 3 stands for the theoretical view that "reciprocal social exchanges" predict absenteeism. The study extends the former "criterion view" on absenteeism. Absenteeism should be regarded not solely as an outcome variable, but also as a predictor of subsequent organizational effects (Breaugh, 1981). A broad discussion and review was first introduced by Goodman et al. (Goodman & Atkin, 1984). Ten years later, Tharenou's landmark study contributed to an interactive view of absenteeism behavior (Nicholson, 1993; Tharenou, 1993). The theoretical question was: Is absence simply an outcome variable, or is it also a potential predictor of subsequent behavior and attitudes on the part of employees and supervisors? Job satisfaction, employee performance, training achievement, supervisory style and absence data were collected at the beginning and at the end of a one-year interval. All test-retest reliabilities for the absence measures were significant at the 5%-level, the coefficients were $r = .48$ for the frequency index (number of absence spells for the one-year period), $r = .46$ for the time lost index (sum of all absence days for the one-year period), and $r = .15$ for certified absence periods (absence spells with medical certification). Cross-lagged regression analyses showed that neither job performance, nor any absenteeism index at time 1 predicted the subscales of leadership behavior "supervisory support", "work facilitation", and "goal emphasis" at time 2 (for scales see Hackman & Oldham, 1974, 1975). On the other hand, non-certified absenteeism and the time lost index predicted employee performance at time 2. However, Tharenou's results contradict the results of previous studies, in which absenteeism was a significant predictor of subsequent supervisor behavior (Szilagyi, 1980a, 1980b). Example 1 and example 2 focus on different origins of the same phenomenon. Though many studies on absenteeism start their introduction with Mowday's statement about absenteeism as a costly personnel phenomenon (Mowday, Porter, & Steers, 1982), the growing research interest cannot be justified by the economic view only. A first look reveals that a wide range of scientific domains, outside psychology, is exploring the phenomenon of absenteeism with different motives. Although based in the domain of research, all investigators follow the same practice-orientated target of reducing absenteeism. Business sciences are the leading domain with the aim of reducing the costs of absenteeism, e.g. by testing sanctions, absenteeism feedback interventions or extended applicant selection procedures (Dilts & Deitsch, 1986; Gaudine & Saks, 2001; Ones, Viswesvaran, & Schmidt, 2003; Poole, 1999). Medical sciences are apparently trying to prevent absenteeism by revealing harmful working conditions or by testing health intervention programs (for an overview see Murphy, 1996). Sociology links individual and group absence behavior with social context variables, such as work-group absence norms (Chadwick-Jones, Nicholson, & Brown, 1982; Gellatly & Luchak, 1998; Narayanan, Menon, & Spector, 1999; Xie & Johns, 2000).

Is there a unifying absence theory? Literature reviews regarding theory development summarize research paradigms rather than widely accepted theoretical frameworks (e. g. Fichman, 1984; Harrison & Martocchio, 1998). Instead of an intense discussion on theory development in absenteeism research (which would go far beyond the scope of this work), an overview of the current research paradigms is presented below. On the one hand, there is a large stock of studies about absenteeism utilizing various methods and methodologies. Johns nevertheless sees great advantages in absenteeism research, regardless of the lack of a unifying theoretical paradigm. He appreciates the wealth of studies as contributing to methodical and methodological diversity (Johns, 1997; 2003, pp 157-158). On the other hand, the same research has been criticized as non-theory based and eclectic (Kaiser, 1998; Nicholson, 1977; Steers & Rhodes, 1978). Others even mentioned that the methods in data management and the data analysis of epidemiological records are non- professional (Reidy, 1991), and that the low return on investment in practical absenteeism research is due to an illegitimate simplification of the criterion (Rosse & Miller, 1984, p. 194). Researchers still controversially discuss the quality of current knowledge about absenteeism. Indeed, the amount of "new" or "stand-alone" theoretical assumptions has become unmanageable, which was already noted in the 80s (Brooke, 1986; Chadwick-Jones et al., 1982; Johns & Nicholson, 1990). In the late 90s, there was no recognizable theory development based on existing theories (for further critiques see Alexanderson, 1998, p. 241; Martinko, Gundlach, & Douglas, 2002, p. 36). However, other reviewers reject this view. In their review of absenteeism research for the twenty years following the Steers and Rhodes model, Harrison and Martoccio conclude that "research on absenteeism is more healthy, robust and cumulative than 20 years ago" (Harrison & Martocchio, 1998, p. 342). The next sections outline the main flows in absenteeism research, referring to the most popular, pertinent studies.

2.1 The individual approach

One of the most provocative and influential paradigms of absenteeism research was the voluntary-involuntary argument from Steers and Rhodes. Regardless of the question as to whether the elements of this dichotomy are the ends of a continuum, this differentiation led to broad research activities on voluntary (or more exactly: motivational) processes in absence behavior. It was an appropriate model for study designs with individual measurement of personality variables and attitudes. Moreover, the authors introduced their postulate as a process model, hypothesizing that actual absenteeism behavior stands in a reciprocal relationship with job attitudes and subsequent attendance motivation. Generally, this conceptual breakthrough opened the field for a research domain in which between-person differences are seen as the reason for absence variance. The problem of the construct validity based on the unclear operationalization of both "ability" (involuntary) and "attendance motivation" (voluntary) (Brooke, 1986; Hammer & Landau, 1981; Kerr & Vos, 1993, p. 180; Steel, 2003) led to a dead end in empirical absenteeism research. Interindividual differences in personality and attitudes are important predictors of subsequent absence behavior. Surprisingly, absenteeism research focusing on individual differences has recently made a dynamic start. In the early 40s Katz et al. mentioned that the reasons for absenteeism may arise from within the person, assuming a higher probability of employee absence when "morale is low" (Katz & Hyman, 1943, p. 20). Herzberg et al. underline the "importance of attacking attitudinal factors in solving this costly problem" (Herzberg et al., 1957, p. 107). In the meantime, the predominant part of current absenteeism research addresses interindividual and intra-individual differences (Johns, 2003, p. 163).

Results from motivational research Early meta-analyses concerned the most striking area of interest of both employers and scientists: the relationship between job satisfaction and absenteeism (Hackett & Guion, 1985; Scott & Taylor, 1985). Dissatisfied employees were hypothesized to be "more absent" than employees who are satisfied with their job. Surprisingly, the mean correlations were apparently low, but the variance across reported correlations was high. Others have argued that the true correlations may be even near zero, because of the fact that probably many more studies with positive correlations were published — leading to an overestimation of real effects in current meta-analyses (Scott & Taylor, 1985, p. 609). In-depth secondary analyses testing numerous moderator variables showed that the job-satisfaction-absenteeism relation was not that simplistic. Job status was identified as moderator: the higher the job status, the higher the correlation between satisfaction and absenteeism (Farrell & Stamm, 1988; Hackett, 1989). Regardless of the rising popularity of multivariate statistical methods, it has been argued that empirical results have yielded little cumulative knowledge regarding the determinants of absenteeism (Brooke & Price, 1989; Kaiser, 1998) and that single predictors, such as job satisfaction, tenure or gender, explain little variance in absenteeism (Mathieu & Kohler, 1990, p. 217).

Further research development The next cognizable step was the development of within-person designs that allow us to observe what circumstances function as a trigger turning a potential influence into a subsequent absence period. However, predicting behavior measures in organizations (e.g. turnover, health, performance, and absence) is inherently difficult (Fichman, 1984, p. 2). Two employees might have had completely different reasons for being absent in Smith's study of attendance on a specific day, one might have taken advantage of the snow storm to avoid an unpleasant meeting in his department; the other might have seized the chance to spend a day with his family. From a phenomenological view, both absence events are the same. Johns and Nicholson propose a "more painstaking investigation, in which ideographic techniques are used to correctly specify the boundaries that are appropriate to explaining episodes and which will enable us to judge when similar explanations are valid for individual actors and episodes" (Johns & Nicholson, 1990, p. 135)). Studies with ideographic designs are extensive and, therefore, rare. Two exceptions are a nurses study, in which absence events were simultaneously matched with absence reasons in a daily diary (Hackett, 1989), and a further experimental study, in which employees rated the probability of reporting sick under specified circumstances. In the latter study, the authors were able to cluster absence profiles (Joseph J. Martocchio, 1994; J. J. Martocchio & Judge, 1994). In a further experimental study by the same authors with university employees, the researchers found dispositional influences on absenteeism attributions in their between- subject analysis. The attribution "life controlled by chance" and "learned helplessness" considerably contributed to external attributions of absenteeism, whereas a within-subject analysis showed that the attribution of external reasons for absenteeism varied remarkably across individuals, with illness as the most important factor (Judge & Martocchio, 1996). Two recent meta-analyses reflect an ongoing trend towards individual-centered approaches in the USA: the use of applicant data (personality traits and attitudes) relevant to absenteeism for personnel selection, in addition to other preemployment tests. Though, the big-five- personality construct failed to predict absenteeism (Salgado, 2002), personality-based integrity tests in assessment interviews achieved a higher (and economically relevant) predictive validity ($r = .33$) for later absenteeism than the overt integrity test did ($r = .16$) (Ones et al., 2003). Biomedical drug screening is another established preemployment test method in large companies and administrative establishments (this is legal in the USA, but illegal in Germany). More than 20 years' experience with the validity of these tests show the high predictability of early illicit drug use for later absenteeism rates of the employees concerned (e. g. Normand, Salyards, & Mahoney, 1990). A study from Harrison et al. represents a methodical link between individual and social approaches and is suitable for connecting the current chapter and the next chapter on sociopsychological approaches. The researchers found a considerably high consistency coefficient ($a = .62$) for self-reported absenteeism across 11 non-overlapping settings. At the ideographic level, absenteeism was associated with perceived social expectations (high values indicate stricter absenteeism policies). Here, the related median correlation coefficient was $r = -.30$ (Harrison & Price, 2003).

2.2 The sociopsychological approach

Absenteeism as a form of human behavior can hardly be understood without accounting for the social context of the employee (Chadwick-Jones et al., 1982; Johns & Nicholson, 1990; Nicholson & Johns, 1985) and some authors even regard the study of social influences as a "more promising avenue" in clarifying inconsistent research findings across studies (Mathieu & Kohler, 1990, p. 217). Recent research has shown that a substantial part of the variance in absenteeism can be explained by influences of a social nature (Johns, 1997; Kaiser, 1998). The following sections provide a short review of the corresponding studies. When researchers and practitioners observe employee absenteeism behavior in a company, they do not simply examine the social influences of the work context, such as coworker support, supervisor behavior, absenteeism policies, group norms etc. Simultaneously, they observe the social influences that lie outside the premises. What does that mean for research? — In a nutshell, this entails restrictions for study designs and the subsequent interpretation of results. The descriptive epidemiological study by Gimeno et al. postulates that there are intercultural differences regarding the possibilities, and acceptance of reporting sick, provided that the risk of becoming ill does not vary considerably between the EU member countries (Gimeno et al., 2004; also see Nicholson & Johns, 1985, p. 399). On the other hand, a cross-national study with 1,772 employees at 14 workplaces in four countries showed the country-independent influence of group cohesion on absenteeism rates: The closer the employees worked together and the better the cohesion ("harmony"), the lower the absence event rates were (in this case, absence events are equal to the "frequency index") (Drago & Wooden, 1992). Interestingly, this effect was moderated by job satisfaction: If job satisfaction was high within a group, absence event rates were apparently low. Low job satisfaction led to higher absence events. The authors conclude that "games" are being played within work groups "with cohesive groups applying pressure on individuals to engage in either high or low absence" (p. 777). This phenomenon of group influence on individual absence behavior was introduced as "absence culture". In the view of Nicholson et al., "absence culture" as a concept was introduced in the early 50s by Hill and Trist (Hill & Trist, 1953, 1955; Nicholson & Johns, 1985, p. 398).

Levels of social influence The origins of social influences on absenteeism range from the work-group level (Geurts, Schaufeli, & Rutte, 1999; Mathieu & Kohler, 1990; Seago, 1996), the department level (Joseph J. Martocchio, 1994; J. J. Martocchio & Judge, 1994), the occupational status (Chadwick-Jones et al., 1982; Farrell & Stamm, 1988; Nicholson & Johns, 1985), and the company level (Schweiger & Denisi, 1991; Tomacci, 1997) up to the national level (Gimeno et al., 2004; Xie & Johns, 2000). (Apparently, many studies concerning social influences on absence - especially absence culture - were conducted in hospitals and other health care settings). Neither Nicholson et al. (Nicholson & Johns, 1985), nor Rhodes et al. (Rhodes & Steers, 1990) formally differ as to possible facets of absence climate according to the level of examination. Employees are exposed to various social/cultural levels: the company, the department, the group, and the individual level. Which level contributes most to the development of an "absence culture" within a group or in individual absence behavior? — A multilevel analysis simultaneously captured group-level absence standards and individual-level absence standards in an underlying "social attribution model". The authors hypothesized that social interaction with the work group and the identity given by the group to the employee interact with the attribution of "acceptable absence levels" (Markham & McKee, 1995). Consequently, the distribution of attribution patterns within and between the groups in five firms of the same company was used as an indicator of the degree of shared meaning for the analysis. The results for the random sample of 800 individuals and 41 supervisory groups showed medium differences in absenteeism rates between supervisory groups ($F = 2.79$; $p < .001$) (which is a basic requirement for further analyses), and small but significant differences between groups concerning perceptions of leadership absenteeism goals ($F = 1.85$; $p < .01$). Correlations between perceived supervisor standards and absenteeism were high with group means as data basis ($r = .50$; $p < .001$). On the other hand, perceived inner-group standards varied significantly between groups ($F = 2.48$; $p < .001$); correlations between the strictness of inner-group standards and absenteeism were not significant. Three main findings emerged: First, perceived supervisor standards overlapped with inner-group and individual standards in this study sample. In other words, work groups explained group members' absenteeism behavior better than individual-level factors. Second, on the department level, no plant effect was observed for any of the analyses. Third, the stability of group sizes did not seem to be associated with subsequent absenteeism (also see Markham, Dansereau, & Alutto, 1982).

Choice of absence measure The kind of absenteeism measure used for analysis seems to be important: A prospective study with bus-drivers showed the influence of group-level absences on subsequent individual absence day sums, but not on individual absence interval counts, which indicates that results concerning the interaction of group absences and individual absences are potentially sensitive to the type of absence measure (Mathieu & Kohler, 1990). Farrell and Stamm noted the same criterion problem as fundamental moderator in their review for the meta-analytic subanalysis of job satisfaction and absenteeism (Farrell & Stamm, 1988).

Job strain, social support and absenteeism Absenteeism is a potential outcome of strain in the workplace. Strain can be regarded as the existence of a stressor over a defined time interval, but also as the non-existence of strain- reducing and stress-reducing factors. Social support can buffer stress and reduce negative health outcomes (Hemingway & Marmot, 1999; Marmot, 1994; Schwarzer & Leppin, 1991). Although assessing health by measuring absenteeism is investigating a secondary rather than the primary outcome, absenteeism research underlines the positive effect of social support on the "secondary" health indicator sickness absence. In their prospective study, Väänänen et al. examined the influence of social support on subsequent absenteeism in 3,895 employees from private industry in Finland. Both coworker support and supervisor support predicted short absenteeism intervals (4–21 days absent) and long absenteeism intervals (>21 days absent). Even after controlling for previous absenteeism rates, demographic variables and further psychological variables, social support explained 5–9 % of absenteeism variance (Väänänen et al., 2003). North et al. examined absenteeism data for more than 10,000 British civil servants and correlated these data with psychosocial workplace variables. In line with the results from the Finnish study, positive social support reduced the probability of absenteeism: After controlling for age, socioeconomic status and further workplace variables, the relative risk (RR) for sickness absence declined from the baseline value of RR = 1 (low support at work) to values between RR = .95 and RR = .81 (high support at work) (also see Marmot, 1994, p. 197; North, Syme, Feeny, Shipley, & Marmot, 1996). Notably, lower grades of employment were associated with lower self-reported social support. In other words, employees with lower educational status seem to be disadvantaged.

Conclusion At the beginning of the present chapter, we asked which level of social influence contributes most to individual absence behavior. Social influences on absenteeism can be regarded as stable background variables. Depending on the study design, these variables may be treated as control variables or moderators. Accordingly, the section on social approaches concludes with a study by Lam et al.: The researchers confine the methodical scope of their cross-national study with Chinese and American workers and argue that the effect of immediate societal context variables in determining psychological reactions (in this case absence behavior) is distal rather than proximal. They conclude that they do not measure cultural differences, but differences in personality, partially influenced by societal variables (Lam, Schaubroeck, & Aryee, 2002, p. 4).

2.3 Economic context

Absenteeism is a problem that occurs across national borders and encompasses all types of industries (Steers & Rhodes, 1984, p. 230). Employees who are sick and whose working capacity is reduced should have the possibility to refrain from work and recover. This is a fundamental achievement of modern welfare states (Alexanderson, 1998). The World Health Organization (WHO) notes that the most widespread negative effect of work on mental health is stress and assumes that 50-60% of all working days lost in the European WHO region are related to stress (WHO, 2004a, 2004b). Mossink has argued that safety and health improvements for workers can bring appealing economic benefits for both companies and societies as a whole, and that financial saving estimations seem to be an effective way to convince decision makers: "What is the value of health, or not being ill?" (Mossink, 2002, p. 12). Besides her overview of company-level assessment methods, she extends the influence of sick leave on society beyond the company, namely, to the health care system, including insurance companies and public or collective funds, customers, colleagues, shareholders and, last but not least, the families of the workers (p. 5). In the early 80s Scott et al. concluded that managers' methods of reducing absenteeism were post hoc, reactive, and punishment-oriented (Scott & Markham, 1982). There is a highly effective example: General Motors reduced absence days by nearly 50% in the early 80s with an „intervention program" that was only based on the strict compliance with (well-known) regulations: In this cooperation project with the United Auto Workers, adherence to three established "guidelines" was enforced. First, compensation-related incentives for casual absences were removed. Instead, fringe benefits were directly linked with hours worked. Second, contractual disciplinary procedures were consequently applied. Third, employees were informed about the costs of absenteeism at the company and the group level (Dilts & Deitsch, 1986, p. 46). Nicholson regards the predominant managerial orientation as the main reason for the "assumptive nature" of absenteeism research and questions the tendency to regard absenteeism behavior as organizational behavior because of the „default registration" of absence data by companies (Nicholson, 1977, p. 237). Besides that critique, it is easy to understand why absenteeism research is mostly associated with economic interests: Usually, the absentee data are provided by organizations supporting or even enabling the underlying studies. Of course, the wish for more detailed insight into the organization-specific absence patterns is common to both the researchers and the organization (also see Hulin, 1984, p. 392). As mentioned before, social influences on absenteeism can be regarded as background variables. Economic background variables refer to the same class of confounders and therefore should either be controlled in an adequate way or considered when interpreting absenteeism results.

3. The problem of control variables and background variables

The preceding sections discussed individual and sociopsychological approaches to absenteeism. Social and economic phenomena can act as serious confounders (third variables). Depending on the research question, researchers strive to find considerable variance in social variables, in order to study their effect or to eliminate their influence. In practice this implies that the presence of third factors can either mask the effects or lead to overestimated results regarding predictors of absenteeism (Clegg, 1983). Generally, the impact of third variables on the specific absence patterns under examination should be considered. Social insurance systems have been discussed as having a latent, but strong, influence on absenteeism behavior in Germany (Salowsky, 1991; also see Steel et al., 1990). Other examples of relatively stable variables or influences are national employment rates and geographical circumstances. The explanatory variance in these variables in respect of absenteeism can only be estimated by large cross-national studies.

Semantic convention Steel et al. link absenteeism research with sociotechnical system theories, assuming that behavioral changes will accompany social-system change (Steel et al., 1990, p. 423). Variables on that level should be defined as background variables with relatively stable characteristics over time (also see Alexanderson, 1998). Contrary to that, variables such as age, gender and tenure are typical control/moderator variables in absenteeism research (Searle, 1989, p. 352). Scores of such potential confounder variables have been employed in statistical analyses - though we find no consistent control of these variables in absenteeism research (Clegg, 1983).

The relation between absenteeism and turnover The phenomenon absenteeism cannot fully be appreciated without considering the impact of background and control variables on absenteeism. In the 40s and 50s, a discussion about the relationship between absenteeism and turnover emerged, which is sufficient to illustrate the potential influence of background variables: Herzberg et al. regard the (voluntary) employee decision to take a day off as a "miniature version" of the more important decision to resign (Herzberg et al., 1957, p. 103). Their progressive withdrawal model assumes that rising absenteeism is a precursor of subsequent turnover and that there is a positive correlation of both measures (p. 105). In contrast, Hill et al. regard absenteeism and turnover as alternative ways to escape dissatisfying working conditions, consequently there is a negative correlation between both phenomena at the same time (Hill & Trist, 1953, p. 360). The scope of these assumptions even includes hazardous behavior: Accidents at work are harmful events for affected employees and a costly phenomenon for employers. It can be rationally argued that employees naturally do not tend to risk their health or even their lives by provoking such accidents. For the voluntary-involuntary argument of absenteeism this statement implies that sickness absence caused by an accident may be interpreted as an indicator of involuntary processes that cannot be controlled by the coworkers. Actually, Hill and Trist even allow for accidents as a probable indicator of voluntary withdrawal intentions. In other words, employees potentially provoke absenteeism via accidents (p. 359). What kind of absenteeism can be measured in empirical studies? — Is it a temporal, masked or morbid kind of absenteeism, resulting from high unemployment rates ? Possible impacts of the background variable "employment rate" are (a) substantially reduced absence rates because of high job insecurity (Leigh, 1985), or (b) increased absence rates as compensating behavior for turnover, because of the lack of job alternatives in the market with low "ease of movement" (Larson, 1985, p. 464). Two recent meta-analyses addressed the absenteeism-turnover topic (Hom, Caranikas-Walker, Prussia, & Griffeth, 1992; Mitra, Jenkins, & Gupta, 1992; for an overview see Rosse & Miller, 1984). Mitra et al. found a corrected mean correlation of $r = .330$ between absenteeism and turnover in 17 studies. Causal testing of the relation of absenteeism and turnover is impossible, unless potential time effects are considered. The hypothesis of turnover as an after-effect of absenteeism can only be tested with (a) longitudinal designs in which the absence measurement period precedes turnover registration, and (b) intra-personal, repeated measurement for each employee (see Zapf, Dormann, & Frese, 1996). The meta-analysis from Mitra et al. satisfies both requirements (Mitra et al., 1992, p. 885). In their moderator analysis, with monthly employment rates for each year of data collection for each study, results showed considerable influence of the moderator employment rates on the correlation between absenteeism and turnover ($r = -.51$; $p = .004$). Correlations between absenteeism and turnover are lower in times of high unemployment (p. 886). Corresponding results from the meta-analytic structural equation models from Hom et al. showed a small, but significant, influence of several forms of unemployment at an early stage in absenteeism-turnover processes: Unemployment moderated the pathways between job satisfaction and withdrawal cognitions (Hom et al., 1992, p. 899). The aforementioned details underline the need to incorporate the background variable employment rate in the interpretation of absence data analyses.

Economical development Economic and market conditions were already mentioned as major influences on employee attendance in the landmark study by Steers and Rhodes (Steers & Rhodes, 1978, p. 397). The researchers included these influences in their process model of employee attendance as "pressures to attend" (p. 393). An epidemiological study with N = 84,319 employees in two counties in Sweden showed no relation between employment rates and long-term sickness absences (>30 days) for women, but a 60% lower absence rate for men in the quartile with the highest unemployment rate compared with the lowest unemployment quartile (Knutsson & Goine, 1998). This result is alarming: If one assumes that unemployment is not a pro-factor for health, this potentially indicates that there is a behavioral adaptation process to job insecurity by the working population. Probably, a part of the long-term sickness absences are masked voluntary absences ("sickness absence abuse"). If this holds true, a reduction in rates would be desirable. In contrast, if employees shorten their rehabilitation time due to fears about loosing their jobs, this would reflect an undesirable and harmful tendency (the latter phenomenon has recently been discussed in the literature as "presenteeism" or "sick but yet at work" (also see Aronsson, Gustafsson, & Dallner, 2000; Chatterji & Tilley, 2002; Koopman et al., 2002)). It is also conceivable that both patterns are present simultaneously. Job-security perceptions seem to play an important role. These perceptions differ widely between countries: A recent European study reported considerable differences in the 25 EU member countries (Fayey, 2004, p. 26). Another epidemiological study within the EU's 15 member countries in the year 2000 showed substantial differences between the types of employment and absenteeism. Even after controlling for individual-level working conditions (e.g. leadership behavior) and country level variables (such as employment rates), full time work was associated with higher absenteeism rates compared with part time work (Benavides, Benach, Diez-Roux, & Roman, 2000). Results from a cross-national study in Australia, New Zealand, Canada and the USA by Drago and Wooden confirmed that absenteeism rates for part-time workers are lower and that there is an inverse relationship between unemployment rates and absenteeism, independent of the business, company and country concerned (Drago & Wooden, 1992).

Workweek schedules It is assumed that employees working under flextime schedules respond more easily to work- life balance demands (Baltes et al., 1999, p. 498; Nord & Costigan, 1973). A recent meta- analysis examined the effects of flextime schedules with different degrees of flexibility (N = 27 studies) and compressed workweek schedules (N = 12 studies; in most cases 4-day workweeks with 10 hours' working time per day) (Baltes et al., 1999). Baseline data were collected before the introduction of the alternative workweek schedule. (Unfortunately, only 13 studies comprised the absenteeism criterion, and only nine studies were conducted with industrial samples — This ratio of industrial to non-industrial studies is characteristic for absenteeism research). In the review by Baltes et al., mean weighted correlations showed a medium-sized positive effect of flextime work schedules in eight of the studies included ($r = .42$; $N = 1,034$) and a null effect for the introduction of compressed workweek schedules in five of the studies ($r < .01$; $N = 507$) (pp 504-506). As noted before, multilevel studies showed inter-country differences in absence patterns. Therefore, it is necessary to take into consideration the country from which the data were obtained. Example 2 in chapter 1.2 reports on results from an epidemiological study in the 15 countries which constituted the European Union up to May 2004. As already reported, the percentage of employees with at least one day of sickness absence per year ranged from 6.7% in Greece to 20.3% in Germany and 24% in Finland. It can be argued that Finland as the "leader" of these statistics must be regarded as a "special candidate" for absenteeism analyses. There is one comparatively large study with a similar approach to workweek schedules from Finland. Interestingly, the influence of "control over working time" (quartiles from low control to high control) in this epidemiological study with municipal employees showed small effects on absenteeism for women, but no effects at all for men after controlling for age and other demographics, health behavior and baseline health (Ala-Mursula, Vahtera, Kivimaeki, Kevin, & Pentti, 2002).

Regional differences The large multilevel analysis by Markham included national-level absence data (monthly median scores) from the Bureau of National Affairs between the years 1976 and 1983, and unemployment data from the U.S. Bureau of Labor Statistics for the same time interval (Markham, 1985). Unemployment data were adjusted for season, absenteeism data were not. Furthermore, Markham introduced the regional level and the organizational level. There was a highly negative correlation between unemployment and absenteeism on the national level, controlled for seasonal effects ($r = -.68$; $p < .0001$). Significant differences in the correlations were found on the regional level between the Northwestern, Southern, Central, and Western regions of the U.S. Consequently, personnel managers and researchers should not only investigate absence patterns on a company level, but also consider that additional regional influences may contribute to the picture (p. 231).

Organizational justice Organizational justice has been intensively discussed as an additional factor in relation to absence. In a U.S.-Chinese study, individual and group perceptions of the fairness of an organization's treatment of employees were examined, together with subsequent behavior such as absenteeism (Lam et al., 2002). Justice was used as a two-dimensional construct, distributive justice as the fairness of the remuneration employees receive, and procedural justice as the perceived fairness of the means used to determine these rewards. A further dimension of the analysis was "power distance", defined as "the extent to which less powerful members of institutions and organizations within a country expect and accept that power is distributed unequally" (also see Hofstede, 1985,

1991, 2001; Lam et al., 2002, p. 6). Results showed that procedural and distributive justice perceptions have considerable influence on absenteeism for both cultures. In every instance, positive estimations of organizational justice were related to lower absenteeism rates. Additionally, these effects were stronger for employees with higher acceptance of power distance, regardless of culture. These results show that sociopsychological variables (measured on the individual level) can have considerable influence on absenteeism behavior across countries and cultural borders.

Occupational class Blue-collar and white-collar industrial workers with different skill levels were examined in a 10-year cohort study by Aro et al. (Aro & Hasan, 1987). Alongside morbidity, biomedical health indicators and health behavior, the researchers collected absenteeism data for the 10- year period (measured as days per year). Occupational class (blue/white-collar, high/low skill) was the main moderator in the statistical analyses. Absenteeism was 2.5 times higher for blue- collar women than for white-collar women and nearly four times higher for semi-skilled blue- collar workers than for highly skilled white-collar men (Aro & Hasan, 1987, p. 65). Other studies did not find any absenteeism-differences between occupational classes: Simulation experiments by Nicholson et al. examined the attributions of employees. A priori arguments for absences (derived from previous open-questions interviews) were provided and had to be judged with regard to their hypothetical impact on absence justifications. Participants were also asked to estimate to what degree they would decide to go to work (or not) in the case of such reasons. Second, the employees stated how frequent these events in fact caused their own absenteeism. Here, the authors did not find any substantial inter-group differences, neither between women and men, nor between blue-collar and white-collar employees (Nicholson & Payne, 1987).

Firm size A further German panel study with occupational status (blue-collar and white-collar) as moderator variable examined the relation of firm size and two absenteeism measures (absence days per year and absence spells per year). Large firms had higher values in both absenteeism criteria. This effect was more significant for women and for blue-collar workers, whereas no effect could be found for white-collar men (Barmby & Stephan, 2000, p. 574). The same panel data for the years 1985-1988 was used to examine the interaction of wages and firm size with absenteeism. A 10% increase in wages reduced the absence day sum by 0.3 days. Employees in larger firms (201-2000 employees) had 1.8 more absence days than employees of firms with less than 201 employees after controlling for wage effects (Winkelmann, 1999).

Methodical critics There is an ongoing discussion regarding the appropriate modeling of confounding variables, such as sociopsychological frameworks, and long-wave influences, such as economic developments that often require decades to change substantially. Alexanderson notes that, one the one hand, "sickness absenteeism is, of course, affected by demography, geography, type of labor market, socioeconomic levels and organization of the local community", but on the other hand this "was seldom taken into account" (Alexanderson, 1998, p. 245; also see Markham, 1985, p. 228). Second, she argues that meta-analyses are in most cases not adequate to answer absenteeism research questions because of "temporal and international dissimilarities" (Alexanderson, 1998, p. 245). What conclusions can be drawn for study designs? — If there is some influence on a higher level than the level of the observed units (e.g. employees of one company in one country at one point of time), it would be methodically impossible to quantify that influence. Consequently, research would depend on large - if not to say, epidemiological multi-national - studies in order to quantify the variance explained by these types of background variables. Moreover, national samples in these cross-national studies would have to reflect a representative cross section. Johns addresses underlying assumptions concerning "climate analyses". He argues that, on the organizational level, theories of climate implicitly assume a higher variance between organizations than within these organizations and, second, that the range of organizational types should be wide (Johns, 1991, p. 84)). Consequently, the "optimal study design" would encompass a sufficient number of companies of each business type nested in large cross- national samples in non-cross-sectional designs. There is an important implication for empirical research: either absenteeism analyses are a „fingerprint" and should therefore be interpretated as a unique phenomenon in an observation unit (e. g. a company), or absenteeism analyses are „epidemiological" and give general information about the associations of absenteeism and predictors. Results of epidemiological absenteeism studies can not replace analyses of the individual case with a specific set of background variables.

Problem-Oriented Behavior in Organizations

Sabine Smolka, Detlev Liepmann, André Beauducel
and Yolanda Ortiz-Deutschmann

Organizational events or processes are traditionally discussed in the context of the entire organizational structure. The importance of the individual is often mini-mized. Prominent examples can be found among the so-called situational approaches or contingency approaches (cf. Kieser, 1999; Kieser & Kubicek, 1992; Liepmann, 1989; 2000). Theoretical conceptualizations of organizational processes remain wanting, in part, due to the complexity of the topic, but also because indi-viduals' contributions to organizational goal attainment have largely been ignored. This is despite the fact that it has long been established that one essential role of leaders is to motivate their co-workers. An examination of behavior in and by organizations should therefore include consideration of individuals and their personality traits (cf. Elke & Wottawa, 2004).

How individual and organizational concepts may be usefully integrated is demonstrated in the concept of *person-job-fit*. Holland (1996) postulates that professions or fields of work are chosen according to the fit of personal and environmental characteristics. Personal qualities may facilitate the execution of certain kinds of tasks. For a new position or job in an organization, the person should be identified who can best develop and use his or her abilities. This kind of fit has been shown to have a positive influence on the effectiveness and motivation of the employee (French, 1978; Sarges, 1995; Holland, 1996; Myer, Becker & Vanderberghe, 2004).

Motivational concepts such as action and state orientation (Kuhl 1982, 1986), and regulatory focus (cf. Higgins, 1997, 1998), which deal with individual strategies in goal pursuit, are highly relevant to organizational psychology. An individual's cognitions about striving toward a goal as well as concomitant reward expectations are important determinants of behavior. Not only must the individual have relevant abilities and skills, he or she must also be motivated to achieve a given goal and maintain that motivation as impediments arise (Brandstaetter & Frey, 2004; Kuhl, 2006). One further behavioral determinant is that the situation offers an opportunity for the behavior to occur. Hence, both the situation and the person must be taken into account (Nerdinger, 2006).

Given this background, the concepts of *action and state orientation* as well as *promotion and prevention motivation* and their contribution to organizational goal attainment will be the focus of further consideration. Kuhl illustrates the concept of action versus state orientation in the framework of his theory of action control (1982, 1984). Higgins developed the concept of promotion-prevention orientation in the framework of his comparatively younger theory of regulatory focus (1997, 1998). The links between these concepts are highly relevant to theory-building, and their integration potentially advantageous. Up to now only Chang and Bott (2004) have attempted to compare and combine the two approaches empirically.

1. Action control

People often fail to achieve their goals in everyday life even when they are motivated. In private and professional life, one is often confronted with tasks to which one has an aversion, or which may even arouse fear. People pursue tasks despite such conflicts, out of a desire for accomplishment or to avoid failure (Rheinberg, 1995). For example, an employee may agonize over a PowerPoint presentation with lots of foreign words that he is required to give in front of his employer and co-workers. He may feel extremely uncomfortable giving the presentation, but may do so if promised a reward such as a promotion if he does well. Important questions derived from this anecdote are: How are intentions translated into action (Kuhl, 1982)? How are plans or projects realized, even when their implementation is hindered by internal or external circumstances? Common colloquial phrases such as "pull yourself together" and "don't fall apart" refer to processes known as *will* or *volition* in the scientific community. The person in our example may hesitate before beginning to implement his intention because he must first overcome his aversion to speaking in a foreign tongue. This is a motivation problem or, perhaps even more so, a problem of will.

An intention does not automatically lead to goal achievement or even to an initiation of action. Sheeran (2002) calls this phenomenon the *intention-behavior gap*. The step of forming an intention helps to demarcate motivational and volitional processes. The motivational phase is reality-oriented; it has to do with the *choice* of goals. The volitional phase, by contrast, is oriented toward the *realization* of goals (Heckhausen, 1989; Brandstaetter & Frey, 2004). Kuhl has strongly emphasized the need to differentiate between these two processes.

In the theory of action control, Kuhl (1982, 1984) assumes that deliberate processes of volitional control enable people to choose from among competing wishes and shield a salient behavioral intention from competing motivational tendencies, thus facilitating goal attainment. An exception to this would be habitual behaviors or externally controlled activities.

Kuhl (1987) refers to the process of strengthening and defending an intention as *action control* or *self-regulation* (Kuhl, 1985), of which there are three distinct forms: self-control, self-regulation, and self-organization. A short vignette of different leadership styles illustrates the differences between these control processes. *Self-control* resembles an authoritarian leadership style. This type is especially advantageous when, for example, something must be handled quickly, or the risk factor is so high that experimenting with different solutions is not possible. *Self-regulation* is characteristic of a democratic leadership style in that several sub-systems participate in the solution to a problem. Of central importance is experi-mentation, through which new ways of problem-solving can be found, when old ways do not lead to the desired end state, and sufficient time and security are not available. *Self-organization* means that individual systems regulate behavior automatically, without a central leader. Any of these three forms of action control may be salient while performing a certain behavior or they may be concurrent (Kuhl, 1994c, 1996).

Kuhl (1987) differentiates six action-control strategies that foster goal achievement by shielding an intention from other competing action tendencies: (1) active attentional selectivity, (2) motivation control, (3) emotion control, (4) en-coding control (5) environment control, and (6) parsimony of information pro-cessing. These self-control strategies become active if a current intention is weak or internal or external obstacles hinder its implementation (Heckhausen & Gollwitzer, 1986).

1.1 Action versus state orientation

Kuhl (1994) defines *state orientation* as an impairment to action occurring primarily in stressful situations. By contrast, people who have an *action-oriented* personality style can tap the full potential of their abilities even in such situations.

In state orientation, Kuhl sees "a condition of reduced volitional efficiency." State oriented persons may be unable to take full advantage of their skills, independent of the extent of their volitional skills. It has been found that people who tend toward a state orientation after an experience of failure have more difficulty detaching themselves emotionally from unpleasant experiences. Kuhl (e.g. 1996) advises that this reduction of action control is grounded in reality and, therefore, does not represent a pathological change in personality. In certain situations, where considering and pausing for reflection is necessary, state orien-tation can be absolutely adaptive. Herrmann & Wortmann (1985) see in state orientation an opportunity to deal with critical or unwanted life events in a way that enables the person to resolve or transcend the problem.

The constructs of action and state orientation differentiate among individuals based on their volitional control and mastery of threatening or unpleasant experiences in the implementation of behavioral intentions (Kuhl, 2001). Action and state orientation indicate cognitive conditions that influence the realization of intentions (Kuhl, 1982). The condition of action orientation fosters the realization of intentions because it pushes for implementing of the intended behavior. By contrast, the state orientation hinders implementation because the person is preoccupied with the constant awareness of recent, past, and future situations (Heckhausen, 1989). Both orientations represent ways to deal with negative and positive emotions (Kuhl, 1983).

1.2 Achievement aspect and situational aspect

Substantial knowledge of the above-mentioned strategies of action control, i.e. an effective development of self-control skills (Kuhl, 1994c), is not a sufficient pre-condition for volitional efficiency: A person can often demonstrate a high degree of self-control, but under stress it may not be fully used or available (Kuhl, 1995). A typical case would be a competitive athlete who trains well, but fails in com-petition. In this case, there is a discrepancy between competence and efficiency (Kuhl, 1994c). The efficiency of action control, as already mentioned, is, according to Kuhl, affected by action- and state orientation (Kuhl, 1982, 1984).

The degree of action or state orientation depends not only on the individual, but also on the situation. For instance, action-oriented individuals may change to a state orientation after repeated negative experiences. State-oriented persons can, under certain conditions (e.g. in a relaxed atmosphere) change to an action orientation, effectively able to use self-control strategies and attain goals. Action-oriented persons with similar abilities in the same type of situation may, by contrast, experience a lessening of their volitional skills (Kuhl, 1994c).

1.3 Empirical findings and their implications for leadership

Important conclusions about organizational leadership may be drawn from Kuhl's theory of action control, as well as from later studies. A manager or leader should first take into account that there are action and state oriented people, and that the dimensions of action-state orientation may depend on the situation. If an employee, for example, shows deficits in achievement, the lessened behavioral efficiency is not necessarily due to a lack of knowledge or abilities. A state-oriented person could have the required knowledge, but be unable to put it into practice because this orientation compromises self-control skills. The inference of a motivational problem due to a lack of interest would be incorrect.

To work against such conditions and to facilitate the transition from a state-oriented to an action-oriented condition, self-control skills as well as the efficiency of utilizing existing competencies can be enhanced.

An experiment that investigated the strategy of active attentional control showed that action-oriented persons, even under stress, created perception filters that filtered out irrelevant information automatically. Hence, one way to assist a state-oriented person would be to create a stress-free, relaxed internal and external environment. Conditions such as these aid state-oriented persons to tap their creative potential. Another method would be to raise the state-oriented person's awareness of other available behavioral alternatives, since knowledge of behavioral options is typically restricted in state-oriented persons. It should be emphasized that a state orientation is not always negative. In practically all professions there are jobs in which a state orientation is important. For instance, in complex situations where there are hidden risks, conscientiousness and caution have an advantage over quick decision-making (Kuhl & Kazén, 2002). Ideally, an individual would be able to switch from one orientation to another, depending on the task at hand.

A new theory, which has arisen from biological-psychological personality research, has been provided by Higgins (1997) with his concept of the regulatory focus. The following section discusses the similarities and differences between regulatory focus and action versus state orientation.

2. Regulatory focus

Early on, Freud (1920) postulated that motivated behavior is regulated by the so-called *pleasure principle*: All humans strive to experience pleasure and avoid pain. This principle, which can also be found in the writing of the ancient Greeks, long dominated the understanding of motivation in many areas of psychology. The simple assumption of the approach and avoidance motivation does not, however, say anything about *how* humans attain pleasure and avoid pain, i.e. what strategies they use to attain their desired goals. Based on the Pleasure Principle, Higgings (1987, 1989) first developed the *theory of self-discrepancy*. In his theory he differentiates between two different, desired conditions, also called *self-guides:*

a) *Ideal self-guides* reflect a person's own ideas and imagination, from which he or she believes how others (or he himself/she herself) want him/her
 to be ideally..

b) *Ought self-guides* represent what the person expects of him/herself (duty and responsibility).

From this it follows that people are led either by *ideal*-orientation or *ought*-orientation toward their goals. According to the Theory of Self-Discrepancy, humans are motivated to reach the desired end state by reducing the discrepancy between their present and desired state. In doing so, they must decide which goal to strive for, which may be guided by either ideal or ought self-guides. Self-regulation based on either an *ideal* or *ought self-guide* leads to a reduction in the discrepancy, although the motivational strategies employed differ (Higgins, 1987, 1998).

Higgins postulates that self-discrepancy represents a specific negative psychological situation, in which every negative situation is connected to particular emotional and motivational conditions. A discrepancy between the present and ideal self reflects a situation in which a positive outcome is absent. It is connected to negative emotions such as sadness, disappointment, and discontent. Ideal self-regulation involves the presence or absence of positive results. The *ought* self-discrepancy, by contrast, represents a situation in which negative outcomes are absent, to which a person reacts with tension and worry. *Ought* self-regulation is based on the presence and absence of negative outcomes or results (Higgins, 1987, 1989). This assumption could be verified in studies by Higgins and Tykocinski (1992).

With the *theory of self-discrepancy* as a basis, Higgins (1987, 1989) developed the *theory of regulatory focus* (1997, 1998). This theory is concerned with *how* people reach specific goals, i.e. strive for pleasant and avoid unpleasant situations. The theory differentiates two fundamentally different forms of self-regulation during goal pursuit:

1) Self-regulation with a promotion focus
2) Self-regulation with a prevention focus

These forms of self-regulation function differently depending on which basic needs are to be fulfilled, such as food and security. In other words, which goals need to be reached. With reference to Higgins's self-discrepancy theory (1987, 1989), two different end-states exist which people may strive to attain: (1) *Ideals* (hopes, wishes, longings, etc.), and (2) *oughts* (duties, responsibilities, safety and security, etc.) Above all, the motivational consequences bring into sharp focus why the pleasure principle is insufficient to assess the true basis of approach and avoidance motivation (Higgins, 1997).

In sum, there are two qualitatively different motivational orientations: the promotion and prevention focus (Higgins, 1998; Friedman & Förster, 2001).

People with a prevention focus are fundamentally motivated by failure and people with a promotion focus are motivated by success (Förster, Grant, Idson & Higgins, 2001).

An important difference between this and related theories such as action versus state orientation (Kuhl, 1994) is that according to the theory of regulatory focus, neither of the two foci generally achieves a superior result. This is because each focus has different advantages and disadvantages (Werth, Denzler & Förster, 2002). In a promotion focus more quantity is produced than in a prevention focus. Empirical studies found that persons with a promotion focus can solve a larger quantity of problems (Crowe & Higgins, 1997). The quality depends greatly on the type of task or job. With tasks that demand precision, people with a prevention focus attain better results, whereas persons with a promotion focus perform better on tasks that require speed or quickness (Foerster, Higgins & Strack, 2000). The concept of Regulatory Focus assumes that it is not a stable personality trait, but that it also can vary depending on the situation. Hence, persons that tend to be promotion oriented, can be prevention oriented in some situations. According to Werth et al. (2002), regulatory foci can also be actively induced. The theory of regulatory focus explains differences in accomplishment, enabling goal pursuit to be optimized by adjusting tasks and demands of the work place towards the chosen self-regulatory focus of the employee.

Promotion focus Self-regulation in combination with the fulfillment of the need for food involves a promotion focus. Individuals concentrate on behaviors and strategies for reaching their *ideals,* i.e. goals, that are tied up with wishes, hopes, and longings (Higgins, 1997). These ideal goals also represent so-called maximal goals, which means people strive to bring about *positive events.* (Idson,

Liberman & Higgins, 2000). Related to this, within self-discrepancy theory (1987, 1989) Higgins also refers to "desired end-states" which reflect personal ideals. The emotions related to reaching an ideal goal are enthusiasm, eagerness, and satis-faction. Eagerness typically continues or intensifies, and motivation increases as the goal is attained. If a positive event does not happen, on the other hand, the person experiences it as a failure. Falling short of an ideal goal manifests itself as disappointment, depression, sadness, etc. Eagerness abates and motivation diminishes (Idson et al., 2000).

Prevention focus Self-regulation in combination with a need for security accompanies the prevention focus. Individuals strive to attain goals such as protection, fulfillment of duty, and responsibility. The prevention focus is to regu-late the presence or absence of such negative events (Higgins, 1998). With respect to the self-discrepancy theory (1986, 1989), Higgins speaks also of desired end-states that reflect personal duties (Higgins, 1997). These so-called "duty goals" re-present minimal goals in which individuals strive to prevent *negative events* from happening (Idson et al., 2000). During goal pursuit, prevention-focused individuals are very *alert*. The absence of negative events is taken as success and is connected to the emotions of relief and feelings of reassurance. As the goal is achieved, alertness diminishes and motivation recedes. On the other hand, the occurrence of negative events indicates a failure. The emotional condition is characterized by anxiety, worry, and a feeling of being threatened and motivation increases (Idson et al., 2000).

Sensitivity for certain situations and events Higgins infers from his findings that people who have activated *ideal* self-guides react more sensitively to situations in which positive events may occur. People, on the other hand, who have activated *ought* self-guides react more sensitively to situations in which negative outcomes may occur (Higgins, Roney, Crowe, Hymes, 1994).

The regulatory focus illustrates a general principle of self-regulation (Higgins & Spiegel, 2004) or the motivational principle that has implications for goals, strategies, emotions, and motivation. It is concerned with *how* people get closer to desired end-states and avoid the undesirable. Differences in emotion, motivation, achievement, etc., can be a function of regulatory focus and can be independent of the pleasure principle. Several studies have found that self-regulation in com-bination with ideals is *motivationally* different from self-regulation in combination with duties (Higgins & Tyocinski, 1992; Higgins et al., 1994; Crowe & Higgins, 1997; Förster, Idson, Higgins, 1998).

2.1 Regulatory fit

The fit between the requirements of a task and regulatory orientation is critical for success. Higgins (2000) calls this concept *regulatory fit*. People who experience such a fit are more motivated to reach their goals. This assumption has already been supported empirically (e.g. Spiegel, Grant-Pillow & Higgins, 2004).

Higgins' (2000) theory of regulatory fit assumes that motivation increases if individuals choose strategies to achieve their goals that are in line with their regulatory orientation, independent of the value of the outcome itself. This congruence is called *regulatory fit*. It causes an enhancement of the value of the activity (Higgins, 2000) and improves achievement (Spiegel, Grant-Pillow, Higgins, 2004). In this context, Higgins formulated five assumptions, which he was able to verify in several studies: (1) People choose strategies that have a greater regulatory fit; in other words, promotion-focused individuals choose promotion strategies instead of prevention strategies - and vice-versa (Crowe & Higgins, 1997). A greater regulatory fit during goal pursuit causes people to have (2) greater motivation (Foerster, Idson, Higgins, 1998), (3) more positive (prospective) feelings regarding a desirable alternative, and more negative feelings about alternatives that are less desirable (4). They evaluate past decisions more positively (Idson et al., 2000) and (5) uprate the monetary value of an object (Higgins & Idson, 2000).

2.2 Empirical studies and their implications for the work place

Risk and creativity Further research (Crowe & Higgins, 1997; Liberman, Idson, Camacho & Higgins, 1999) has revealed that individuals with a promotion focus, in comparison to those with a prevention focus, choose strategies involving more risk. They are more often confronted with change. Individiuals with a prevention focus, by contrast, are risk-averse, and prefer low-risk, conservative strategies; they strive for stability. If an employee must make a high-risk decision, he/she should - from the perspective of the company - put him/herself into a prevention focus. This would help minimize the risk taken. By contrast, in a situation where innovative problem-solving is called for, promotion-focused individuals are more likely to succeed. It is therefore important for a company to create a definite compatibility between requirements and tasks (Friedman & Foerster, 2001).

Crowe & Higgins (1997) investigated the influence of regulatory focus on creativity. The test person was given a task in which all the alternatives generated by probands were correct solutions to a problem. Individuals with a promotion focus, compared to individuals with a prevention focus, generated many different alternatives. People with a prevention focus, by contrast, offered the fewest number of alternatives. Their intention was to avoid mistakes. A cognitive style that em-braces risk promotes creativity; a risk-aversion blocks it. (Friedman & Foerster, 2001).

Feedback A further important aspect, which can be illuminated by the theory of regulatory focus, is *feedback*. Which consequences or effects do positive and negative feedback have on people? Does everyone react to feedback? What role does regulatory focus play? Studies have found that feedback plays different roles for individuals with a promotion and prevention focus. Those with a promotion focus, who are primarily motivated by the occurrence and duration of positive events, are especially sensitive to positive feedback.

Successful responses or feedback lead to a heightening of promotion motivation. The "goal looms larger" effect becomes stronger, the closer the person gets to goal achievement. Prevention-focused people, who are motivated by the occurrence negative events, react strongly to negative feedback (Förster et al., 1998, 2001).

The finding that promotion-focused people can be motivated by success and prevention-focused people by failure, can be advantageous in devising leadership strategies. Assuming supervisors can assess the focus of the workers, they can, through appropriate feedback, motivate their employees to a high level (Werth et al., 2002).

Leadership As explained in the preceding section, the insights on regulatory focus have clear consequences for leadership. The way tasks are formulated has a significant influence on the strategy that employees choose in carrying these out. Words such as "be innovative, try things out, mistakes aren't bad" stimulate promotion strategies. Workers would be creative, although not unduly preoccupied with their actions. In contrast, an assignment with words such as "A careful and accurate procedure is important", or "please, no mistakes" evokes a prevention strategy. In this case, employees would be very careful, but less creative. Leaders should be mindful of the effect their word-choices have on the foci of the workers, and the resulting consequences.

Also with regard to the goals and objectives of their employees, leaders should take into account their varying foci. If a person is prevention-focused, he or she associates rather minimal goals with work: making a living and meeting the requirements of the job. A promotion-focused person strives in his or her work for maximal goals such as promotion, career opportunities, and increased skills. Neither one nor the other focus is better than the other one. For the best results it is therefore important for leaders to articulate goals in a way that creates a "fit", so that employees can choose the appropriate strategy. Ideally, either the focus should fit the task or the task should fit the focus.

3. Integrative concept

Chang and Bott (2004) developed a concept of the integration of the dimensions of action and state-orientation (Kuhl, 1982, 1984) with the motivational orient-tations of the promotion and prevention focus (Higgins, 1997, 1998). The study design was based on the Rubicon model of action phases (Gollwitzer, 1990; Heckhausen, 1989; Heckhausen & Gollwitzer, 1986, 1987).

The basis of the concept is the rapid development of social-cognitive concepts regarding motivation and goal achievement. As can be seen in approach-avoidance motives (e.g., Carver & Scheier, 1998) and in the promotion-prevention-focus (e.g., Higgins, 1998), the *self-image* is central to this framework. Results of empirical studies provide support for the assumption that the self-concept has consequences for the individual motivational focus, which can be either chronic (e.g. Higgins et al., 1997) or situational (e.g. Freitas, Liberman, Salovey & Higgins, 2002). The authors criticize the fact that studies addressing this issue have a tendency to con-centrate on consequences of the "selves" (self-activation) for merely one or two elements in the goal-striving process, instead of analyzing the process holistically. Chang and Bott (2004) notice in this regard that up to now there has been little attempt to integrate motives with the dispositional, individual differences in moti-vation.

The aim of their study is to analyze the *joint effects of promotion and prevention focus and action and state orientation on individual goal pursuit process in the framework of the model of action phases.*

The two regulatory foci, therefore, result from an activation of various "selves"; by contrast, the constructs of action and state orientation represent stable moti-vational constructs.

3.1   Theoretical background

The theoretical background of the study of Chang and Bott is the *theory of action control (Kuhl, 1982, 1984)*, the *self-discrepancy theory (Higgins, 1987, 1989)*, *the theory of regulatory focus (Higgins, 1997, 1998)* as well as the *Rubicon model of action phases (Gollwitzer, 1990; Heckhausen, 1989; Heckhausen & Gollwitzer, 1986, 1987)*.

The study describes a concept that integrates the dimensions of promotion and prevention focus of the regulatory focus with that of action and state orientation in the framework of the model of action phases. In particular, the authors raise a debate about the model of action phases. The study tested the effects of regulatory focus and action-state orientation on the time individuals spend considering alternatives and memorizing information about the options.

The cover story for the probands was that the study was investigating the ability to follow instructions when folding origami objects.

All participants received the same task, but under two different conditions: in (a) the promotions focus condition they were told that they could win $25 in a lottery if they folded 80% of the objects correctly. In (b) the prevention focus condition they were told they could not participate in the lottery and win $25 if they folded even 1 of the 5 origami objects incorrectly. Assignment to the different test conditions was randomized.

Regardless of condition, the test persons could decide between two sets of origami patterns – animals and objects. Even though both patterns had the same degree of difficulty, the persons were informed of the advantages and disadvantages of the origami patterns. Then, the participants were given 20 minutes for folding five origami objects.

The following psychometric variables were assessed:

Predictors:
(1) *action-state orientation*
    This dimension was assessed with the HAKEMP 90 (Kuhl, 1994c), which involves 12 items for the three dimensions preoccupation, hesitation and volatility.
(2) *demographic variables* (age, sex, etc.)
(3) *goal acceptance* and *commitment* as control variables

Dependent variables:
(4) *time* the test persons needed for pondering the advantages and disadvantages of different sets of origami patterns. The participants were asked to remember the advantages and disadvantages. After finishing the task, they were asked if they withdrew at any of the origami patterns and if yes at which one.
(5) *overall performance:*
    The overall number of correctly folded origami objects

There follows a summary of the results of the study:

1) Withdrawal mediated the interaction between hesitation and the test condition according to the effect of overall performance. The more action-oriented the proband was, the weaker the tendency to withdraw from the task. This led to better overall accomplishment.
2) The participants saw the experiment as a task with only one goal. The more action-oriented the probands were – as characterized by hesitation – the less often they withdrew from attempting an origami pattern, especially when they had a promotion focused condition.
3) Withdrawal had negative effects on overall performance.
4) The time needed for considering alternatives reflects both a deliberative and a planning mindset (Chang & Bott, 2004).

Altogether, these findings *support* the concept of integration of action and state orientation with the regulatory focus dimensions within the model of behavioral phases. Chang and Bott (2004) point out that an exact analysis of the suggested relationships is necessary (l.c.). Herrmann, Liepmann, & Otto (1986) have already mentioned comparable considerations in the context of an overall problem-solving concept. They refer to correlations between individual problem-solving skills and dimensions of action orientation in the range of $r = .18$ to $.43$.

3.2   Empirical questions

Chang and Bott (2004) are the first to develop a concept in which the two theories are integrated - the constructs of action and state orientation, and promotion and prevention focus. Their results (the more action-oriented the person was, the more improbable was a withdrawal from an origami pattern, especially when in the promotion-focused condition.) seem to imply that with Kuhl's dimensions of action and state orientation, Higgins's dimension of promotion and prevention focus could be partially predicted. From this we can assume that action-oriented persons are more likely to choose a promotion strategy, state-oriented persons by contrast would choose a prevention strategy.

Emanating from the theories of Kuhl and Higgins described above, as well as from the integrative concept of Chang and Bott (2004), the present study aims to investigate the correlation of action control and regulatory focus. It does not replicate the study of Chang and Bott. The central question is, rather, to what extent the two concepts covary, or whether they are independent. This will be evaluated using a bivariate correlation and a dimension analysis.

4. Method

Sample The study involved 1,006 job entrants from the ages of 15 to 28 (594 male and 412 female participants). The dimensions were assessed using paper-pencil-questionnaires. The male test subjects, with a mean age of 19.7, were on average half a year younger than the female subjects at 20.4 years.

Instruments The questionnaires HAKEMP 90 (Kuhl, 1994c) and a German version of the rfq (regulatory focus questionnaire; Higgins, Friedman, Harlow, Idson, Ayduk & Taylor, (2001) were used to assess the constructs that were relevant in the context of this study, i.e. *action and state orientation* as well as *promotion and prevention focus,* respectively. Higgins et al. (2001) report internal consistency estimates of $a = .73$ for the (a) promotion scale and $a = .80$ for the (b) prevention scale. These values cannot be replicated in the present study.

The scales of the HAKEMP 90 selected for this study were (a) action and state orientation subsequent to failure (HOM / LOM) and (b) prospective action- and state orientation (HOP / LOP).

5. Results

The covariations of the four dimensions are shown in Table 1. The bivariate analyses show noticeable covariations between both dimensions of the Regulatory Focus and the two scales of action control. The dimension Action Orientation subsequent to failure is positively related to Prevention Focus with $r=.03$ and to Promotion Focus with $r=.23$. The prospective orientation shows results of $r = .15$ with the Prevention Focus, and $r = .37$ with the Promotion

Focus. A differentiation in dependence of the genders (see Table 1) does not indicate a conspicuous deviation.

Altogether it can be said that a stronger action orientation (subsequent to failure) tends to be associated with a distinct promotion focus, and vice-versa. The prospective orientation yields stronger relations. Here, the correlations for the entire sample, as well as the sub-samples, show with $r = .37$ an acceptable result.

Table 1: **Correlations between action-state orientation and the regulatory focus**

	Action-State Orientation *(subsequent to failure)*			Action-State Orientation *(prospective)*		
	all	women	men	all	women	men
Promotion Focus	.23	.22	.21	.37	.37	.37
Prevention Focus	.03	.03	.05	.15	.13	.18

The conspicuous covariations were inducement for the conduction of factor analyses with the four dimensions "action-state orientation subsequent to failure", "action-state orientation prospective", "promotion focus", and "prevention focus." (cf. Table 2).

Table 2: **Loadings and communalities of four dimensions**

	communalities	loadings
Action-State Orientation/prospective	.640	.800
Promotion Focus	.494	.703
Action-State Orientation/failure	.448	.669
Prevention Focus	.109	.330

Eigenvalue = 1,69; 42,26% explained variance

With 42% of explained variance, only one factor with an eigenvalue of > 1.0 can be identified. The dimension promotion (regulatory focus) shows, with a loading of .33, only a minor connection to an overall factor "problem-oriented behavior," while the first three aspects allow a definite identification (cf. Herrmann, Liepmann & Otto; 1986).

Discussion of results Altogether, the assumption that the scales of action and state orientation and scales of regulatory focus assess partially comparable content is supported. The bivariate analyses show systematic covariations which, in turn, demand a theoretical discussion. The *sub-group analysis* in relation to gender provides systematically similar structures.

If regulatory focus is regarded as a dependant dimension, approach and avoidance behavior can be predicted through action and state orientation.

Action and state orientation and the regulatory focus appear to be empirically partially dependant dimensions and are, thus, in a limited way applicable for prognostic prospects.

Lastly, we can state that:

1. The realization of intention, i.e. a predisposition to action vs. reflection, depends on the dimension action versus state orientation.
2. The dimension promotion versus prevention focus, by contrast target motivation: It describes whether an individual's actions are more strongly characterized by striving for a desired state or by the prevention of an undesired state.

References

Adler, S., & Weiss, H. (1981). Cognitive complexity and the structure of implicit leadership theories. *Journal of Applied Psychology, 66*, 69-78.

Ala-Mursula, L., Vahtera, J., Kivimaeki, M., Kevin, M. V., & Pentti, J. (2002). Employee control over working times: Associations with subjective health and sickness absences. *Journal of Epidemiology and Community Health, 56*, 272-278.

Alban-Metcalfe, R. J. & Alimo-Metcalfe, B. (2000). An analysis of the convergent and discriminant validity of the transformational leadership questionnaire. *International Journal of Selection and Assessment, 8*, 158-175.

Alderfer, C. P. (1969). An empirical test of a new theory of human needs. *Organizational Behavior and Human Performance, 4*, 143-175.

Alexanderson, K. (1998). Sickness absence: a review of performed studies which focused on levels of exposures and theories utilized. *Scandinavian Journal of Social Medicine, 26*, 241-249.

Alimo-Metcalfe, B. & Alban-Metcalfe, R. J. (2001). The development of a new transformational leadership questionnaire. *Journal of Occupational and Organizational Psychology, 74*, 1-27.

Amthauer, R., Brocke, B., Liepmann, D., & Beauducel, A. (1999). *Intelligenz-Struktur-Test 2000 (I-S-T 2000)*. Göttingen: Hogrefe.

Amthauer, R., Brocke, B., Liepmann, D., & Beauducel, A. (2001). *I-S-T 2000R Manual*. Göttingen: Hogrefe.

Anderson, C. A., & Lindsay, J. J. (1998). The development, perseverance, and change of naive theories. *Social Cognition, 16*, 8-30.

Antonakis, J., Avolio, B. J., & Sivasubramaniam, N. (2003). Context and leadership: An examination of the nine-factor full-range leadership theory using the Multifactor Leadership Questionnaire. *Leadership Quarterly, 14*, 261-295.

Antonakis, J. & House, R. J. (2002). The full-range leadership theory: The way forward. In B. J. Avolio & F. J. Yammarino (Eds.), *Transformational and charismatic leadership: the road ahead* (pp. 3-34). Amsterdam: JAI.

Antoni, C. & Bungard, W. (1989). Beanspruchung und Belastung. In E. Roth (Hrsg.), *Enzyklopädie der Psychologie*, (S. 431-485). Göttingen: Hogrefe.

Antonovsky, A. (1987). *Unraveling the mystery of health. How people manage stress and stay well*. San Francisco, CA: Jossey-Bass.

Aro, S., & Hasan, J. (1987). Occupational class, psychosocial stress and morbidity. *Annals of Clinical Research, 19* (2), 62-68.

Aronsson, G., Gustafsson, K., & Dallner, M. (2000). Sick but yet at work. An empirical study of sickness presenteeism. *Journal of Epidemiology Community Health, 54*, 502-509.

Arvey, R. D., Bouchard, T. J., Segal, N. L., & Abraham, L. M. (1989). Job satisfaction: Environmental and genetic components. *Journal of Applied Psychology, 74*, 187-192.

Atkin, R. S., & Goodman, P. S. (1984). Methods of defining and measuring absenteeism. In P. S. Goodman & R. S. Atkin (Eds.), *Absenteeism* (1 ed., pp. 47-109). San Francisco: Jossey-Bass.

Audas, R., & Goddard, J. (2001). Absenteeism, seasonality, and the business cycle. *Journal of Economics and Business, 53*, 405-419.

Aust,B. & Ducki, A. (2004). Comprehensive health promotion interventions at the workplace: Experiences with health circles in Germany. *Journal of Occupational Health Psychology, 9*, 258 – 270.

Avolio, B. J. (1999). *Full leadership development: Building the vital forces in organizations.* Thousand Oaks: Sage Publications.

Avolio, B. J. & Bass, B. M. (2002). *Developing potential across a full range of leadership.* Mahwah, N. J.: Lawrence Erlbaum Associates.

Avolio, B. J. & Bass, B. M. (2004). *Multifactor Leadership Questionnaire.* Manual and Sampler Set. (3rd ed.) Redwood City: Mind Garden, Inc.

Avolio, B. J. & Yammarino, F. J. (2002a). Introduction to, and overview of, transformational and charismatic leadership. In B. J. Avolio & F. J. Yammarino (Eds.), *Transformational and charismatic leadership: The road ahead* (pp. VIII-XXIII).

Avolio, B. J. & Yammarino, F. J. (2002b). *Transformational and charismatic leadership: The road ahead.* Amsterdam: JAI.

Avolio, B. J. (1999). *Full leadership development: Building the vital forces in organizations.* Thousand Oaks: Sage Publications.

Axtell, C., Wall, T., Stride, C., Pepper, K., Clegg, C., Gardner, P., et al. (2002). Familiarity breeds content: The impact of exposure to change on employee openness and well-being. *Journal of Occupational and Organizational Psychology, 75,* 217-231.

Badura, B. & Ritter, W. (1998). Qualitätssicherung in der betrieblichen Gesundheitsförderung. In E. Bamberg, A. Ducki, & A.-M. Metz (Hrsg.), *Handbuch Betriebliche Gesundheitsförderung* (S. 17-36). Göttingen: Hogrefe.

Bagozzi, R. P. (1978). Salespeople performance and satisfaction as a function of individual difference, interpersonal, and situational factors. *Journal of Marketing Research, 15,* 517-531.

Baldwin, T. T. & Padgett, M. (1993). Management development: A review and commentary. *International Review of Industrial and Organizational Psychology, 8,* 35-85.

Baltes, B. B., Briggs, T. E., Huff, J. W., Wright, J. A., & Neuman, G. A. (1999). Flexible and compressed workweek schedules: a meta-analysis of their effects on work-related criteria. *Journal of Applied Psychology, 84,* 496-513.

Baltes, B. B., & Parker, C. P. (2000). Reducing the effects of performance expectations on behavioral ratings. *Organizational Behaviour and Human Decision Processes, 82,* 237-267.

Bamberg, E., Ducki, A., & Metz, A.-M. (1998). Handlungsbedingungen und Grundlagen der betrieblichen Gesundheitsförderung. In E. Bamberg, A. Ducki, & A.-M. Metz (Hrsg.), *Handbuch der betrieblichen Gesundheitsförderung,* (S. 17-36). Göttingen: Hogrefe.

Bamberg, E. & Metz, A.-M. (1998). Intervention. In E. Bamberg, A. Ducki, & A.-M. Metz (Hrsg.), *Handbuch Betriebliche Gesundheitsförderung,* (S. 177-209). Göttingen: Hogrefe.

Barling, J. & Griffiths, A. (2003). A history of occupational health psychology. In J. C. Quick & L. E. Tetrick (Eds.), *Handbook of occupational health psychology,* (pp. 19 - 33). Washington, DC: American Psychological Ass.

Barling, J., Weber, T., & Kelloway, E. K. (1996). Effects of transformational leadership training on attitudinal and financial outcomes: A field experiment. *Journal of Applied Psychology, 81,* 827-832.

Barmby, T., & Stephan, G. (2000). Worker absenteeism: why firm size may matter. *Manchester School, 68,* 568-577.

Baron, R. M., & Kenny, D. A. (1986). The moderator-mediator variable distinction in social psychological research: conceptual, strategic, and statistical considerations. *Journal of Personality and Social Psychology, 51,* 1173-1182.

Bass, B. M. (1985). *Leadership and performance beyond expectations.* New York: Free Press.

Bass, B. M. (1997). Does the transactional-transformational leadership paradigm transcend organizational and national boundaries? *American Psychologist, 52,* 130-139.

Bass, B. M. (1998). *Transformational leadership: Industrial, military and educational impact.* Mahway, NJ: Lawrence Erlbaum Associates.

Bass, B. M. (1999). Two decades of research and development in transformational leadership. *European Journal of Work and Organizational Psychology, 8,* 9-32.

Bass, B. M. & Avolio, B. J. (1994). *Improving organizational effectiveness through transformational leadership.* Thousand Oaks: Sage.

Bass, B. M. & Avolio, B. J. (1999). *Training Full Range Leadership.* Redwood City: Mind Garden, Inc.

Bass, B. M. & Avolio, B. J. (2000). *MLQ Multifactor Leadership Questionnaire.* Redwood City: Mind Garden.

Bass, B. M., & Avolio, B. J. (2005). *Training Full Range Leadership.* (J. Rowold, J. Radstaak, Trans.). Redwood City, CA: Mindgarden. (Original Work published 1999).

Bass, B. M., & Riggio, R. E. (2006). *Transformational leadership.* Mahwah, NJ: Lawrence Erlbaum.

Bass, B. M. & Steidlmeier, P. (1999). Ethics, character, and authentic transformational leadership behavior. *Leadership Quarterly, 10,* 181-217.

Bearden, W. O., & Netemeyer, R. G. (1999). *Handbook of Marketing Scales.* London: Thousand Oaks.

Beauducel, A., Brocke, B., & Liepmann, D. (2001). Perspectives on fluid and crystallized intelligence: facets for verbal, numerical, and figural intelligence. *Personality and Individual Differences, 30,* 977-994.

Behling, O. & Law, K. S. (2000). *Translating questionnaires and other research instruments: Problems and solutions.* Thousand Oakes, CA: Sage.

Benavides, F. G., Benach, J., Diez-Roux, A. V., & Roman, C. (2000). How do types of employment relate to health indicators? Findings from the Second European Survey on working conditions. *Journal of Epidemiology and Community Health, 54,* 494-501.

Bertua, C., Anderson, N., & Salgado, J. F. (2005). The predictive validity of cognitive ability tests: A UK meta-analysis. *Journal of Occupational and Organizational Psychology, 78,* 387-409.

Blackburn, M. L., & Neumark, D. (1993). Omitted-ability bias and the increase in the return of schooling. *Journal of Labor Economics, 11,* 521-544.

Boudreau, J. W., Boswell, W. R., Judge, T. A., & Bretz, R. D. (2001). Personality and cognitive ability as predictors of job search among employed managers. *Personnel Psychology, 54,* 25-50.

Brandstätter, V. & Frey, D. Motivation zu Arbeit und Leistung. In H. Schuler (Hrsg.) (2004). *Enzyklopädie der Psychologie* (S.295-341). Göttingen: Hogrefe.

Breaugh, J. A. (1981). Predicting absenteeism from prior absenteeism and work attitudes. *Journal of Applied Psychology, 66,* 555-560.

Brooke, P. P. (1986). Beyond the Steers and Rhodes model of employe attendance. *Academy of Management Journal, 11,* 345-361.

Bresnen, M. J. (1995). All things to all people? Perceptions, attributions, and constructions of leadership. *Leadership Quarterly, 6,* 495-513.

Brown, D. J., Scott, K. A., & Lewis, H. (2004). Information processing and leadership: A review and implications for application. In R. Sternberg, J. Antonakis, & A. T. Cianciolo (Eds.), *The nature of leadership* (pp. 125-147). Thousand Oaks, CA: Sage.

Brooke, P. P., & Price, J. L. (1989). The determinants of employee absenteeism: An emprical test of a causal model. *Journal of Occupational Psychology, 62,* 1-19.

Bryman, A. (1987). The generalizability of implicit leadership theory. *Journal of Social Psychology, 127,* 129-141.

Bunce, D. (1997). What factors are associated with the outcome of individual-focused worksite stress management interventions? *Journal of Occupational and Organizational Psychology, 70*, 1-17.

Bunce, D., & West, M. A. (1996). Stress management and innovation interventions at work. *Human Relations, 49*, 209-231.

Burns, J. M. (1978). *Leadership.* New York: Harper & Row.

Busch, C. (1998). Streßmanagement und betriebliche Gesundheitsförderung. In E. Bamberg, A. Ducki, & A.-M. Metz (Hrsg.), *Handbuch Betriebliche Gesundheitsförderung. Arbeits- und organisationspsychologische Konzepte,* (S. 97-110). Göttingen: Hogrefe.

Buunk, B. P., De Jonge, J., Ybema, J. F., & De Wolff, J. (1998). Psychosocial aspects of occupational stress. In P. J. D. Drenth, H. Thierry, & C. J. d. Wolff (Eds.), *Handbook of work and organizational psychology,* (pp. 145-182). Hove: Psychology press.

Calder, B. J. (1977). An attribution theory of leadership. In B. Staw & G. Salancik (Eds.), *New directions in organizational behavior* (pp. 179-204). Chicago: St. Clair.

Carver, C. S. & Scheier, M. F. (1998). *On the self-regulation of behavior.* Cambridge University Press.

Cataldo, M. F. & Coates, T. J. (Eds.) (1986). *Health and industry: A behavioral medicine perspective.* New York: Wiley.

Cattell, R. B. (1963). Theory of fluid and crystallized intelligence: A critical experiment. *Journal of Educational Psychology, 54*, 1-22.

Chadwick-Jones, J. K., Brown, C. A., Nicholson, N., & Sheppard, C. (1971). Absence measures: Their reliability and stability in an industrial setting. *Personnel Psychology, 24*, 463- 470.

Chadwick-Jones, J. K., Nicholson, N., & Brown, C. (1982). *Social psychology of absenteeism.* New York: Praeger Publishers.

Chang, C.-H., & Bott, J. P. (2004). *An Integration of Promotion/Prevention Focus and Action-State Orientation.* Paper presented at the 19th Annual Meeting of the Society for the Industrial and Organizational Psychology, Chicago.

Chapman, L. J., & Chapman, J. P. (1969). Illusory correlation as an obstacle to the use of valid psychodiagnostic signs. *Journal of Abnormal Psychology, 74*, 271-280.

Chatterji, M., & Tilley, C. J. (2002). Sickness, absenteeism, presenteeism, and sick pay. *Oxford Economic Paper, 54*, 669-687.

Cherulnik, P. D. (1995). Physical appearance, social skill, and performance as a leadership candidate. *Basic and Applied Social Psychology, 16*, 287-295.

Cherulnik, P. D., Turns, L. C., & Wilderman, S. K. (1990). Physical appearance and leadership: Exploring the role of appearance-based attribution in leader emergence. *Journal of Applied Social Psychology, 20*, 1530-1539.

Chong, L. M. A., & Thomas, D. C. (1997) Leadership perceptions in cross-cultural context: Pakeha and Pacific Islanders in New Zealand. *Leadership Quarterly, 8*, 275-293.

Clegg, C. W. (1983). Psychology of employee lateness, absence, and turnover: A methodological critique and an empirical study. *Journal of Applied Psychology, 68*, 88-101.

Cohen, J. (1988). *Statistical power analysis for the behavior science.* New York: Erlbaum Hillsdale.

Cohen, S., Kamarck, T., & Mermelstein, R. (1983). A global measure of perceived stress. *Journal of Health and Social Behavior, 24*, 385-396.

Colarelli, S. M., Dean, R. A., & Konstans, C. (1987). Comparative effects on personal and situational influences on job outcomes of new professionals. *Journal of Applied Psychology, 72*, 558-566.

Conger, J. A. & Kanungo, R. N. (1987). Toward a behavioral theory of charismatic leadership in organizational settings. *Academy of Management Review, 12*, 637-647.

Conger, J. A. & Kanungo, R. N. (1988). *Charismatic leadership. The elusive factor in organisational effectiveness.* San Francisco: Jossey-Bass.

Conger, J. A. & Kanungo, R. N. (1992). Perceived behavioral attributes of charismatic leadership. *Canadian Journal of Behavioural Science, 24,* 86-102.

Conger, J. A. & Kanungo, R. N. (1994). Charismatic leadership in organizations - perceived behavioral-attributes and their measurement. *Journal of Organizational Behavior, 15,* 439-452.

Conger, J. A. & Kanungo, R. N. (1998). *Charismatic leadership in organizations.* Thousand Oaks: Sage.

Conger, J. A., Kanungo, R. N., & Menon, S. T. (2000). Charismatic leadership and follower effects. *Journal of Organizational Behavior, 21,* 747-767.

Conger, J. A., Kanungo, R. N., Menon, S. T., & Mathur, P. (1997). Measuring charisma: Dimensionality and validity of the Conger-Kanungo scale of charismatic leadership. *Canadian Journal of Administrative Sciences, 14,* 290-302.

Connelly, M. S., Gilbert, J. A., Zaccaro, S. J., Threfall, K. V., Marks, M. A., & Mumford, M. D. (2000). Exploring the relationship of leadership skills and knowledge to leader performance. *Leadership Quarterly, 11,* 65-85.

Cox, T., Griffiths, A., & Rial-Gonzalez, E. (2000). *Research on work-related stress.* European Agency for Safety and Health at Work, Luxemburg.

Crowe, E. & Higgins, E. T. (1997). Regulatory Focus and Strategic Inclinations: Promotion and Prevention in Decision-Making. *Organizational Behavior and Human Decision Processes, 69,* 117-132.

Csikszentmihalyi, M. (1988). The flow experience and its significance for human psychology. In M. Csikszentmihalyi & I. S. Csikszentmihalyi (Eds.), *Optimal experience: Psychological studies of flow in consciousness* (pp. 15-35). New York: Cambridge University Press.

Day, D. V., & Lord, R. G. (1992). Expertise and problem categorization: The role of expert processing in organizational sense-making. *Journal of Management Studies, 29,* 35-47.

De Jonge, J., Dormann, C., Janssen, P.P.M., Dollard, M.F., Landeweerd, J.A., & Nijhuis, F.J.N. (2001). Testing reciprocal relationships between job characteristics and psychological well-being: A cross-lagged structural equation model. *Journal of occupational and organizational psychology, 74,* 29-46.

Deluga, R. J. (1995). The relationship between attributional charismatic leadership and organizational citizenship behavior. *Journal of Applied Social Psychology, 25,* 1652-1669.

Den Hartog, D. N., House, R. J., Hanges, P. J., Ruiz-Quintanilla, S. A., & Dorfmann, P. W. (1999). Culture specific and cross-culturally generalizable implicit leadership theories: Are attributes of charismatic/transformational leadership universally endorsed? *Leadership Quarterly, 10,* 219-256.

Diener, E., & Fujita, F. (1995). Resources, personal strivings, and subjective well-being: a nomothetic and idiographic approach. *Journal of Personality and Social Psychology, 68,* 926-935.

Dilts, D. A., & Deitsch, C. R. (1986). Absentee workers back on the job: the case of GM. *Practical Business, 29,* 46-51.

Domsch, M. & Regnet, E. (1990). Personalentwicklung für weibliche Fach- und Führungskräfte. In M. Domsch & E. Regnet (Eds.), *Weibliche Fach- und Führungskräfte* (pp. 101-123). Stuttgart: Schäffer.

Drago, R., & Wooden, M. (1992). The determination of labour absence: Economic factors and workgroup norms across countries. *Industrial and Labor Relations Review, 45,* 764-778.

Ducki, A. (1998a). Allgemeine Prozessmerkmale betrieblicher Gesundheitsförderung. In: Bamberg, E., Ducki, A. & Metz, A.-M. (1998) (Hrsg.), *Handbuch Betriebliche Gesundheitsförderung* (S. 135-143). Göttingen: Hogrefe.

Ducki, A. (1998b). Ressourcen, Belastungen und Gesundheit. In E. Bamberg, A. Ducki, & A.-M. Metz (Hrsg.), *Handbuch Betriebliche Gesundheitsförderung*, (S. 145-153). Göttingen: Hogrefe.

Ducki, A. (2000). *Diagnose gesundheitsförderlicher Arbeit: eine Gesamtstrategie zur betrieblichen Gesundheitsanalyse.* Zürich: vdf Hochschulverlag AG an der ETH.

Ducki, A., Jenewein, R., & Knoblich, H.-J. (1998). Gesundheitszirkel - Ein Instrument der Organisationsentwicklung. In E. Bamberg, A. Ducki, & A.-M. Metz (Hrsg.), *Handbuch betriebliche Gesundheitsförderung*, (S. 267-281). Göttingen: Hogrefe.

Dumdum, U. R., Lowe, K. B., & Avolio, B. J. (2002). A meta-analysis of transformational and transactional leadership correlates of effectiveness and satisfaction: An update and extension. In B. J. Avolio & F. J. Yammarino (Eds.), *Transformational and charismatic leadership: the road ahead* (pp. 35-66). Amsterdam: JAI.

Dvir, T., Eden, D., Avolio, B. J., & Shamir, B. (2002). Impact of transformational leadership on follower development and performance: A field experiment. *Academy of Management Journal, 45*, 735-744.

Eden, D., & Leviatan, U. (1975). Implicit leadership theory as a determinant of the factor structure underlying supervisory behavior scales. *Journal of Applied Psychology, 60*, 736-741.

Eden, D., Geller, D., Gewirtz, A., Gordon-Terner, R., Inbar, I., Liberman, M., Pass, Y., Salomon-Segev, I., & Shalit, M. (2000). Implanting Pygmalion leadership style through workshop training: Seven field experiments. *Leadership Quarterly, 11*, 171-210.

Elke, G. & Wottawa, H. (2004). Persönlichkeits- und differenzialpsychologische Grundlagen. In Schuler, H. (Hrsg.) (2004). *Enzyklopädie der Psychologie* (S. 249-293). Göttingen: Hogrefe.

Elke, G., Neumann, B., & Schuld, C. (1990). Personalführungskonzepte in innovativen Unternehmen - Eine Studie [Leadership concepts in innovative companies – a study]. In S. Hoefling & W. Butollo (Eds), *Psychologie für Menschenwürde und Lebensqualität. Aktuelle Herausforderung und Chancen für die Zukunft.* Bericht über den 15. Kongress für Angewandte Psychologie des Berufsverbandes Deutscher Psychologen, München 1989 (Vol 2, pp. 215-226). Bonn, Germany: Deutscher Psychologen Verlag.

Ellis, A. (1977). *Die rational-emotive Therapie.* München: Urban & Schwarzenberg.

Emrich, C. G. (1999). Context effects in leadership perception. *Personality and Social Psychology Bulletin, 25*, 991-1006.

Engle, E. M., & Lord, R. G. (1997). Implicit theories, self-schemas, and leader-member-exchange. *Academy of Management Journal, 40*, 988-1010.

Epitropaki, O., & Martin, R. (2004). Implicit leadership theories in applied settings: Factor structure, generalizability, and stability over time. *Journal of Applied Psychology, 89*, 293-310.

Epitropaki, O., & Martin, M. (2005). From ideal to real: A longitudinal study of the role of implicit leadership theories on leader-member exchanges and employee outcomes. *Journal of Applied Psychology, 90*, 659-676.

Eskildsen, J. K., Kristensen, K., & Westlund, A. H. (2003). The effect of employee characteristics on intrinsic work motivation and job satisfaction. Results from the Nordic employee index. In A. Neely, A. Walters, & R. Austin (Eds.). *Performance Measurement and Management 2002: Research and Action* (pp. 181-188). Boston.

Fahrmeir, L., Hamerle, A., & Tutz, G. (1996). *Multivariate statistische Verfahren [Multivariate statistical analysis]*. Berlin, Germany: De Gruyter.

Farkas, G., & Vicknair, K. (1996). Appropriate tests of racial wage discrimination require controls for cognitive skill: Comment on Cancio, Evans and Maume. *American Sociological Review, 61*, 691-706.

Farrell, D., & Stamm, C. L. (1988). Meta-analysis of the correlates of employee absence. *Human Relations, 41*, 211-227.

Fayey, T. (2004). Employment, education and skills. In European Foundation for the Improvement of Living and Working Conditions (Ed.), *Quality of life in Europe* (pp. 23-32). Luxembourg: European Foundation for the Improvement of Living and Working Conditions.

Felfe, J. (2002). *Organizational development and leadership*. Frankfurt/M.: Verlag Peter Lang.

Felfe, J. (2005). Personality and romance of leadership. In B. Schyns & J.R. Meindl (Eds.), *Implicit leadership theories: Essays and explorations* (pp.199-226). Greenwich, CT: Information Age Publishing.

Felfe, J., Liepmann, D., & Resetka, H.-J. (1996). *Skalen zur Organisationsdiagnose*. Freie Universität Berlin.

Felfe, J. & Six, B. (2006). *Die Relation von Arbeitszufriedenheit und Commitment*. In L. Fischer (Hrsg.), Arbeitszufriedenheit (S. 37 - 60). Göttingen: Hogrefe.

Felfe, J., Tartler, K., & Liepmann, D. (2004). Advanced research in the field of transformational leadership. *Zeitschrift für Personalforschung, 18*, 262-288.

Fichman, M. (1984). A theoretical approach to understanding employee absence. In P. S. Goodman & R. S. Atkin (Eds.), *Absenteeism* (1 ed., pp. 1-46). San Francisco: Jossey-Bass.

Fiedler, F. E. (1967). *A theory of leadership effectiveness*. New York, NY: McGraw-Hill.

Fielding, J. E. (1979). Preventive medicine and the bottom line. *Journal of Occupational Medicine, 21*, 79-88.

Fielding, J. E. (1982). Effectiveness of employee health improvement programs. *Journal of Occupational Medicine, 24*, 907-916.

Fiol, C. M., & Huff, A. S. (1992). Maps for managers: Where are we? Where do we go from here? *Journal of Management Studies, 29*, 267-286.

Fischer, N. (1993). *Leading self-directed work teams: A guide to developing new team leadership skills*. New York: McGraw-Hill.

Förster, J., Idson, L. C., & Higgins, E. T. (1998). Approach and Avoidance Strength During Goal Attainment: Regulatory Focus and the „Goal Looms Larger" Effect. *Journal of Personality and Social Psychology, 75*, 1115-1131.

Förster, J., Grant, H., Idson, L. C., & Higgins, E. T. (2001). Success/failure feedback, expectancies, and approach (Avoidance motivation: How regulatory focus moderates classic relations). *Journal of Experimental Social Psychology, 37*, 253-260.

Förster, J., Higgins, E. T., & Strack, F. (2000). When stereotype disconfirmation is a personal threat: How prejudice and Prevention Focus moderate incongruency effects. *Social Cognition, 18*, 178-197.

Foti, R. J. (1983). *Prototypes and scripts: The effects of alternative methods of processing information on rating accuracy*. Unpublished dissertation: The University of Akron.

Fox, J. B., & Scott, J. F. (1943). Absenteeism: management's problem. *Business research studies* (no. 29)/ Publication of the Graduate School of Business Adminstration, 30(4).

Frese, M., Beimel, S., & Schoenborn, S. (2003). Action training for charismatic leadership: Two evaluations of studies of a commercial training module on inspirational communication of a vision. *Personnel Psychology, 56*, 671-698.

Frehr, H.-U. (1994a). *Total Quality Management – Unternehmensweite Qualitätsverbesserung*. München: Hanser.

Frehr, H.-U. (1994b). Total Quality Management. In W. Masing (Hrsg.), *Handbuch Qualitätsmanagement* (3.Aufl., S. 31-48). München: Hanser.

Frese, M. & Semmer, N. (1991). Streßfolgen in Abhängigkeit von Moderatorvariablen: Der Einfluß von Kontrolle und sozialer Unterstützung. In S. Greif, E. Bamberg, & N. Semmer (Hrsg.), *Psychischer Streß am Arbeitsplatz*, (S. 135-153). Göttingen: Hogrefe.

Frese, M. & Zapf, D. (1994). Action as the Core of Work Psychology: A German Approach. In H. C. Triandis, M. D. Dunnette, & L. M. Hough (Eds.), *Handbook of industrial and organizational psychology*, (pp. 271-340). Palo Alto: Consulting psychologists press.

Freitas, A. L., Liberman, N., Salovey, P., & Higgins, E. T. (2002). When to Begin? Regulatory Focus and Initiating Goal Pursuit. *Personality and Social Psychology Bulletin, 28*, 121-130.

Freud, S. (1920). *Jenseits des Lustprinzips*. Leipzig: Internationaler Psychoanalytischer Verlag.

Friczewski, F. (1994). Gesundheitszirkel als Organisations- und Personalentwicklung: Der "Berliner Ansatz". In G. Westermayer, B. Bähr (Eds.), *Betriebliche Gesundheitszirkel*, (S. 14- 24). Göttingen: Verlag für Angewandte Psychologie.

Friczewski, F., Jenewein, R., Lieneke, A., Schiwon-Spies, L. & Westermayer, G. (1989). Betriebliche Gesundheitszirkel: Primärprävention streßbezogener Erkrankungen am Arbeitsplatz. *Psychomed, 1*, 140-143.

Fried, Y., Haynes Slowik, L., Ben-David, H. A., & Tiegs, R. B. (2001). Exploring the relationship between workspace density and employee attitudinal reactions: An integrative model. *Journal of Occupational and Organizational Psychology, 74*, 359-372.

Friedman, R. S. & Förster, J. (2001). The Effects of Promotion and Prevention Cues on Creativity. *Journal of Personality and Social Psychology, 81*, 1001-1013.

Gallup (2003). *Das Engagement am Arbeitsplatz sinkt weiter: Nur noch 12 Prozent der MitarbeiterInnen sind hierzulande engagiert im Job - Der gesamtwirtschaftliche Schaden liegt in Milliardenhöhe*. Press release. The Gallup Organization.

Ganzach, Y. (1998). Intelligence and job satisfaction. *Academy of Management Journal, 41*, 526-539.

Ganzach, Y., & Pazy, A. (2001). Within occupation sources of variance in incumbent perception of job complexity. *Journal of Occupational and Organizational Psychology, 74*, 95-108.

Gardell, B. (1978). Arbeitsgestaltung, intrinsische Arbeitszufriedenheit und Gesundheit. In M. Frese, S. Greif & N. Semmer (Eds.), *Industrielle Psychopathologie*. Bern: Huber.

Gardner, W. I., & Avolio, B. (1998). The charismatic relationship: A dramaturgical perspective. *Academy of Management Review, 23*, 32-58.

Gaudine, A. P., & Saks, A. M. (2001). Effects of an absenteeism feedback intervention on employee absence behavior. *Journal of Organizational Behavior, 22*, 15-29.

Gellatly, I. R., & Luchak, A. A. (1998). Personal and organizational determinants of perceived absence norms. *Human Relations, 51*, 1085-1102.

Genser, B. (1978). Erziehungswissen von Eltern [Knowledge of parents on education]. In K.A. Schneewind & H. Lukesch (Hrsg.). *Familiäre Sozialisation. Probleme, Ergebnisse, Perspektiven* (pp. 27-43). Stuttgart: Klett-Cotta.

Gerhart, B. (2005). The (affective) dispositional approach to job satisfaction: sorting out the policy implications. *Journal of Organizational Behavior, 26*, 79-97.

Gerstner, C. R., & Day, D. V. (1994). Cross-cultural comparison of leadership prototypes. *Leadership Quarterly, 5*, 121-134.

Gerstner, C. R. & Day, D. V. (1997). Meta-analytic review of leader-member exchange theory: Correlates and construct issues. *Journal of Applied Psychology, 82*, 827-844.

Geurts, S. A. & Gründemann, R. (1999). Workplace stress and prevention in Europe. In M. Kompier, & C. Cooper (Eds.), *Preventing stress, improving productivity*, (pp. 9-32). London & New York: Routledge.

Geurts, S. A., Schaufeli, W. B., & Rutte, C. G. (1999). Absenteeism, turnover intention and inequity in the employment relationship. *Work Stress, 13*, 253-267.

Gimeno, D., Benavides, F. G., Benach, J., & Amick, B. C. (2004). Distribution of sickness absence in the European Union countries. Journal of *Occupational and Environmental Medicine, 61*, 867-869.

Gluminski, I. & Stangel-Meseke, M. (1993). Der handlungstheoretische Ablaufplan – eine Strukturierungshilfe für Fragen der betrieblichen Bildungsbedarfsanalyse. *Zeitschrift für Personalforschung, 7*, 50-63.

Glynn, M. A. (1998). Situational and dispositional determinants of managerial satisfaction. *Journal of Business and Psychology, 13*, 193-209.

Glynn, M. A. (1999). On leveraging individual intellect in organizations: A study of the work perceptions of the highly intelligent. In J. F. Porac & R. Garud (Eds.). *Advances in managerial cognition and organizational information processing: Cognition, knowledge and organizations* (pp. 31-56). Elsevier Science.

Gollwitzer, P. M. (1990). Action phases and mind sets. In E.T. Higgins & R. M. Serpentine (Eds.), *Handbook of motivation and cognition: Foundations of social behavior* (Vol. 2, pp. 53-92). New York: Guilford Press.

Goodman, P. S., & Atkin, R. S. (1984). *Absenteeism* (1 ed.). San Francisco: Jossey-Bass.

Goodwin, V. L., Wofford, J. C, & Boyd, N. C. (2000). A laboratory experiment testing the antecedents of leader cognitions. *Journal of Organizational Behavior, 21*, 769-788.

Graen, G. B. & Uhl-Bien, M. (1995). Relationship-based approach to leadership: Development of leader-member exchange (LMX) theory of leadership over 25 years: applying a multi-domain perspective. *Leadership Quarterly, 6*, 219-247.

Graham, S., Wedman, J. F., & Garvin-Kester, B. (1994). Manager coaching skills: What makes a good coach? *Performance Improvement Quarterly, 7*, 81-94.

Graves, L. M., & Powell, G. N. (1982). Sex differences in implicit theories of leadership: An initial investigation. *Psychological Reports, 50*, 689-690.

Grebner, S., Semmer, N. K., Faso, L. L., Gut, S., Kälin, W., & Elfering, A. (2003). Working conditions, well-being, and job-related attitudes among call centre agents. *European Journal of Work and Organizational Psychology, 12*, 341-366.

Greif, S., Bamberg, E., & Semmer, N. K. (Hrsg.), (1991). *Psychischer Streß am Arbeitsplatz.* Göttingen: Hogrefe

Haccoun, R. R., & Jeanrie, C. (1995). Self reports of work absence as a function of personal attitudes towards absence, and perceptions of the organisation. *Applied Psychology: An International Review, 44*, 155-170.

Hacker, W. (1978). *Allgemeine Arbeits- und Ingenieurpsychologie. Psychische Struktur und Regulation von Arbeitstätigkeiten.* Berlin: Deutscher Verlag für Wissenschaften.

Hackett, R. D. (1989). Work attitudes and employee absenteeism: A synthesis of the literature. *Journal of Occupational Psychology, 62*, 235-248.

Hackett, R. D., & Guion, R. M. (1985). A reevaluation of the absenteeism-job satisfaction relationship. *Organizational Behavior & Human Decision Processes, 35*, 340-381.

Hackman, J. R., & Oldham, G. R. (1974). *The job diagnostic survey: an instrument for the diagnosis of jobs and the evaluation of redesign projects* (Tech. Rep. No. 4): Yale University, New Haven, NJ.

Hackman, J. R., & Oldham, G. R. (1975). Development of the Job Diagnostic Survey. *Journal of Applied Psychology, 60*, 159-170.

Hackman, J. R., & Oldham, G. R. (1976). Motivation through the design of work: test of a theory. *Organizational Behavior and Human Performance, 16*, 250-279.

Hackman, J. R. & Oldham, G.R. (1980). *Work redesign*. Reading, MA: Addison Wesley.

Hackmann, J. R. & Wageman, R. (2005). A theory of team coaching. *Academy of Management Review, 30*, 269-287.

Hall, D. T., Seibert, K. W., & Hollenbeck, G. P. (1999). Behind closed doors: What really happens in executive coaching. *Organizational Dynamics, 29*, 39-53.

Halverson, S. K., Murphy, S. E., & Riggio, R. E. (2004). Charismatic leadership in crisis situations: A laboratory investigation of stress and crisis. *Small Group Research, 35*, 495-514.

Hammer, T. H., & Landau, K. (1981). Methodological issues in the use of absence data. *Journal of Applied Psychology, 66*, 574-581.

Harrison, D. A., & Martocchio, J. J. (1998). Time for absenteeism: A 20-year review of origins, offshoots, and outcomes. *Journal of Management, 24*, 305-350.

Harrison, D. A., & Price, K. H. (2003). Context and consistency in absenteeism: studying social and dispositional influences across multiple settings. *Human Resource Management Review, 13*, 203-225.

Heckhausen, H. (1989). *Motivation und Handeln*. Berlin: Springer-Verlag.

Heckhausen, H. & Gollwitzer, P.M.(1986). Information processing before and after the formation of an intent. In F. Klix & H. Hagendorf (Eds.). *In memoriam Herrmann Ebbinghaus: Synopsium on the structure and function of human memory* (pp. 1071-1082). Amsterdam: Elsevier/North Holland.

Heckhausen, H. & Gollwitzer, P. M. (1987). Thought contents and cognitive functioning in motivational versus volitional states of mind. *Motivation and Emotion, 11*, 101-120.

Heinitz, K. & Rowold, J. (2007) Gütekriterien einer deutschen Adaptation des Transformational Leadership Inventory (TLI). *Zeitschrift für Arbeits- und Organisationspsychologie, 51*, 1-15.

Hemingway, H., & Marmot, M. (1999). Psychosocial factors in the aetiology and prognosis of coronary heart disease: systematic review of prospective cohort studies. *British Medical Journal, 318*, 1460-1467.

Herman, J. B. (1973). Are situational contingencies limiting job attitude-job performance relationships? *Organizational Behavior & Human Performance, 10*, 208-224.

Herrmann, C., Liepmann, D. & Otto, J. (1986). The relationsship between test anxiety, problem solving and action control. In R. Schwarzer, H.M. van der Ploeg, C.D. Spielberger (Eds.): *Advances in Test Anxiety Research*, (Vol. V, pp. 87-96). Lisse: Swets & Zeitlinger.

Herrmann, C. & Wortmann, C. B. (1985). Action control and coping process. In Kuhl, J. & Beckmann, J. (Eds.) *Action and control: From cognition to behavior*. (pp. 151-180). Springer, New York.

Herzberg, F., Mausner, B., Peterson, R. O., & Capwell, D. F. (1957). *Job attitudes. A review of research and opinions*. Pittsburg: Psychological Service of Pittsburg.

Hewstone, M. (1983). *Attribution Theory: Social and Functional Extensions*. Oxford: Blackwell.

Higgins, E. T. (1987). Self-Discrepancy Theory: A theory relating self and affect. *Psychological Review, 94*, 319-340.

Higgins, E. T. (1989). Self-Discrepancy Theory: What patterns of self-beliefs cause people to suffer? In L. Berkowitz (Eds.), *Advances in experimental social psychology*, (Vol. 22, pp. 93-136). New York: Academic Press.

Higgins, E. T. (1997). Beyond pleasure and pain. *American Psychologist, 52*, 1280-1300.

Higgins, E. T. (1998). Promotion and prevention: Regulatory focus as a motivational principle. In M. P. Zanna (Eds.). *Advances in experimental social psychology,* (Vol. 30, pp. 1-46). New York: Academic Press.

Higgins, E. T. (2000). *Making a good decision: Value from „fit".* American Psychological Association Award Address, Washington, DC.

Higgins, E. T., Friedman, R. S., Harlow, R. E., Idson, L. C., Ayduk, O. N., Taylor, A. (2001). Achievement orientations from subjective histories of success: Promotion pride versus prevention pride. *European Journal of Social Psychology, 31,* 3-23.

Higgins, E. T. & Idson, L. C. (2000). *Fit as added value.* Unpublished manuscript. Co-lumbia University, New York.

Higgins, E. T. & Spiegel, S. (2004). *Promotion and prevention strategies for self-regulation: A motivated cognition perspective.* Verfügbar unter: *http://www.columbia.edu/cu/ psychology/higgins/papers/higginsspiegel/2004/doc* [10.12.06].

Higgins, E. T. & Tykocinski, O. (1992). Self-discrepancies and biographical memory: Personality and cognition at the level of psychological situation. *Personality and Social Psychology Bulletin, 18,* 527-535.

Higgins, E. T., Roney, C., Crowe, E., & Hymes, C. (1994). Ideal versus ought predilections for approach and avoidance: Distinct self-regulatory systems. *Journal of Personality and Social Psychology, 66,* 276-286.

Holland, J. L. (1996). Exploring careers with a typology: What we have learned and some new directions. *American Psychologist, 51,* 397-406.

Hill, J. M. M., & Trist, E. L. (1953). A considerartion of industrial accidents as a means of withdrawal from the work situation. *Human Relations, 6,* 357-380.

Hill, J. M. M., & Trist, E. L. (1955). Changes in accidents and other absences with length of service. *Human Relations, 8,* 121-152.

Hillmann, L. W., Schwandt, D. R., & Bartz, D. E. (1990). Enhancing staff members' performance through feedback and coaching. *Journal for Management Development, 71,* 40-52.

Hofstede, G. (1985). The interaction between national and organizational value systems. *Journal of Management Studies, 22,* 347-357.

Hofstede, G. (1991). *Cultures and organizations: Software of the mind.* London: McGraw-Hill.

Hofstede, G. (2001). *Culture's consequences: Comparing values, behaviors, institutions and organizations across nations* (2 ed.). Sage Publications, Inc.

Hogg, M. A. (2001). A social identity theory of leadership. *Personality and Social Psychology Review, 5,* 184-200.

Holling, H., Preckel, F., & Vock, M. (2004). Intelligenzdiagnostik. *Kompendien Psychologische Diagnostik,* Band 6. Goettingen: Hogrefe.

Hom, P. W., Caranikas-Walker, F., Prussia, G. E., & Griffeth, R. W. (1992). A meta-analytical structural equations analysis of a model of employee turnover. *Journal of Applied Psychology, 77,* 890-909.

Hoojiberg, R., & Schneider, M. (2001). Behavioral complexity and social intelligence: How executive leaders use stakeholders to form systems perspective. In S.J. Zaccaro & R.J. Klimoski (Eds.), *The nature of organizational leadership: Understanding the performance imperatives confronting today's leadership* (pp. 104-131). San Francisco: Jossey-Bass.

House, R. J. (1977). A 1976 Theory of charismatic leadership. In J. G. Hunt & L. L. Larson (Eds.), Leadership: *The cutting edge* (pp. 121-145). Carbondale: Southern Illinois University Press.

House, R. J. (1997). The social scientific study of leadership: quo vadis? *Journal of Management, 23,* 409-473.

House, R. J. (2004). A path-goal theory of leader effectiveness. *Administrative Science Quarterly, 16*, 321-338.

Howell, J. M. & Avolio, B. J. (1992). The ethics of charismatic leadership: Submission or liberation? *Academy of Management Executive, 6*, 43-54.

Hudson, P., Miller, S., Salzberg, C., & Morgan, R. (1994). The role of per coaching in teacher education programs. *Teacher Education and Special Education, 17*, 224-235.

Hulin, C. L. (1984). Suggested directions for defining, measuring, and controlling absenteeism. In P. S. Goodman & R. S. Atkin (Eds.), *Absenteeism* (1 ed., pp. 391-420). San Francisco: Jossey-Bass.

Hunt, J. G. & Peterson, M. F. (1997). International and cross-cultural leadership research. *Leadership Quarterly, 8*, 201-202.

Idson, L. C., Liberman, N., & Higgins, E. T. (2000). Distinguishing Gains from Nonlosses and Losses from Nongains: A Regulatory Focus Perspective on Hedonic Intensity. *Journal of Experimental Social Psychology, 36*, 252-274.

Ivancevich, J.M., Matteson, M.T., Freedman, S.M., & Phillips, J.S. (1990). Worksite Stress Management Interventions. *American Psychologist, 45*, 252-261.

Jacobs, P. & Chovil, A. (1983). Economic evaluation of corporate medical programs. *Journal of Occupational Medicine, 25*, 273-278.

Jacobson, E. (1996). *Entspannung als Therapie. Progressive Relaxation in Theorie und Praxis*. München: Pfeiffer.

Jacobson, B. H., Aldana, S. G., Goetzel, R. Z., Vardell, K. D., Adams, T. B., & Pietras, R. J. (1996). The relationship between perceived stress and self-reported illness-related absenteeism. *American Journal of Health Promotion, 11*, 54-61.

Janssen, J. & Laatz, W. (1999). *Statistische Datenanalyse mit SPSS für Windows*. Berlin: Springer.

Johns, G. (1978). Attitudinal and nonattitudinal predictors of two forms of absence from work. *Organizational Behavior and Human Decision Processes, 22*, 431-444.

Johns, G. (1991). Substantive and methodological constraints on behavior and attitudes in organizational research. *Organizational Behavior and Human Decision Processes, 49*, 80-104.

Johns, G. (1994). How often were you absent? A review of the use of self-reported absence data. *Journal of Applied Psychology, 79*, 574-591.

Johns, G. (1997). Contemporary research on absence from work: Correlates, causes and consequences. In C. L. Cooper & I. T. Robertson (Eds.), *International Review of Industrial and Organizational Psychology* (1 ed., pp. 115-173). West Sussex, UK: Wiley.

Johns, G. (2003). How methodological diversity has improved our understanding of absenteeism from work. *Human Resource Management Review, 13*, 157-184.

Johns, G., & Nicholson, N. (1990). The meanings of absence: New strategies for theory and research. In L. L. Cummings & B. M. Staw (Eds.), *Evaluation and employment in organizations* (pp. 207-252). Greenwich, CT: JAI Press.

Johnson, J. V. & Hall, E. M. (1988). Job strain, work place social support, and cardiovascular disease: a cross-sectional study of a random sample of the Swedish working population. *American Journal of Public Health, 78*, 1336-1342.

Johnson, J. V., Hall, E. M., & Theorell, T. (1989). Combined effects of job strain and social isolation on cardiovascular disease morbidity and mortality in a random sample of the Swedish male working population. *Scandinavian Journal of Work, Environment and Health, 15*, 271-279.

Jones, J. W., Barge, B. N., Steffy, B. D., Fay, L. M., Kunz, L. K., & Wuebker, L. J. (1988). Stress and medical malpractice: Organizational risk assessment and intervention. *Journal of Applied Psychology, 73*, 727-735.

Judge, T. A. (2005). *Psychological leadership research: The state of the art.* Paper presented at the 4th conference of the German Psychological Association, section I/O Psychology, Bonn, Germany.

Judge, T. A., Bono, J. E., Thoresen, C. J., & Patton, G. K. (2001). The job satisfaction-job performance relationship: A qualitative and quantitative review. *Psychological Bulletin, 127,* 376-407.

Judge, T. A., Heller, D., & Mount, M. K. (2002). Five-factor model of personality and job satisfaction: A meta-analysis. *Journal of Applied Psychology, 87,* 530-541.

Judge, T. A., & Martocchio, J. J. (1996). Dispositional influences on attributions concerning absenteeism. *Journal of Management, 22,* 837-861.

Judge, T. A. & Piccolo, R. F. (2004). Transformational and transactional leadership: A meta-analytic test of their relative validity. *Journal of Applied Psychology, 89,* 755-768.

Jungkunz, D. (1996). Zufriedenheit von Auszubildenden mit ihrer Berufsausbildung. *Zeitschrift für Berufs- und Wirtschaftspädagogik, 92,* 405-415.

Kämmerer, A. (1983). *Die therapeutische Strategie "Problemlösen". Theoretische und empirische Perspektiven ihrer Anwendung in der kognitiven Psychotherapie.* Münster: Aschendorff.

Kahn, W. A. (1990). Toward an agenda for business ethics research. *Academy of Management Review, 15,* 311-328.

Kaiser, C. P. (1998). What do we know about employee absence bahavior? An interdisciplinary interpretation. *Journal of Socioeconomics, 27,* 79-96.

Kalimo, R., & Vuori, J. (1990). Work and sense of coherence: Resources for competence and life satisfaction. *Behavioral Medicine, 16,* 76-89.

Kampa-Kokesch, S. & Anderson, M. Z. (2001). Executive coaching: A comprehensive review of the literature. *Consulting Psychology Journal: Practice and Research, 53,* 205-228.

Karasek, R. A. (1979). Job demands, job decision latitude and mental strain: implications for job redesign. *Administrative Science Quarterly, 24,* 285-308.

Karasek, R. A. (1985). *Job Content Questionnaire and user's guide.* Lowell: University of Massachusetts Lowell, Department of Work Environment.

Katz, D., & Hyman, H. (1943). Industrial morale and public opinion methods. *International Journal of Opinion & Attitude Research, 1,* 13-20.

Keller, T. (1999). Images of the familiar: Individual differences and implicit leadership theories. *Leadership Quarterly, 10,* 423-448.

Kenney, R. A., Blascovich, J., & Shaver, P. R. (1994). Implicit leadership theories: Prototypes for new leaders. *Basic and Applied Social Psychology, 15,* 409-437.

Kenney, R. A., Schwartz-Kenney, B. M., & Blascovich, J. (1996). Implicit leadership theories: Defining leaders described as worthy of influence. *Personality and Social Psychology Bulletin, 22,* 1128-1143.

Kerr, J. H., & Vos, M. C. (1993). Employee fitness programmes, absenteeism and general well-being. *Work Stress, 7,* 179-190.

Kersten, G. (1994). Fehlermöglichkeits- und Fehlereinflussnahme (FMEA). In W. Masing (Hrsg.), *Handbuch Qualitätsmanagement* (3.Aufl., S. 469-490). München, Wien: Hanser.

Kieser, A. (Hrsg.) (1999). *Organisationstheorien.* Stuttgart: Kohlhammer (3. Aufl.)

Kieser, A. & Kubicek, H. (1992). *Organisation.* Berlin: De Gryter. (3. Aufl.)

Kilburg, R. R. (2001). Facilitating intervention adherence in executive coaching: A model and methods. *Consulting Psychology Journal: Practice and Research, 53,* 251-267.

Knutsson, A., & Goine, H. (1998). Occupation and unemployment rates as predictors of long term sickness absence in two Swedish counties. *Social Science & Medicine, 47,* 25-31.

Komaki, J. L. (1998). *Leadership from an operant perspective.* New York: Routledge.

Konrad, E. (2000). Implicit leadership theories in Eastern and Western Europe. *Social Science Information, 39,* 335-347.

Konrad, E., & Kranjcec, R. (1997). A comparison of implicit leadership theories of managers and students. *Review of Psychology, 4,* 41-47.

Konst, D., Vonk, R., & Van Der Vlist, R. (1999). Inferences about causes and consequences of behavior of leaders und subordinates. *Journal of Organizational Behavior, 20,* 261-271.

Koopman, C., Pelletier, K. R., Murray, J. F., Sharda, C. E., Berger, M. L., Turpin, R. S., et al. (2002). Stanford Presenteeism Scale: Health status and employee productivity. *Journal of Occupational and Environmental Medicine, 44,* 14-20.

Kristensen, K., Juhl, H. J., & Eskildsen, J. K. (2003). Models that matter. *International Journal of Business Performance Management, 5,* 91- 106.

Krystek, U. & Müller-Stewens, G. (1990). Grundzüge einer strategischen Frühaufklärung. In D. Hahn & B. Taylor (Hrsg.), *Strategische Unternehmungsplanung.* Heidelberg, Wien: Physika-Verlag.

Kuhl, J. (1982). Handlungskontrolle als metakognitiver Vermittler zwischen Intention und Handeln: Freizeitaktivitäten bei Hauptschülern. *Zeitschrift für Entwicklungspsychologie und Pädagogische Psychologie, 14,* 141-148.

Kuhl, J. (1983). *Motivation, Konflikt und Handlungskontrolle.* Berlin: Springer-Verlag.

Kuhl, J. (1984). Volitional aspects of achievement and learned helplessness: Toward a comprehensive Theory of Action Control. In B. A. Maher (Eds.), *Progress in experimental personality research,* (Vol. 13, pp. 99-171). New York: Academic Press.

Kuhl, J. (1985). Volitional Mediators of Cognition-Behavior Consistency; Self-Regulatory Processes and Action Versus State Orientation. In J. Kuhl. & J. Beckmann (Eds.), *Action Control: From Cognition to Behavior* (pp. 101-128). Heidelberg: Springer-Verlag.

Kuhl, J. (1986). Motivation and Information Processing. A New Look at Decision Making, Dynamic Change, and Action Control. In Sorrentino, R. M. & Higgins, E. T. (Eds.), *Handbook of Motivation and Cognition* (pp. 404-434). Chichester: Wiley & Sons.

Kuhl, J. (1987). Action control: The maintenance of motivational states. In F. Halisch & J. Kuhl (Eds.), *Motivation, Intention and Volition* (pp. 279-291). Berlin: Springer-Verlag.

Kuhl, J. (1990). Handlungs- und Lageorientierung. In W. Sarges (Hrsg.), *Managementdiagnostik.* (S. 247-252) Göttingen: Hogrefe.

Kuhl, J. (1995). *Wille, Freiheit und Verantwortung: Alte Antimonien aus experimentalpsychologischer Sicht* (Forschungsbericht Nr. 13). Universität Osnabrück.

Kuhl, J. (1996). Wille und Freiheitserleben: Formen der Selbststeuerung. In: J. Kuhl & H. Heckhausen (Hrsg.), *Enzyklopädie der Psychologie: Motivation, Volition und Handlung* (Serie IV, Band 4, S. 665-765). Göttingen: Hogrefe.

Kuhl, J. (2001). *Motivation und Persönlichkeit. Interaktionen psychischer Systeme.* Göttingen: Hogrefe.

Kuhl, J. (2006). Individuelle Unterschiede in der Selbststeuerung. In Heckhausen, J. & Heckhausen, J. (Hrsg.). *Motivation und Handeln* (S. 303-329). Heidelberg: Springer.

Kuhl, J. (ohne Jahresangabe). *Kurzanweisung zum Fragebogen HAKEMP. Handlungskontrolle nach Erfolg, Misserfolg und prospektiv.* Osnabrück: Universität. Fachbereich Psychologie, Abteilung für Differentielle Psychologie und Persönlichkeitsforschung. Göttingen: Hogrefe.

Kuhl, J. & Kazén, M. (2002). Handlungs- und Lageorientierung: Wie lernt man seine Gefühle zu steuern? In Stiensmeier-Pelster, J. & Rheinsberg, F. (2002). *Diagnostik von Selbstkonzept, Lernmotivation und Selbstregulation* (S.201- 219). Göttingen: Hogrefe.

Leigh, J. P. (1985). The effects of unemployment and the business cycle on absenteeism. *Journal of Economics and Business, 37,* 159-170.

Lam, C., & Chan, F. (1988). Job satisfaction of sheltered workshop clients. *Journal of Rehabilitation, 12,* 51-54.

Lam, S. S. K., Schaubroeck, J., & Aryee, S. (2002). Relationship between organizational justice and employee work outcomes: a cross-national study. *Journal of Organizational Behavior, 23,* 1-18.

Landy, F. J., Vasey, J. J., & Smith, F. D. (1984). Methodological problems and strategies in predicting absence. In P. S. Goodman & R. S. Atkin (Eds.), *Absenteeism* (1 ed., pp. 111-157). San Francisco: Jossey-Bass.

Larson, J. R. (1982). Cognitive mechanisms mediating the impact of implicit theories of leader behavior on leader behaviors ratings. *Organizational Behavior and Human Performance, 29,* 129-140.

Larson, E. W. (1985). Employee absenteeism: the role of ease of movement. *Academy of Management Journal, 28,* 464-471.

Laske, O. E. (1999). An integrated model of developmental coaching. *Consulting Psychology Journal: Practice and Research, 51,* 139-159.

Laucken, U. (1973). *Naive Verhaltenstheorie. Ein Ansatz zur Analyse des Konzeptrepertoires, mit dem im alltäglichen Lebensvollzug das Verhalten der Mitmenschen erklärt und vorhergesagt wird.* Stuttgart, Germany: Klett.

Lazarus, R. S. (1966). *Psychological stress and the coping process.* New York: McGraw Hill.

Lazarus, R. S. & Launier, R. (1981). Streßbezogene Transaktion zwischen Person und Umwelt. In J. R. Nitsch (Hrsg.), *Streß. Theorien, Untersuchungen und Maßnahmen,* (S. 213-295). Bern: Huber.

Leary, M. R. (1989). Self-presentational processes in leadership emergence and effectiveness. In R.A. Giacalone & P. Rosenfeld (Eds.), *Impression management in the organization* (pp. 363-374). Hillsdale, NJ: Lawrence Erlbaum.

LeFevre, J. (1988). Flow and the quality of experience during work and leisure. In M. Csikszentmihalyi & I. S. Csikszentmihalyi (Eds.), Optimal experience: *Psychological studies of flow in consciousness* (pp. 15-35). New York: Cambridge University Press.

Leitner, K. (1993). Auswirkungen von Arbeitsbedingungen auf die psychosoziale Gesundheit. *Zeitschrift für Arbeitswissenschaft, 47,* 98-107.

Leitner, K. (1999). Kriterien und Befunde zu gesundheitsgerechter Arbeit - Was schädigt, was fördert die Gesundheit? In R. Oesterreich & W. Volpert (Hrsg.), *Psychologie gesundheitsgerechter Arbeitsbedingungen,* (S. 63-139). Bern: Huber.

Leitner, K., Volpert, W., Greiner, B., Weber, W. G., & Hennes, K. (1987). *Analyse psychischer Belastung in der Arbeit. Das RHIA-Verfahren.* Köln: TÜV Rheinland.

Liberman, N., Idson, C., Camacho, C. J. & Higgins, E. T. (1999). Promotion and pre-vention choices between stability and change. *Journal of Personality and Social Psychology, 77,* 1135-1145.

Liepmann, D. (1989). Fragen zu einer empirischen Unternehmenskulturforschung. In H. Merkens, W. Dürr, F. Schmidt & D.Liepmann D. (Hrsg.), *Wertvorstellungen in Unternehmenskulturen,* (S. 61-82). Baltmannsweiler: Pädagogischer Verlag.

Liepmann, D. (2000) (Hrsg.). *Motivation, Führung und Erfolg in Organisationen.* Frankfurt am Main. Lang.

Liepmann, D. & Felfe, J. (1997). Betriebliche Gesundheitsförderung. In R. Schwarzer (Hrsg.), *Gesundheitspsychologie* (2. Auflage, S. 535-551). Göttingen: Hogrefe.

Liepmann, D. & Felfe, J. (2002). Gesundheitsförderung in der Arbeit. In R. Schwarzer, M. Jerusalem & H. Weber (Hrsg.), *Gesundheitspsychologie von A bis Z.* (S. 163-166). Göttingen: Hogrefe.

Lin, P.-C., & Shih, M.-M. (1997). Implicit leadership theories and leader's behaviour: The elementary school principals in Taipei. *Journal of Education and Psychology, 20*, 71-90.

Ling, W., Chia, R. C., & Fang, L. (2000). Chinese implicit leadership theory. *The Journal of Social Psychology, 140*, 729-739.

Lippmann, E. (2005). *Coaching: Angewandte Psychologie für die Beratungspraxis*. Berlin: Springer.

Lipsett, L., & Wilson, J. W. (1954). Do suitable interests and mental ability lead to job satisfaction? *Educational and Psychological Measurement, 14*, 373-380.

Locke, E. A. (1976). The nature and causes of job satisfaction. In M. D. Dunette (Ed.). *Handbook of Industrial and Organizational Psychology*, (pp. 1297-1349). Chicago: Rand McNelly.

Locke, E. A. & Latham, G. P. (2002). Building a practically useful theory of goal setting and task motivation: A 35-year odyssey. *American Psychologist, 57*, 705-717.

Loher, B. T., Noe, R. L., Moeller, N. J., & Fitzgerald, M. P. (1978). A meta- analysis of the relation of job characteristics to job satisfaction. *Journal of Applied Psychology, 70*, 280-289.

Lord, R. G. (1985). An information processing approach to social perceptions, leadership and behavioral measurement in organizations. *Research in Organizational Behavior, 7*, 20-48.

Lord, R. G., Brown, D. J., Harvey, J. L., & Hall, R. J. (2001). Contextual constraints on prototype generation and their multilevel consequences for leadership perceptions. *Leadership Quarterly, 12*, 311-338.

Lord, R. G., & Emrich, C. G. (2001). Thinking outside the box by looking inside the box: Extending the cognitive revolution in leadership research. *Leadership Quarterly, 11*, 551-579.

Lord, R. G., Foti, R. J., & De Vader, C. L. (1984). A test of leadership categorization theory: Internal structure, information processing, and leadership perceptions. *Organizational Behavior and Human Performance, 34*, 343-378.

Lord, R. G., Foti, R. J., & Philips, R. S. (1982). A theory of leadership categorization. In J.G. Hunt, U. Sekaran & C. Schriesheim (Eds.), *Leadership: Beyond established views* (pp. 104-121). Carbondale, IL: Southern Illinois University Press.

Lord, R. G., & Maher, K. J. (1991). Cognitive theory in industrial and organizational psychology. In M. D. Dunnette & L. E. Hough (Eds.), *Handbook of industrial and organizational psychology*, (Vol. 2, pp. 1-62). Palo Alto: Consulting Psychologists Press.

Lounsbury, J. W., Gibson, L. W., Steel, R. P., Sundstrom, E. D., & Loveland, J. L. (2004). An investigation of intelligence and personality in relation to career satisfaction. *Personality and Individual Differences, 37*, 181- 189.

Luthans, F., Hodgetts, R. M., & Rosenkrantz, S. A. (1988). *Real managers*. Cambridge, MA: University Press.

Luthans, F. & Peterson, S. J. (2003). 360-degree feedback with systematic coaching: Empirical analysis suggests a winning combination. *Human Resource Management, 42*, 243-256.

Macdonald, S. & Wells, S. (1994). The prevalence and characteristics of employee assistance, health promotion and drug testing programs in Ontario. *Employee Assistance Quarterly, 10*, 25-55.

Mackenzie, R.A. (1991). *Die Zeitfalle. Sinnvolle Zeiteinteilung und Zeitnutzung*. Heidelberg: Sauer.

MacKenzie, S. B., Podsakoff, P. M., & Rich, G. A. (2004). Transformational and transactional leadership and salesperson performance. *Journal of the Academy of Marketing Science, 29*, 115-134.

Manuso, J. S. J. (Ed.) (1983). *Occupational clinical psychology*. Westport: Praeger.

Markham, S. E. (1985). An investigation of the relationship between unemployment and absenteeism: a multilevel approach. *Academy of Management Journal, 28*, 228-234.

Markham, S. E., Dansereau, F., & Alutto, J. A. (1982). Group size and absenteeism rates: A longitudinal analysis. *Academy of Management Journal, 25*, 921-927.

Markham, S. E., & McKee, G. (1995). Group absence behavior and standards: a multilevel analysis. *Academy of Management Journal, 38*, 1174-1190.

Marmot, M. (1994). Work and other factors influencing coronary health and sickness absence. *Work Stress, 8*, 191-201.

Marmot, M., Siegrist, J., Theorell, T., & Feeney, A. (1999). Health and the psychosocial environment at work. In M. Marmot & R. G. Wilkinson (Eds.), *Social Determinants of Health*, (pp. 105-127). Oxford: University Press.

Martin, R., & Epitropaki, O. (2001). Role of organizational identification on implicit leadership theories (ILTs), transformational leadership and work attitudes. *Group Processes and Intergroup Relations, 4*, 247-262.

Martinko, M. J., Gundlach, M. J., & Douglas, S. C. (2002). Toward an integrative theory of counterproductive workplace behavior: a causal reasoning perspective. *International Journal of Selection and Assessment, 10*, 36-50.

Martocchio, J. J. (1994). The effects of absence culture on individual absence. *Human Relations, 47*, 243-262.

Martocchio, J. J., & Judge, T. A. (1994). A policy-capturing approach to individuals' decisions to be absent. *Organizational Behavior and Human Decision Processes, 57*, 358-386.

Mathieu, J. E., & Kohler, S. S. (1990). A cross-level examination of group absence influences on individual absence. *Journal of Applied Psychology, 75*, 217-220.

Matthews, A. M., Lord, R. G., & Walker, J. B. (1990). *The development of leadership perceptions in children*. Unpublished manuscript: University of Akron.

Maurer, T. J., & Lord, R. G. (1991). An exploration of cognitive demands in group interaction as a moderator of information processing variables in perceptions of leadership. *Journal of Applied Social Psychology, 21*, 821-839.

McElroy, J. C. (1991). Attribution theory applied to leadership: Lessons from presidential politics. *Journal of Managerial Issues, 3*, 90-106.

McGregor, D. (1960). *The human side of enterprise*. New York: McGraw-Hill.

Meindl. J. R. (1990). On leadership: An alternative to the conventional wisdom. *Research in Organizational Behavior, 12*, 159-203.

Meindl, J. R. (1995). The romance of leadership as a follower-centric theory: A social construction approach. *Leadership Quarterly, 6*, 329-341.

Meindl, J. R., & Ehrlich, S. B. (1987). The romance of leadership and the evaluation of organizational performance. *Academy of Management Journal, 30*, 91-109.

Meindl, J. R., & Ehrlich, S. B: (1988). *Developing a romance of leadership scale*. Silver Anniversary Proceedings. Eastern Academy of Management Meetings. Washington, DC, May.

Meindl, J. R., Ehrlich, S. B., & Dukerich, J. M. (1985). The romance of leadership. *Administrative Science Quarterly, 30*, 78-102.

Michalos, A. C. (1985). Multiple discrepancies theory (MDT). *Social Indicators Research, 16*, 347-413.

Mitchell, T. R., Larsen, J. R., & Green, S. G. (1977). Leader behaviour, situational moderators, and group performance: An attributional analysis. *Organizational Behaviour and Human Performance, 18*, 254-268.

Mitra, A., Jenkins, J. D., & Gupta, N. (1992). A meta-analytic review of the relationship between absence and turnover. *Journal of Applied Psychology, 77*, 879-889.

Mittag, W. & Jerusalem, M. (1997) Evaluation von Präventionsprogrammen. In R. Schwarzer (Hrsg.), *Gesundheitspsychologie* (2. Auflage, S. 595-611). Göttingen: Hogrefe.

Mohr, G. (1986). *Die Erfassung psychischer Befindensbeeinträchtigungen bei Industriearbeitern.* Frankfurt: Lang.

Mohr, G., Rigotti, T., & Müller, A. (2003). *Die Erfassung psychischer Befindensbeeinträchtigungen: Irritation.* [Onlinedokument] http://www.uni-leipzig.de/~apsycho/irritation_NEU.htm.

Mohr, G. & Semmer, N.K. (2002). Arbeit und Gesundheit: Kontroversen zu Person und Situation. *Psychologische Rundschau, 53*, 77-84.

Mossink, J. C. M. (2002). *Understanding and performing economic assessments at the company level* (Vol. 2). Geneva: World Health Organization.

Mowday, R. T., Porter, L. W., & Steers, R. M. (1982). *Employee-organization linkages. The psychology of commitment, absenteeism, and turnover.* New York: Academic Press.

Mumford, M. D., Marks, M. A., Connelly, M. S., Zaccaro, S. J., & Reiter-Palmon, R. (2000). Development of leadership skills: Experience and timing. *Leadership Quarterly, 11*, 87-114.

Munz, D. C., Kohler, J. M., & Greenberg, C. L. (2001). Effectiveness of a comprehensive worksite stress management program: combining organizational and individual interventions. *International Journal of Stress Management, 8*, 49-62.

Murphy, L. R. (1996). Stress management in work settings: a critical review of the health effects. *American Journal of Health Promotion, 11*, 112-135.

Murphy, L. R. (Ed.) (1995). *Job stress interventions.* Washington: American Psychological Association

Murphy, M. R., & Jones, A. P. (1993). The influence of performance cues and observational focus on performance rating accuracy. *Journal of Applied Social Psychology, 23*, 1523-1545.

Narayanan, L., Menon, S., & Spector, P. (1999). A cross-cultural comparison of job stressors and reactions among employees holding comparable jobs in two countries. *International Journal of Stress Management, 6*, 197-212.

Nathan, P. E. (1984). Johnson & Johnson's "Live-for-Life": A comprehensive positive lifestyle change program. In J. D. Matarazzo, S. M. Weiss, J. A. Herd, N. E. Miller & S. M. Weiss (Eds.), *Behavioral health: A handbook of health enhancement and disease prevention* (pp. 1064-1070). New York: Wiley.

Nerdinger, F. W. (2006). Motivierung. In Schuler, H. (Hrsg.), (2006). *Lehrbuch der Personalpsychologie* (2. überarb. Auflage, S. 385-408). Göttingen: Hogrefe.

Neubauer, W. (1982). Dimensionale Struktur der impliziten Führungstheorie bei Vorgesetzten. *Psychologie und Praxis, 26*, 1-11.

Neubauer, W. (1986). Implizite Führungstheorien und Führungserfahrung bei Vorgesetzten. In K. Daumenlang & J. Sauer (Hrsg.), *Aspekte psychologischer Forschung.* Festschrift zum 60. Geburtstag von Erwin Roth (pp. 70-95). Göttingen: Hogrefe.

Nicholson, N. (1977). Absence behavior and attendance motivation: a conceptual synthesis. *Journal of Management Studies, 14*, 231-252.

Nicholson, N. (1993). Absence - There and back again. *Journal of Organizational Behavior, 14*, 288-290.

Nicholson, N., Brown, C. A., & Chadwick-Jones, J. K. (1976). Absence from work and job satisfaction. *Journal of Applied Psychology, 61*, 728-737.

Nicholson, N., & Johns, G. (1985). The absence culture and the psychological contract - Who's in control of absence. *Academy of Management Journal, 10*, 397-407.

Nicholson, N., & Payne, R. (1987). Absence from work: explanations and attributions. *Applied Psychology: An International Review, 36*, 121-132.

Noe, R. A. & Colquitt, J. A. (2002). Planning for training impact: Principles of training effectiveness. In K.Kraiger (Ed.), *Creating, Implementing, and Managing Effective Training* (pp. 53-79). San Francisco, CA: Jossey-Bass.

Nord, W. R., & Costigan, R. (1973). Worker adjustment to the four-day week: a longitudinal study. *Journal of Applied Psychology, 58*, 60-66.

Normand, J., Salyards, S. D., & Mahoney, J. J. (1990). An evaluation of preemployment drug testing. *Journal of Applied Psychology, 75*, 629-639.

North, F. M., Syme, S. L., Feeny, A., Shipley, M., & Marmot, M. (1996). Psychosocial work environment and sickness absence among British civil servants: The Whitehall II study. *American Journal of Public Health, 86*, 332-340.

Nye, J. I. (2002). The eye of the follower - Information processing effects on attribution regarding leaders of small groups. *Small Group Research, 33*, 337-360

Nye, J. I., & Forsyth, D. R. (1991). The effects of prototype biases on leadership appraisal: A test of leadership categorization theory. *Small Group Research, 22*, 360-375.

Oesterreich, R. (1981). *Handlungsregulation und Kontrolle.* München, Wien, Baltimore: Urban und Schwarzenberg.

Oesterreich, R. (1998). Die Bedeutung arbeitspsychologischer Konzepte der Handlungs-regulationstheorie für die betriebliche Gesundheitsförderung. In E. Bamberg, A. Ducki, & A.-M. Metz (Hrsg.), *Handbuch Betriebliche Gesundheitsförderung.*, (S. 75-94). Göttingen: Hogrefe.

Oesterreich, R. (1999). Konzepte zu Arbeitsbedingungen und Gesundheit - Fünf Erklärungsmodelle im Vergleich. In R. Oesterreich & W. Volpert (Hrsg.), *Psychologie gesundheitsgerechter Arbeitsbedingungen*, (S. 141-215). Bern: Huber.

Offermann, L. R., Kennedy, J. K. Jr., & Wirtz, P.W. (1994). Implicit leadership theories: Content, structure, and generalizability. *Leadership Quarterly, 5*, 43-58.

Oldham, G. R., Kulik, C. T., & Stepina, L. P. (1991). Physical environments and employee reactions: Effects of stimulus screening and job complexity. *Academy of Management Journal, 34*, 929-938.

Olivero, G., Bane, K. D., & Kopelman, R. E. (1997). Executive coaching as a transfer of training tool: Effects on productivity in a public agency. *Public Personnel Management, 26*, 461-469.

Ones, D. S., Viswesvaran, C., & Schmidt, F. L. (2003). Personality and absenteeism: A meta-analysis of integrity tests. *European Journal of Personality, 17*, 19-38.

Ott, B. (1980). *Arbeitszufriedenheit bei Jugendlichen in der Ausbildung.* Unpublished doctoral dissertation, Humboldt University of Berlin, Germany.

Paoli, P., & Merllié, D. (Eds.) (2001). *Third European survey on working conditions 2000. In European Foundation for the Improvement of Living and Working Conditions.* Luxembourg: European Foundation for the Improvement of Living and Working Conditions.

Parkes, K. R. (1994). Personality and coping as moderators of work stress processes: models, methods and measures. *Work & Stress, 8*, 110-129.

Parkes, K. R., Mendham, C. A., & Rabenau, C. (1994). Social support and the demand-discretion model of job stress: Tests of additive and interactive effects in two samples. *Journal of vocational behavior, 44*, 91-113.

Pastor, J. C. (1998). *The social construction of leadership: A semantic and social network analysis of social representation of leadership.* Unpublished doctoral dissertation: State University of New York at Buffalo.

Pfeffer, J. (1977). The ambiguity of leadership. *Academy of Management Review, 2,* 104-112.

Phillips, J. S., & Lord, R. G. (1981). Causal attributions and perceptions of leadership. *Organizational Behavior and Human Performance, 28,* 143-163.

Phillips, J. S., & Lord, R. G. (1982). Schematic information processing and perceptions of leadership in problem-solving groups. *Journal of Applied Psychology, 67,* 486-492.

Phillips, J. S., & Lord, R. G. (1986). Notes on the practical and theoretical consequences of implicit leadership theories for the future of leadership measurement. *Journal of Management, 12,* 31-41.

Pillai, R., & Meindl, J. R. (1998). Context charisma: A "meso" level examination of the relationship of organic structure, collectivism, and crisis to charismatic leadership. *Journal of Management, 24,* 643-671.

Pocock, S. J. (1974). Daily variation in sickness absence. *Applied Statistics, 23,* 375-391.

Podsakoff, N. P., MacKenzie, S. B., Moorman, R. H., & Fetter, R. (1990). Transformational leader behaviors and their effects on followers' trust in leader, satisfaction, and organizational citizenship behaviors. *Leadership Quarterly, 1,* 107-142.

Podsakoff, P. M., MacKenzie, S. B., & Bommer, W. H. (1996). Transformational leader behaviors and substitutes for leadership as determinants of employee satisfaction, commitment, trust, and organizational citizenship behaviors. *Journal of Management, 22,* 259-298.

Poole, C. J. (1999). Can sickness absence be predicted at the pre-placement health assessment? *Occupational Medicine, 49,* 337-339.

Powell, G. N., Butterfield, D. A., & Parent, J. D. (2002). Gender and managerial stereotypes: Have the times changed? *Journal of Management, 28,* 177-193.

Preiser, S. (1989). *Zielorientiertes Handeln. Ein Trainingsprogramm zur Selbstkontrolle.* Heidelberg: Asanger.

Prideux, S. & Ford, J. E. (1987). Management development: competencies, teams, learning contracts and work experience based learning. *Management Development, 7,* 13-21.

Rauen, C. (2003). *Coaching.* Göttingen: Hogrefe.

Reidy, A. (1991). Questioning the status quo: sickness absence research so far claims more than it should. *Social Science & Medicine, 31,* 421-432.

Rennenkampff, A.v., Kühnen, U., & Sczesny, S. (2003). Die Attribution von Führungskompetenz in Abhängigkeit von geschlechtsstereotyper Kleidung. In U. Rasero (Hrsg.), *Gender – from costs to benefits* (pp. 170-182). Wiesbaden, Germany: Westdeutscher Verlag.

Resch, M. (2003). *Analyse psychischer Belastungen. Verfahren und ihre Anwendungen im Arbeits- und Gesundheitsschutz.* Bern: Huber.

Rheinberg, F. (1995). *Motivation.* Stuttgart: Kohlhammer.

Rhodes, S. R., & Steers, R. M. (1990). *Managing employee absenteeism.* Menlo Park: Addison-Wesley.

Riese, I. (1998). *Evaluation eines Gesundheitszirkels - eine quasiexperimentelle Felduntersuchung.* Unveröffentlichte Diplomarbeit. Technische Universität Berlin, Fachbereich Maschinenbau und Produktionstechnik, Institut für Psychologie.

Robertson, I. T. (1990). Behavior modelling: its record and potential in training and development. *British Journal of Management, 1,* 117-125.

Rosch, E. (1978). Principles of categorization. In E. Rosch & B. Lloyd (Eds.), *Cognition and Categorization* (pp. 27-48). Hillsdale, NJ: Lawrence Erlbaum Associates.

Rosenstiel, L. v., Nerdinger, F. W., Spieß, E., & Stengel, M. (1989). *Führungsnachwuchs im Unternehmen.* München: Beck.

Rosse, J. G., & Miller, H. E. (1984). Relationship between absenteeism and other employee behaviors. In P. S. Goodman & R. S. Atkin (Eds.), *Absenteeism* (1 ed., pp. 194-228). San Francisco: Jossey-Bass.

Rossi, P. H., Freeman, H. E. & Lipsey, M. W. (1999). *Evaluation: A systematic approach.* (6th ed.) Thousand Oaks, CA; Sage.

Rothwell, W. J. & Kazanas, H. C. (1994). Management development: The state of art as perceived by HRD professionals. *Performance Improvement Quarterly, 4,* 40-59.

Rowold, J. (2004a). *Deutsche Übersetzung der Conger & Kanungo Scales (CKS) charismatischer Führung.* http://wwwpsy.uni-muenster.de/inst2/hell/rowold/cks.pdf [Online].

Rowold, J. (2004b). *MLQ-5X. German translation of Bass & Avolio's Multifactor Leadership Questionnaire.* Redwood City: Mind Garden.

Rowold, J. (2005). *Multifactor Leadership Questionnaire. Psychometric properties of the German translation by Jens Rowold.* Redwood City: Mind Garden.

Rowold, J. & Heinitz, K. (2007) Transformational and charismatic leadership: Assessing the convergent, divergent and criterion validity of the MLQ and the CKS. *Leadership Quarterly, 18,* 121-133.

Rowold, J. & Rowold, G. (2006). Zur Wirksamkeit des Kollegialen Team Coachings: Ergebnisse einer zweijährigen Längsschnittstudie. In *Das Kollegiale Team Coaching: Hintergründe und Anwendungen* (in press).

Rush, M. C., & Russell, J. E. (1988). Leader prototypes and prototype-contingent consensus in leader behavior descriptions. *Journal of Experimental Social Psychology, 24,* 88-104.

Rush, M. C., Phillips, J. S., & Lord, R. G. (1981). The effects of temporal delay in rating on leader behaviour descriptions: A laboratory investigation. *Journal of Applied Psychology, 66,* 722-727.

Rush, M. C., Thomas, J. C., & Lord, R. G. (1977) Implicit leadership theory: A potential threat to the internal validity of leader behavior questionnaires. *Organizational Behavior and Human Performance, 20,* 93-110.

Saksvik, P.O., Nytro, K., Dahl-Jor Gensen, C., & Mikkelsen, A. (2002). A process evaluation of individual and organizational occupational stress and health interventions. *Work & Stress, 16,* 37-57.

Salgado, F. J. (2002). The big five personality dimensions and counterproductive behaviors. *International Journal of Selection and Assessment, 10,* 117-125.

Salowsky, H. (1991). *Fehlzeiten: Eine Bilanz nach 20 Jahren Lohnfortzahlungsgesetz* (1 ed.). Köln: Deutscher Instituts-Verlag.

Sarbin, T., Taft, R. & Bailey, D. (1960). *Clinical inference and cognitive theory.* New York: Holt, Rinehart & Winston.

Schein, E. H. (1969). *Process consultation: Its role in organization development.* Reading, MA: Addison-Wesley.

Schein, V. E. (1973). The relationship between sex role stereotypes and requisite management characteristics. *Journal of Applied Psychology, 57,* 95-100.

Schein, V. E. (2001). A global look at psychological barriers to women's progress in management. *Journal of Social Issues, 57,* 675-688.

Schein, V. E., & Mueller, R. (1992). Sex role stereotypes and requisits management characteristics: A cross cultural look. *Journal of Organizational Behavior, 13,* 439 - 447.

Schein, V. E., Mueller, R., Lituchy, T., & Liu, J. (1996). Think manager-think male: A global phenomenon? *Journal of Organizational Behavior, 17,* 33-41.

Schilling, J. (2001). *Wovon sprechen Führungskräfte, wenn Sie von Führung sprechen? Eine Analyse subjektiver Führungstheorien.* Hamburg, Germany: Verlag Dr. Kovac.

Schmidt, F. L., & Hunter, J. E. (1998). The validity and utility of selection methods in personnel psychology: Practical and theoretical implications of 85 years of research findings. *Psychological Bulletin, 124,* 262-274.

Schmidt, F. L., & Hunter, J. E. (2000). Select on intelligence. In E. A. Locke (Ed.), *Handbook of principles of organizational behaviour* (pp. 3-14). Oxford, England: Blackwell.

Schultz, J.H. (1932). *Das Autogene Training.* Stuttgart: Thieme.

Schulz, H. & Koch, U. (2002). Evaluation. In R. Schwarzer, Jerusalem, M & Weber, H. (Hrsg.), *Gesundheitspsychologie von A bis Z.* (S. 105-108). Göttingen: Hogrefe.

Schwarzer, R. (Hrsg.) (1997). *Gesundheitspsychologie.* (2. Aufl.) Göttingen: Hogrefe.

Schwarzer, R., & Leppin, A. (1991). Social support and health: A theoretical and empirical overview. *Journal of Social and Personal Relationships, 8,* 99-127.

Schweiger, D. M., & Denisi, A. S. (1991). Communication with employees following a merger: A longitudinal field experiment. *Academy of Management Journal, 34,* 110-135.

Schyns, B., & Meindl, J. R. (2005). An overview of implicit leadership theories and their application in organization practice. In B. Schyns & J. R. Meindl (Eds.), *Implicit leadership theories: Essays and explorations.* Greenwich, CT: Information Age Publishing.

Schyns, B., Meindl, J. R., & Croon, M. A. (2004). *The romance of leadership scale: Structural validations in different countries and contexts.* Proceedings of the First Conference on Cross-Cultural Leadership and Management Studies. Seoul, June 10-12.

Scott, K. D., & Markham, S. E. (1982). Absenteeism control methods: A survey of practices and results. *Personnel Administration, 24,* 425-431.

Scott, K. D., & Taylor, G. S. (1985). An examination of conflicting findings on the relationship between job satisfaction and absenteeism: A meta-analysis. *Academy of Management Journal, 28,* 599-612.

Sczesny, S. (2003). A closer look beneath the surface: Various facets of the think manager-think male stereotypes. *Sex Roles, 47,* 353-363.

Seago, J. A. (1996). Work group culture, stress, and hostility. Correlations with organizational outcomes. *Journal of Nursing Administration, 26,* 39-47.

Searle, S. J. (1989). Sickness absence. In H. A. Waldron (Ed.), *Occupational health practice* (3 ed., pp. 341-368). London: Butterworths.

Sethi, A. S., Caro, D. H. J. & Schuler, R. S. (1987). *Strategic management of technostress in information society.* Lewiston, NY/Toronto: Hogrefe Inc.

Semmer, N. (1997). Streß. In H. Luczak & W. Volpert (Hrsg.), *Handbuch Arbeitswissenschaft,* (S. 332-339). Stuttgart: Schäffer-Poeschel.

Semmer, N. (2003a). Individual differences, work, stress and health. In M. J. Schabracq, J. A. M. Winnubst, & C. L. Cooper (Eds.), *The Handbook of Work and Health Psychology,* (pp. 83 – 120). West Sussex: John Wiley & Sons Ltd.

Semmer, N. (2003b). Job stress interventions and organization of work. In J. C. Quick & L. E. Tetrick (Eds.), *Handbook of occupational health psychology,* (pp. 325-353). Washington, DC: American Psychological Ass.

Semmer, N. & Dunckel, H. (1991). Streßbezogene Arbeitsanalyse. In S. Greif, E. Bamberg, & N. Semmer (Hrsg.), *Psychischer Streß am Arbeitsplatz, (S. 57 – 90).* Göttingen: Hogrefe.

Semmer, N., Zapf, D., & Greif, S. (1996). "Shared job strain": A new approach for assessing the validity of job stress measurements. *Journal of occupational and organizational psychology, 69,* 293-310.

Semmer, N. K. (1984). *Streßbezogene Tätigkeitsanalyse. Psychologische Untersuchung von Streß am Arbeitsplatz.* Weinheim: Beltz.

Shultz, K. S. (1994). Attributions for success and failure of men and women in leadership positions. *Psychological Reports, 75,* 1307-1312.

Sims, H. P., & Lorenzi, P. (1992). *The new leadership paradigm: Social learning and cognition in organizations.* Newbury Park: Sage.

Singer, M. (1989). Implicit leadership theory: Are results generalizable from student to professional samples? *The Journal of Social Psychology, 130,* 407-408.

Seltzer, J. & Bass, B. M. (1990). Transformational leadership: Beyond initiation and consideration. *Journal of Management, 16,* 693-703.

Shamir, B., House, R. J., & Arthur, M. B. (1993). The motivational effects of charismatic leadership: A self-concept based theory. *Organization Science, 4,* 577-594.

Shamir, B., Zakay, E., Breinin, E., & Popper, M. (1998). Correlates of charismatic leader behavior in military units: Subordinates' attitudes, unit characteristics, and superiors' appraisals of leader performance. *Academy of Management Journal, 41,* 387-409.

Sheeran, P. (2002). Intention-behavior relations: A conceptual and empirical review. In W. Stroebe & M. Hewstone (Eds.), *European Review of Social Psychology,* (Vol. 12, pp. 1-36). New York: Wiley.

Sims, H. R., Szilagyi, A., & Keller, R. (1979). The measurement of job characteristics. *Academy of Management Journal, 26,* 195-212.

Six, B., & Felfe, J. (2004). Einstellungen und Werterhaltungen. In H. Schuler (Ed.), *Enzyklopädie der Psychologie. Organisationspsychologie 1 -Grundlagen und Personalpsychologie* (S. 597-672). Göttingen: Hogrefe.

Slesina, W. (2001). Evaluation betrieblicher Gesundheitszirkel. In H. Pfaff & W. Slesina (Hrsg.), *Effektive betriebliche Gesundheitförderung. Konzepte und methodische Ansätze zur Evaluation und Qualitätssicherung,* (S. 75 – 96). Weinheim/München: Juventa.

Slusher, M. P., & Anderson, C. A. (1987). When reality monitoring fails: The role of imagination in stereotype maintenance. *Journal of Personality and Social Psychology, 52,* 653-662.

Smith, F. J. (1977). Work attitudes as predictors of attendance on a specific day. *Journal of Applied Psychology, 62,* 16-19.

Smith, J. A., & Foti, R. J. (1998). A pattern approach to the study of leader emergence. *Leadership Quarterly, 9,* 147-160.

Smither, J. W., London, M., Flautt, R., Vargas, Y., & Kucine, I. (2002). Can working with an executive coach improve multisource feedback ratings over time? A quasi-experimental field study. *Personnel Psychology, 56,* 23-44.

Snyder, M., Tanke, E. D., & Berscheid, E. (1977). Social perception and interpersonal behaviour: On the self-fulfilling nature of social stereotypes. *Journal of Personality and Social Psychology, 35,* 656-666.

Sochert, R. (1999). *Gesundheitsbericht und Gesundheitszirkel - Evaluation eines integrierten Konzepts betrieblicher Gesundheitsförderung.* Bremerhaven: Wirtschaftsverlag NW.

Spiegel, S., Grant-Pillow, H., & Higgins, E. T. (2004). How regulatory fit enhances motivational strength during goal pursuit. *European Journal of Social Psychology 34,* 39-54.

Staehle, W. (1999). *Management: Eine verhaltenswissenschaftliche Perspektive* (8. Aufl.). München: Vahlen

Stankov, L. (2000). The theory of fluid and crystallized intelligence. New findings and recent developments. *Learning and Individual Differences, 12,* 1-3.

Steel, R. P. (2003). Methodological and operational issues in the construction of absence variables. *Human Resource Management Review, 13,* 243-251.

Steel, R. P., Shane, G. S., & Kennedy, K. A. (1990). Effects of social-system factors on absenteeism, turnover, and job performance. *Journal of Business and Psychology, 4,* 423-430.

Steers, R. M., & Rhodes, S. R. (1978). Major influences on employees attendance: a process model. *Journal of Applied Psychology, 63,* 391-407.

Steers, R. M., & Rhodes, S. R. (1984). Knowledge and speculation about absenteeism. In P. S. Goodman & R. S. Atkin (Eds.), *Absenteeism* (1 ed., pp. 229-275). San Francisco: Jossey-Bass.

Stern, E., & Guthke, J. (2001). *Perspektiven der Intelligenzforschung.* Lengerich: Pabst Science Publishers.

Sternberg, R. J. (1999). *Cognitive Psychology.* Yale: Harcourt Brace.

Stewart, G. (2002). Uncovering implicit leadership beliefs: Variation between information technology (IT) executives and business executives in a public service agency. *International Journal of Organisational Behaviour, 5,* 163-179.

Stogdill, R. (1969). Validity of leader behavior descriptions. *Personnel Psychology, 22,* 153-158.

Stone, E. F., Stone, D. L., & Gueutal, H. G. (1990). Influence of cognitive ability on response to questionnaire measures: measurement precision and missing response problems. *Journal of Applied Psychology, 75,* 418-427.

Szilagyi, A. D. (1980a). Causal inferences between leader reward behaviour and subordinate performance, absenteeism, and work satisfaction. *Journal of Occupational Behavior, 53,* 195-204.

Szilagyi, A. D. (1980b). Reward behavior by male and female leaders: A causal inference analysis. *Journal of Vocational Behavior, 16,* 59-72.

Tharenou, P. (1993). A test of reciprocal causality for absenteeism. *Journal of Organizational Behavior, 14,* 269-287.

Theorell, T. & Karasek, R. A. (1996). Current issues relating to psychosocial job strain and cardiovascular disease research. *Journal of Occupational Health Psychology, 1,* 9-26.

Thomas, A. M. (1998). *Coaching in der Personalentwicklung.* Bern: Huber.

Tiedens, L. Z. (2001). Stereotypes about sentiments and status: Emotional expectations for high-status group members. *Journal of Personality & Social Psychology, 80,* 86-94.

Tomacci, T. (1997). *The relationship between perceptions of organizational culture and the job satisfaction of male and female middle managers.* U San Francisco, US, 1.

Towler, A. J. (2003). Effects of charismatic influence training on attitudes, behavior, and performance. *Personnel Psychology, 56,* 363-381.

Turnley, W. H., & Bolino, M. C. (2001). Achieving desired images while avoiding undesired images: Exploring the role of self-monitoring in impression management. *Journal of Applied Psychology, 86,* 351-360

Väänänen, A., Toppinen-Tanner, S., Kalimo, R., Mutanen, P., Vahtera, J., & Peiro, J. M. (2003). Job characteristics, physical and psychological symptoms, and social support as antecedents of sickness absence among men and women in the private industrial sector. *Social Science and Medicine, 57,* 807-824.

Van der Doef, M. & Maes, S. (1999). The Job Demand-Control(-Support) Model and psychological well-being: a review of 20 years of empirical research. *Work & Stress, 13,* 87-114.

Van der Klink, J. J .L., Blonk, R. W. B., Schene, A. H., & van Dijk, F. J. H. (2001). The benefits of interventions for work-related stress. *American Journal of Public Health, 91,* 270-277.

Van der Sluis-den Dikken, L. & Hoeksema, L. H. (2001). The palette of management development. *Journal of Management Development, 20,* 168-179.

Van Velsor, E., Leslie, J. B., & Fleenor, J. W. (2001). *Choosing 360. A guide to evaluating multi-rater feedback instruments for management development.* Greensboro, NC: Center for Creative Leadership.

Volpert, W. (1987b). Psychische Regulation von Arbeitstätigkeiten. In U. Kleinbeck & J. Rutenfranz (Hrsg.), *Arbeitspsychologie. Enzyklopädie der Psychologie, Themenbereich D, Serie III, Band 1*, (S. 1-42). Göttingen: Hogrefe.

Vroom, V. & Yetton, P. (1973). *Leadership and decison-making*. Pittsburgh, PA: University Press.

Warner, E. W. & Murt, H. A. (1985). Economic incentives and health behavior. In J. C. Rosen & L. J. Solomon (Eds.), *Prevention in health psychology* (pp. 236-274). Hanover, NH/London: University Press of New England.

Weber, M. (1972). *Wirtschaft und Gesellschaft. Grundrisse de verstehenden Soziologie*. Tübingen: Mohr-Siebeck.

Weiss, H. M., & Adler, S. (1981). Cognitive complexity and the structure of implicit leadership theories. *Journal of Applied Psychology, 66*, 69-78.

Werth, L., Denzler, M. & Förster, J. (2002). Was motiviert wen? Woraus der Fokus liegt, entscheidet über den Erfolg. *Wirtschaftspsychologie, 2*, 5-12.

Westermayer, G. (1995). Welche Einsichten können aus der Arbeit mit Gesundheitszirkeln gewonnen werden? In R. Buch (Hrsg.), *Betriebliche Gesundheitsförderung* (S. 74-86). Berlin: FU Berlin Referat für Weiterbildung.

Westermayer, G. (1998). Organisationsentwicklung und betriebliche Gesundheitsförderung. In E. Bamberg, A. Ducki, & A.-M. Metz (Hrsg.), *Handbuch Betriebliche Gesundheitsförderung*, (S. 119-132). Göttingen: Hogrefe.

Westermayer, G. & Bähr, B. (Hrsg.) (1994). *Betriebliche Gesundheitszirkel*. Göttingen: Hogrefe.

WHO (1993). *Ottawa-Charta zur Gesundheitsförderung* (Nachdruck der Fassung von 1986). Hamburg: Verlag für Gesundheitsförderung.

WHO. (2004a). *Briefing for the WHO European ministerial conference on mental health in Helsinki*, January 2005, online publication.

WHO. (2004b). *WHO concerned about absence from work due to stress-related conditions*: preparation for the WHO European ministerial conference on mental health in Helsinki in January 2005, online publication.

Wilbur, C. S., Hartwell, T. D. & Piserchia, P. V. (1986). The Johnson & Johnson "LIVE FOR LIFE" Program: Its organization and evaluation plan. In M. F. Cataldo & T. J. Coates (Eds.), *Health and industry: A behavioral medicine perspective* (pp. 338-350). New York: Wiley.

Wilk, S. L., Desmarais, L. B., & Sackett, P. R. (1995). Gravitation to jobs commensurate with ability: Longitudinal and cross-sectional tests. *Journal of Applied Psychology, 80*, 79-85.

Winkelmann, R. (1999). Wages, firm size and absenteeism. *Applied Economics Letters, 6*, 337-341.

Wofford, J. C., & Goodwin, V. L. (1994). A cognitive interpretation of transactional and transformational leadership theories. *Leadership Quarterly, 5*, 161-186.

Wofford, J. C., Goodwin, V. L. & Whittington, J. L. (1998). A field study of a cognitive approach to understanding transformational and transactional leadership. *Leadership Quarterly, 9*, 55-84.

Wofford, J. C., Joplin, J. R., & Comforth, B. (1996). Use of simultaneous verbal protocols in analysis of group leaders' cognitions. *Psychological Reports, 79*, 847-858.

Woodall, J. (2005). International management development. In T. Edwards & C. Rees (Eds.), *International HRM: A Critical Introduction* (pp. 34-58). London: Pearson.

Xie, J.-L. & Johns, G. (1995). Job scope and stress: Can job scope be too high? *Academy of Management Journal, 38*, 188-1309.

Xie, J. L., & Johns, G. (2000). Interactive effects of absence culture salience and group cohesiveness: A multi-level and cross-level analysis of work absenteeism in the Chinese context. *Journal of Occupational and Organizational Psychology, 73*, 31-52.

Yammarino, F. J. & Bass, B. M. (1990). Transformational leadership and multiple levels of analysis. *Human Relations, 43*, 975-995.

Yorges, S. L., Weiss, H. M., & Strickland, O. L. (1999). The effect of leader outcomes on influence, attributions, and perceptions of charisma. *Journal of Applied Psychology, 84*, 428-436.

Yukl, G. (1988). *Development and validation of the managerial practice questionnaire* (Technical Report). Albany, NY: State University of New York.

Yukl, G. (1999). An evaluation of conceptual weaknesses in transformational and charismatic leadership theories. *Leadership Quarterly, 10*, 285-305.

Yukl, G. (2002). *Leadership in organizations.* (5th ed.) Upper Saddle River, NJ: Prentice Hall.

Yukl, G. & Van Fleet, D. (1992). Theory and research on leadership in organizations. In M.D.Dunnette & L. M. Hough (Eds.), *Handbook of industrial and organizational Psychology* (pp. 147-197). Palo Alto, CA: Consulting Psychologist Press.

Zapf, D. & Dormann, C. (2001). Gesundheit und Arbeitsschutz. In H. Schuler (Hrsg.), *Lehrbuch der Personalpsychologie*, (S. 559-587). Göttingen: Hogrefe.

Zapf, D., Dormann, C., & Frese, M. (1996). Longitudinal studies in organizational stress research: a review of the literature with reference to methodological issues. *Journal of Occupational Health Psychology, 1*, 145-169.

Zapf, D. & Semmer, N. K. (2004). Stress und Gesundheit in Organisationen. In H. Schuler (Hrsg.), *Enzyklopädie der Psychologie, Themenbereich D, Serie III, Band 3 Organizationspsychologie* (2. Aufl., S. 1007-1053). Göttingen: Hogrefe.

WIRTSCHAFTSPSYCHOLOGIE

HERAUSGEGEBEN VON DETLEV LIEPMANN

www.peterlang.de

Claudia Zuleta Luksic

Transformational Leadership and Commitment

A Study in Bolivia

Frankfurt am Main, Berlin, Bern, Bruxelles, New York, Oxford, Wien, 2006.
164 pp., num. tab., 5 graf.
Wirtschaftspsychologie. Edited by Detlev Liepmann. Vol. 13
ISBN 978-3-631-54901-8 · pb. € 34.–*

In this book various application-oriented facets are interlinked. Transnational concepts are touched upon and it is basically assumed that deviating behavioral patterns on an individual level can be pinpointed in varying contexts. The practical relevance is founded on the fact that in Latin America, few studies have been published to date that emphasize the systematic reproduction of organizational behaviour from the point of view of transformational leadership. The reference to distinctive cultural as well as regional features is delved into in much more detail whilst doing research on this topic. This is underscored by the references of numerous (Anglo-American) authors who even state that there is a paradigm shift due to the concept of transformational leadership.

Contents: Practical relevance of transformational leadership · Information about Bolivia · Social indicators and economic rates · Charismatic leadership · Transactional and transformational leadership · Antecedents and outcomes of commitment · Empirical analysis for a Bolivian sample · Transformational leadership as a cultural specific phenomenon

Frankfurt am Main · Berlin · Bern · Bruxelles · New York · Oxford · Wien
Distribution: Verlag Peter Lang AG
Moosstr. 1, CH-2542 Pieterlen
Telefax 00 41 (0) 32 / 376 17 27

*The €-price includes German tax rate
Prices are subject to change without notice
Homepage http://www.peterlang.de